1619

A reporte of the manner of proceeding
in the General assembly convented at
James citty in Virginia, July. 30. 1619.
consisting of the Governo[r] the counsell
of Estate, and two Burgesses elected out
of eache Incorporation, and plantation; &
being dissolued the 4th of August next ensuing

First Sir George Yeardley knight Governo[r] & Captaine
generall of Virginia, hauing sente his sumons all over
the Country, aswell to invite those of the Counsell of Estate
that were absente, as also for the Election of Burgesses
there were chosen and appeared

For James citty
    Captaine William Powell,
    Ensigne William Spense.
For Charles citty.
    Samuel Sharpe,
    Samuel Jordan.
For the citty of Henricus
    Thomas Dowse,
    John Polentine
For Kiccowtan
    Captaine William Tucker,
    William Capp.
For Martin-Brandon Capt. John Martins plantation
    M[r]. Thomas Davis
    M[r]. Robert Stacy.
For Smythes hundred
    Captaine Thomas Graues,
    M[r]. Walter Shelley.

141

FRONTISPIECE—The General Assembly was the first representative governing body in America, convened at Jamestown, July 30–August 4, 1619. John Pory's Report of the Proceedings of the General Assembly. Permission from the National Archives, UK.

1619

Jamestown

AND THE FORGING OF

American Democracy

JAMES HORN

BASIC BOOKS

New York

Basic Books
Hachette Book Group
1290 Avenue of the Americas, New York, NY 10104
www.basicbooks.com

Printed in the United States of America

First Edition: October 2018

Published by Basic Books, an imprint of Perseus Books, LLC, a subsidiary of Hachette Book Group, Inc. The Basic Books name and logo is a trademark of the Hachette Book Group.

The Hachette Speakers Bureau provides a wide range of authors for speaking events. To find out more, go to www.hachettespeakersbureau.com or call (866) 376-6591.

The publisher is not responsible for websites (or their content) that are not owned by the publisher.

Print book interior design by Amy Quinn.

Library of Congress Cataloging-in-Publication Data

Names: Horn, James P. P., author.
Title: 1619: Jamestown and the Forging of American Democracy / James Horn.
Other titles: One thousand six hundred nineteen | Sixteen nineteen | Jamestown and the Forging of American Democracy
Description: First edition. | New York: Basic Books, [2018] | Includes bibliographical references and index.
Identifiers: LCCN 2018001108| ISBN 9780465064694 (hardcover) | ISBN 9781541698802 (ebook)
Subjects: LCSH: Jamestown (Va.)—History—17th century. | Jamestown (Va.)—Politics and government—17th century. | Colonists—Virginia—Jamestown—History—17th century. | African Americans—Virginia—Jamestown—History—17th century. | Slavery—Virginia—History—17th century. | Democracy—United States—History.
Classification: LCC F234.J3 H65 2018 | DDC 975.5/425102—dc23
LC record available at https://lccn.loc.gov/2018001108

ISBNs: 978-0-465-06469-4 (hardcover), 978-1-5416-9880-2 (ebook)

LSC-C

10 9 8 7 6 5 4 3 2 1

For Sally, Liz, Ben, and Alice,
with love

If a nation expects to be ignorant and free . . .
it expects what never was and never will be.

   —*Thomas Jefferson*

Contents

Author's Note

FOR THE CONVENIENCE OF THE READER, I HAVE ALTERED THE spelling and punctuation of historical passages to make them conform to modern conventions but have retained original capitalization to offer an impression of the original sources. No substantive changes of any sort have been made to direct quotations.

Introduction

1619

Along the banks of the James River, Virginia, during an oppressively hot spell in the middle of summer 1619, two events occurred within a few weeks of each other that would profoundly shape the course of history. Convened with little fanfare or formality, the first gathering of a representative governing body anywhere in the Americas, the General Assembly, met from July 30 to August 4 in the choir of the newly built church at Jamestown. Following instructions from the Virginia Company of London, the colony's financial backers, the meeting's principal purpose was to introduce "just Laws for the happy guiding and governing of the people." The assembly sat as a single body and was made up of the governor, Sir George Yeardley, his four councilors, and twenty-two burgesses chosen by the free, white, male inhabitants of every town, corporation, and large plantation throughout the colony.[1]

A few weeks later, a battered English privateer, the *White Lion,* entered the Chesapeake Bay and anchored off Point Comfort, a small but thriving maritime community at the mouth of the James River that was the first port of call for oceangoing ships. While roving in the Caribbean, the ship, together with its companion, the *Treasurer,* had been involved in a fierce battle with a Portuguese slaver bound for Veracruz. Victorious, the two privateers pillaged the Portuguese vessel and sailed away northward carrying dozens of enslaved Africans. Running short of water and provisions, they headed for the nearest English haven, Virginia, where a couple of weeks later the prominent planter John Rolfe reported that the *White Lion* had "brought not anything but 20. and odd Negroes," who were *"bought"* (my italics) for food supplies. The *Treasurer* entered the James River a few days later but opted to leave quickly, possibly after clandestinely selling some of the African captives on board. Forcibly transported from West Central Africa (modern-day Angola), they were the first Africans to arrive in mainland English America.[2]

No one in Virginia in 1619 or in the years following could have possibly grasped the importance of what had occurred. Settlers understood that the assembly allowed them to have a hand in governing themselves, but they were motivated more by opportunities to approve laws sent by the Virginia Company from London and to propose their own legislation rather than by abstract concepts of self-government or subjects' rights and liberties. Equally, no documented discussion took place in the colony about the morality of owning and enslaving Africans. Deliberations in future general assemblies at Jamestown, as mirrored later in colonial legislatures across English America, focused far more on policing measures against Africans and protecting the rights of masters than on the rights of the enslaved or ethical considerations. Slavery, African and Indian, together with a broad spectrum of white non-freedom—apprenticeships, convict labor, and serfdom—were simply taken for granted in the emerging Atlantic world of the time and elicited little comment.[3]

Yet the coincidence of the meeting of the first representative government and arrival of the first enslaved Africans in the summer of 1619 was portentous. Historians have argued that the rise of liberty and equality in America, America's democratic experiment, was shadowed from its beginning by its dark obverse: slavery and racism. Slavery in the midst of freedom, Edmund Morgan writes, was the central paradox of the birth of America. The rapid expansion of opportunities for Europeans was made possible only by the enslavement and exploitation of African and Indian peoples. Non-Europeans were consigned to a permanent underclass excluded from the benefits of white society, while Europeans profited enormously from the fruits of the labors of those they oppressed. Arguably, then, 1619 marks the inception of the most important political development in American history, the rise of democracy, and the emergence of what would in time become one of the nation's greatest challenges: the corrosive legacy of racial stereotypes that continues to afflict our society today.[4]

—•—

DESPITE THE SIGNIFICANCE OF 1619 AND SURROUNDING years, this period is almost entirely unknown to the public. Insofar as any attention has been given to early Virginia, the dominant narrative portrays Jamestown as an unqualified disaster, little more than a "dismal and fraught" precursor of the successful godly settlements in New England where, so it goes, America's story really begins. For the nation at large, Plymouth in 1620 or the founding of the Puritan colony of Massachusetts a decade later exerts a far greater influence on our collective historical memory than the founding of Virginia in 1607 or the events of 1619. This is especially perplexing considering that what took place in early Jamestown had far-reaching implications for all English colonies that followed in Virginia's wake, as well as eventually on the creation of the United States itself.[5]

Owing to numerous setbacks, the Virginia colony struggled in its early years, leading the Company to introduce wholesale reforms in an effort to save the colony from collapse. Still largely an experimental period in England's empire-building trajectory, the import of 1619 derives from the consequential philosophical and political assumptions that guided the reforms, though they in turn led to unforeseen and tragic outcomes that ultimately brought an end to the project. Instigated by the highly respected parliamentarian and leader of the Virginia Company, Sir Edwin Sandys (pronounced *Sands*), propertied white males in the colony were granted remarkable political freedoms as well as opportunities to share in the running of their own affairs. In addition, plans were put in place to promote a harmonious society where diverse peoples and religious groups would live together side by side in peace to their mutual benefit. Because so many influential parliamentary leaders were involved with the Company, proposals for Virginia were informed by the wide-ranging political debates taking place simultaneously at James I's court and in Parliament, which linked developments in the fledgling colony to domestic and international issues of momentous consequence. By 1619, the Virginia Company was recognized by many in high political circles as a laboratory for some of the most advanced constitutional thinking of the age.

Company leaders grounded their efforts to establish a godly and equitable society in the philosophical theory of the commonwealth. The term *commonwealth,* or the "common weal," emerged in Europe in the late fifteenth and sixteenth centuries and brought together a variety of political and economic precepts that highlighted the common good of the people. Particular emphasis was given to the importance of wise and noble rulers and mixed government—a salutary balance of monarchy, aristocracy, and democracy—as well as Christian morality, prosperity, and social well-being. Linked to Renaissance humanist ideas, statesmen and intellectuals believed that the application of rational approaches to government and social and economic organization would encourage the improvement of societies and the human condition. Where better to test these ideals than the New World? In Virginia, commonwealth theory guided the leadership's approach to every facet of the emerging colony, including government, the rule of law, protections for private property, the organization of the local economy, and relations with the Powhatans, the Indian peoples whose territories surrounded English settlements. The great reforms introduced in 1619, therefore, were all-encompassing, not directed simply toward the creation of a legislative body.[6]

Embracing diversity was also integral to the Virginia Company's plans. "Multitudes" of settlers were to be drawn from all ranks of society and from all parts of the country. England's first mass Atlantic migration, which was initiated by the Company, underlined the Company's desire to translate large sections of English society to the growing colony. But settlement of the colony would not only depend on immigrants from England; Sandys and his supporters were committed also to incorporating Indian peoples into their newly reformed commonwealth as full members of society, an ambition without precedent in the New World. Symbolized by the conversion of Pocahontas, daughter of the Powhatan chieftain, to Anglicanism and her marriage to gentleman-planter John Rolfe at Jamestown, the Company aspired to bring the entire Powhatan people to Protestantism and the Church of England—a necessary precondition for their conversion to English ways and absorption into English Virginia.

Enslaved Africans, however, were not part of Sandys's plans for the colony. The rapid spread of tobacco husbandry in the colony after 1614 dismayed Company leaders, who promoted a mixed economy based on a wide variety of natural commodities and manufactured goods that they anticipated would offer plenty of work for settlers and create broad-based economic equality across the colony. Slaves would be unnecessary. Instead, white workers and converted Indian peoples would provide the workforce as self-sufficient and equal members of their communities, thereby strengthening relations between the English and Powhatans.[7]

WITHIN A FEW YEARS, SANDYS'S DREAM OF A MODEL AMERI-can commonwealth had been shattered. A series of disasters, including a massive attack by Powhatan warriors that killed hundreds of settlers, political intrigue involving the king and his ministers, and deep divisions among Company leaders in London, ultimately led to the Company's collapse. The colony survived, however, which attested to the commercial success of preceding years, but after 1625 in the absence of Company rule, a quite different society emerged from that promoted by Sandys. A commonwealth was founded on the well-being of the people as a whole, not the few; this was a fundamental principle emphasized by classical philosophers of Greece and Rome as well as by leading statesmen of the sixteenth and early seventeenth centuries. Sandys and other Company officers adopted initiatives they believed would stimulate prosperity for broad sections of society and sought to prevent wealthy planters from gaining excessive influence in the colony. These measures involved limitations on the powers of the governor and his councilors, an emphasis on the rule of law, and the founding of the General Assembly, which was created specifically to represent the majority of settlers, not only the rich. The Company's wholehearted support of reformed Anglicanism and Christian morality encouraged neighborly support and care for others as well as individual piety and moral discipline.

Following the Company's demise, efforts and legislation put in place to encourage the common good and a widespread equality of interests were quickly abandoned. Even before the collapse of the Company, conspicuous disparities in wealth had begun to surface. Soon after tobacco became established as the colony's principal commodity, a boom in the price of tobacco leaf on the London market enabled a small group of planters and government officials to become extremely rich by steadily amassing land and laborers. After the Powhatan attack of 1622 that nearly destroyed the colony, racial stereotypes demonizing the Indians were quickly adopted by settlers to justify the slaughter of Indian peoples and appropriation of their territory. Huge areas of prime agricultural lands were taken up by settlers, creating the first English land rush in America. Some Powhatan captives were enslaved and joined Africans in bondage; other Indian peoples moved out of the region beyond the reach of settlers.[8]

The Company's commonwealth project was also condemned by critics for being dangerously egalitarian. Captain John Bargrave, a prominent merchant-planter, wrote forcefully that the "mouth of equal liberty must needs be stopped," denouncing what he saw as the overt populist tendencies among Company leaders, including Sandys. "Extreme liberty," he warned, was more perilous to the political and social order than "extreme tyranny." Political leadership, lauded among the responsible, propertied classes, was not deemed suitable for the poor and landless who comprised the vast majority of people in early modern society. It was axiomatic among the upper classes that poor people's lack of independence, property, and education disqualified them from prominent roles in society. In Virginia, where poor workers made up a far higher percentage of the total population than in England, political power rapidly became concentrated in the hands of small groups of wealthy planters who, largely autonomous in their own localities and insulated from close oversight by English government officials three and a half thousand miles away, became accustomed to a freedom of action unthinkable at home.

While Virginia and the American colonies were attractive to countless middle-class British immigrants and other Europeans during the seventeenth century precisely because of the perceived benefits of political and economic liberty, those very freedoms permitted the wholesale and largely unchecked exploitation of lower-class whites, Africans, and Indians. For most poor English settlers, crossing the Atlantic to Virginia or other colonies was a gamble of heroic proportions whereby a fortunate few might succeed in vastly improving their material condition through luck, hard work, and timing, but the great majority did not. For the mass of Indian and African peoples, of course, even the faintest glimmer of hope of personal improvement was denied them. Slavery and inequality thus arose as synchronic opposites of liberty and opportunity, products of the same political and economic forces.

———

AT THE DAWN OF THE BRITISH EMPIRE IN AMERICA, IT WAS unclear how colonies would evolve. Would they be little more than "pirate nests," as feared by successive Spanish ambassadors in London, or develop as fishing stations and trading posts such as those founded in Newfoundland by different nations or along the Hudson River by the Dutch? Or would they become stable and prosperous British settlements that would eventually spread across the entire northern continent?

Virginia was the first of England's settlements in America to persist and ultimately flourish. The great reforms of 1619 that took place at Jamestown had an enduring influence on the development of Virginia and British America and heralded the opening of an extended Anglo-American examination of sovereignty, individual rights, liberty, and constitutionalism that would influence all Britain's colonies. Representative government spread outward across the continent, beginning the vital democratic experiment that has characterized American society down to our own times. Concurrently, Virginia's early adoption of slavery and dispossession of Indian peoples reflected and reinforced racial attitudes that began the highly discriminatory processes that have stigmatized society ever since. Such were the conflicted origins of modern America.[9]

One

Jamestown

We hope to plant a nation,
Where none before hath stood.

—*Richard Rich* (1610)

That no man blaspheme God's holy name upon pain
of death, or use unlawful oaths, taking the name of
God in vain . . . upon pain of severe punishment for
the first offense so committed, and for the second to
have a bodkin thrust through his tongue.

—*Laws Divine, Moral, and Martial* (1609–1611)

JAMESTOWN WAS UNASHAMEDLY A COMMERCIAL VENTURE.
Founded by royal charter in April 1606, the Virginia Company was the latest of a number of trading companies that had blossomed during the previous half century, evidence of the growing wealth and global reach of English, especially London's, merchants. "*All* Kingdoms," an anonymous writer

pointed out to the secretary of state, Robert Cecil, Earl of Salisbury, "are maintained by Rents or Traffic [trade], but especially by the latter, which in maritime places most flourish by means of Navigation." Companies enabled sovereigns to promote overseas expansion and commerce while at the same time adopting the convenient fiction that they had little direct involvement in the creation of empire.[1]

Led by some of the ablest merchants and statesmen of the day and inspired by a generation of promoters of American colonies, the Virginia Company set out to create a burgeoning transatlantic trade by the establishment of permanent settlements in the Chesapeake Bay and New England regions. Company leaders, including Cecil, were confident that thriving industries could be established in America and products exported back to England, thereby lessening the country's dependence on imports from Europe and elsewhere. To ensure they had the best possible workers, the Company recruited skilled artisans from England and overseas: Italian glassworkers; Polish and German experts in the production of industrial commodities and valuable minerals; vignerons from Languedoc, France, to cultivate the colony's vines that had been recently imported from the Canaries. The men were said to be skilled also in the manufacture of silk. John Pory, writing from Jamestown to Sir Edwin Sandys, treasurer and chief promoter of the Company, was especially enthusiastic about the colony's potential for producing wine (he was reputed to be a heavy drinker). Once vineyards were established, he believed Virginia would yield enough wine to "lade all the ships that come" with vintages as good as those of France and Spain.[2]

John Pory was a perceptive man. Educated at Gonville and Caius College, Cambridge, and connected to the highest ranks of English society, he combined a gift for languages with a taste for travel and diplomacy, having spent several years in Europe and the Levant. As the recently appointed secretary of Virginia, he painted a vivid picture of Jamestown's fledgling society for Company leaders in London. English plows and cattle, he remarked at the end of September 1619, would soon bring the "Colony to perfection." The land was marvelously fertile and once tilled would support both a plentiful crop of wheat and abundant Indian corn in a single year. The planting of mulberry trees would lead to a thriving silk industry, while cattle and other livestock were increasing quickly and would be a steady source of income for planters. By adapting English husbandry practices to the new conditions, Pory had no doubt that settlers would "produce miracles out of this earth," which in turn would supply ample provisions for the hundreds of new arrivals the Company was sending over.[3]

Already, considerable fortunes were being made. Tobacco cultivation had spread rapidly over the previous five years as a growing number of colonists took up prime lands along the James River valley and discovered the benefit of the lucrative cash crop. "All our riches for the present do consist in tobacco," Pory commented wryly, so that even "our Cow-keeper here of James City on Sundays goes accoutered [dressed] all in fresh flaming silks, and a wife of one that in England had professed the black art not of a scholar but of a collier of Croydon, wears her rough beaver hat with a fair pearl hatband and a silken suit." With tobacco commanding high prices in London, one man had made a profit of £200 in a year from just his own labor. Planters with the help of their field-workers could make much more; a man with six servants had earned £1,000 from one crop, an extraordinary sum considering that a common day laborer in England might earn only £12 annually. Although such returns were unusual, they were nevertheless possible. Here, seemingly, were opportunities for ordinary people to get rich by their own hard work and for the wealthy and well placed to become richer still. No better example could be found than the new governor himself. Sir George Yeardley had first arrived in the colony a decade earlier with little more than his sword, Pory commented, but when in London shortly before returning to Jamestown, he and his lady had spent a small fortune to furnish his forthcoming voyage. It would not be long before the governorship of Virginia, he wrote, would be worth as much as the highly lucrative office of lord deputy of Ireland.[4]

The colony was changing dramatically. Several years earlier, Virginia could count only a few hundred settlers living in a half dozen small English settlements, but by the spring of 1620, more than two dozen communities had been established from the mouth of the James River to the falls a hundred miles upriver, and the settler population had quadrupled. Tens of thousands of acres had been taken up by private investors who—with the Company's blessing—were encouraged to transport their own laborers to the colony, thereby adding to the flow of new arrivals and rapid expansion of settlement. As a consequence of new initiatives introduced by Company leader Edwin Sandys, the country was flourishing, the English were at peace with local Indian peoples, the Powhatans, and Virginia appeared destined for a period of prolonged stability and prosperity.[5]

The abundance and prosperity described by Pory were a far cry from the disasters that had blighted Jamestown's first decade. Among these were the heavy loss of life, lengthy hostilities against the Powhatans, and a desperate lack of profitable returns to investors. Jamestown might well have become another "lost colony" alongside Roanoke had not the immensely influential Earl of Salisbury, the London merchant prince Sir Thomas Smythe, and other prominent leaders, including Sandys, decided to intervene and thoroughly overhaul the organization of the Company and colony in 1608–1609. This first phase of reform was in some respects a foreshadowing of their later attempts to build a true commonwealth—for example, in their emphasis on converting the Indians to the Church of England—but was completely different in regard to governing and leadership. What was required, the Company believed, was the enforcement of law and order by an authoritarian government in Virginia led by an all-powerful lord governor and captain general.

In retrospect, a military regime and martial law proved necessary to sustain the colony through the coming years of war and the immediate aftermath, yet it was not at all conducive to the development of an expansive civilian society necessary for growth and prosperity in postwar Virginia. The formidable challenges of the first ten years played a key role in shaping the comprehensive reforms launched by Sir Edwin Sandys and his supporters in 1619.

IN THE WINTER OF 1606, THE LEADERS OF THE FIRST EXPEDI-
tion to Virginia received a series of detailed instructions,
which illustrate the high hopes of the Company on the eve of
the venture. The colony was to be governed by a small council of prominent settlers appointed by the Company. Once
they arrived in Virginia, they would elect a "president" from
among their own number who would oversee the colony for
up to a year. The leaders of the expedition were ordered to
ensure their initial settlement was located on a prominent
river about a hundred miles from the ocean, a precaution to
reduce the risk of attack from the sea by a hostile enemy,
notably Spain, and to position settlers close to the mountains
inland, where the discovery of a passage might lead them
through the North American landmass to the Pacific Ocean,
believed to be only a few hundred miles from the Atlantic
coast. Settlers were also instructed to take advantage of trade
with Indian peoples from surrounding regions and to search
for any existing gold or silver mines.[6]

In the context of the times, these aspirations were quite
realistic. The belief that North America had vast riches yet
to be discovered was commonplace in Europe by the mid-
sixteenth century. Spectacular Spanish discoveries and the
pillaging of Indian peoples in the Caribbean, Middle America,
and South America had confirmed the existence of enormous
wealth in new lands (new to Europeans). A century earlier,
the English had been among the first European nations to
cross the Atlantic but missed the opportunity to capitalize on
their discoveries of the North American mainland, much to
the exasperation of early promoters such as Richard Eden.
Had we not lacked "manly courage," he complained, "it

might happily have come to pass that that rich treasury called *Perularia* (which is now in Spain in the city of Seville, and so named for that in it is kept the infinite riches brought thither from the newfound land of Peru) might long since had been in the Tower of London, to the king's great honor and wealth of this his realm."

During the sixteenth century, Spanish explorers and then the French and English had eagerly turned their gaze upon the northern continent, convinced that just as Mexico and Peru had yielded great treasures, so in time would North America. The Spanish had searched in vain for riches in the southeast and southwest, the French in Florida and the far north, and the English in mid-Atlantic and northern lands. In the 1570s, Martin Frobisher had prospected for gold on Meta Incognita (southern shore of Baffin Island) in the Arctic Ocean, and in the 1580s Sir Walter Ralegh had sponsored three large-scale voyages to the island of Roanoke and adjacent lands on the coast of North Carolina. These efforts had come to nothing. Fifteen years later, at the beginning of the new century, the Virginia Company was determined to try again, this time searching along the shores of the Chesapeake Bay and inland.[7]

Despite seemingly promising beginnings, Jamestown settlers were unable to find a passage to the Pacific Ocean, gold or silver in the mountains, or wealth of any kind other than the natural produce of the country. Within days in August 1607, following the return to London of one of the expedition's leaders, Captain Christopher Newport, rumors that gold had been discovered in Virginia spread like wildfire around the city, only to be followed just as rapidly by news that the samples of ore brought back by Newport were worthless. "Silver and gold they have none," a well-placed commentator noted simply.[8]

Disappointing as the news was for the Company, information that arrived in the spring of 1608 indicated the colony was on the brink of collapse. Disease had carried off the majority of the original 104 men and boys during the previous summer and fall, and the leadership had splintered into bitterly divided factions. Tensions had been high ever since the original voyage to the colony when, a few months after departing England, Captain John Smith, one of the principal leaders, was arrested for challenging the authority of other officers and attempting to make himself "king." He was cast into the brig and confined below decks for much of the voyage. Following further disruption, he narrowly avoided being hanged when the expedition made landfall on the island of Nevis in the West Indies.[9]

Seven months later at Jamestown, another mutiny occurred. The first president of the colony, Captain Edward Maria Wingfield, a veteran of wars in Ireland and the Netherlands, was overthrown by three members of the council on the grounds that he was unworthy to serve and an atheist. In turn, he accused those who had plotted against him of forsaking "His Majesty's Government" and of planning to establish a *"Parliament"* (my italics), evidently believing his ousters sought to convene a popular government wherein even the lowliest would have a voice—a most dangerous leveling precedent. Wingfield alleged that the new president, John Ratcliffe, and his supporters, including Smith, had overthrown the legitimate authority and imposed a brutal regime of arbitrary rule, threatening and beating anyone who opposed them. By way of an example, he reported that James Read, a blacksmith, who had been condemned to be hanged for striking Ratcliffe, saved himself from the gallows by accusing Captain George Kendall, also recently deposed from the council, of treason. Despite little evidence to prove his guilt, Kendall was convicted a few days later and summarily shot to death. If "this whipping, lawing, beating, and hanging in Virginia" was known in England, Wingfield protested, referring to the breakdown of any semblance of law and order, "I fear it would drive many well-affected minds from this honorable action."[10]

———

WHETHER OR NOT THE COMPANY'S LEADERS BELIEVED WINGfield's self-justifications, they recognized that within less than a year the colony had degenerated into a half-starved mutinous rabble and the enterprise was in grave danger of foundering. They determined that the colony needed to be thoroughly remodeled. To that end, Company leaders petitioned the king, James I, to grant them extensive new powers.[11] Their first charter of 1606, which had established the Company, was superseded by a new charter of May 1609, that reorganized the Company as "the Treasurer and Company of Adventurers and Planters of the City of London for the First Colony in Virginia." Henceforth, the enterprise was to be governed by a treasurer, who was the leading officer, a ruling council, and ordinary members (called *adventurers*) who would convene regularly in weekly and quarterly meetings. Sir Thomas Smythe, a powerful London merchant and statesman who had played a prominent role in the Virginia venture since its inception, was appointed treasurer, the foremost officer of the Company. Members nominated candidates from among their own ranks to form a new council, which together with the treasurer comprised the standing administration of the Company. Endowed with authority to establish "all manner of laws, directions, instructions, forms and ceremonies of government and magistracy" necessary for the colony, the Company council's jurisdiction was limited, in theory, only by the important caveat that such ordinances should "as near as conveniently may be, be agreeable to the laws, statutes, government and policy of this our realm of England."[12]

Policy and general oversight of the colony remained firmly located in London under the authority of the Company, but to ensure that Virginia was governed effectively and law and order restored, the Company created a new position, an "absolute Governor," who would rule in the colony. Sir Thomas West, twelfth Baron De La Warr, a high-ranking nobleman and soldier, was appointed the colony's first lord governor and captain general, supported by Sir Thomas Gates, another veteran of the wars in Ireland and Europe, who would serve as lieutenant governor. Although the governor would be assisted by an advisory council in the colony of his own choosing, the Company made it clear that he could not be overruled or removed by it.

Under the new regime, the governor or his deputy were given extensive civil and military powers, including authority to enforce martial law and to supplement, revise, or interpret any laws in force in the colony at their own discretion.

Mindful of the frequent challenges to former leaders at Jamestown, governors were instructed to deploy a strong personal guard both to "beget reverence to [for] your authority" and to remind colonists to "obey the gravity of those laws under which they were born." In matters of civil justice, he was advised to act more like a chancellor than a judge, "rather upon the natural right and equity than upon the niceness and letter of the law which [might be] perplexing in this tender body." The Company encouraged him to "discreetly" combine "a summary and arbitrary way of justice" with more traditional forms of magistracy as is best suited "for you and that place."[13]

The outcome was the colony's first legal code, the *Laws Divine, Moral, and Martial,* drafted by William Strachey, the newly appointed secretary of the colony, and expanded by Gates and then his successor Sir Thomas Dale. It laid out in plain language the duties of settlers and soldiers and itemized punishments for transgressions. The "Divine" and "Moral" components of the code emphasized obedience to God and church. Settlers were to attend services twice daily, in the morning and evening, summoned by the tolling of the church bells. Anyone who did not attend divine service or persistently blasphemed God's holy name or called into question the reputation of a preacher or minister would be punished by whipping, having their tongues bored through with a bodkin (a long, blunt needle), or by death. With regard to serious crimes—treason, murder, the rape of English or Indian women, theft, embezzlement of Company property, trading with the Indians without permission, or running away to the Indians—the punishment was also death.

Measures aimed at regulating relationships with the Indians were a reflection of the Company's continuing hope
to convert the Powhatans to Christianity and English ways.
Other transgressions such as slandering the Company or its
leaders, killing livestock, and fornication carried the penal-
ties of whippings, branding, loss of ears, galley service, which
meant serving at the oars of longboats, and pleas for forgiveness in front of the congregation assembled in church. Additional sections set out the martial laws, pertaining to military
service and therefore the great majority of men, which carried equally severe punishments. By these means, Gates and
Dale determined not only to restore order but also to bring
about the moral reform of their men and settlers generally.
Jamestown and other garrisons to be established along the
James River were to be ruled by military laws as well as strict
religious principles.[14]

To achieve their plans, Smythe and his advisors completely overhauled the Company's financial organization and
created a joint stock enterprise whereby anyone prepared to
invest in the general stock or to put themselves forward to go
to the colony in person was eligible to join the venture. Company's leaders cast their recruitment campaign far and wide
throughout England. In the spring, they issued a newssheet
to be distributed in London that encouraged skilled artisans
and tradesmen to join them. Even at this early stage, the
Company promoted a range of skills to create a productive
and diversified economy in Virginia. Efforts were made to attract men and women as well as foreign workers "of whatever
craft they may be," who were instructed to make their way
to Smythe's city house to register for the voyage. In return

for signing up, prospective settlers were promised dwelling houses, vegetable gardens and orchards, as well as food and clothing at the Company's expense, together with a share in the division of land after seven years.

Appeals for financial support were forwarded to city and merchant leaders around England. Contrary to the true state of affairs, letters sent by the Company to merchants throughout the country in early 1609 described in rosy hues the achievements of early settlers in creating a firm foundation for the colony's future prosperity. They had discovered a bounteous country that was "safe from any danger of the Savages or other ruin that may threaten us." Letters listed examples of the many valuable commodities available in Virginia and potential industries that would be established, and expressed "no improbable hope" of finding rich mines.

The success of the campaign can be measured by the alacrity with which members of the aristocracy and gentry, merchants, and ordinary working men and women joined the venture. By the time the Company received royal approval for its new charter, 55 London mercantile and guild companies and 619 individuals had invested in the Company, thousands of pounds had been raised, and hundreds of colonists had been recruited. Fundamental organizational and financial reforms had been put in place that would persist throughout the Company's management of the colony.[15]

Company leaders summarized their objectives to Lieutenant Governor Sir Thomas Gates shortly before he left for Jamestown. Four major priorities were identified that they believed would lead to continuing investment and commercial success: (1) the discovery of either "the south seas or royal [valuable] mines"; (2) trading with Indian peoples near and far who were accessible by water; (3) tribute from local Indians; and (4) the production of natural commodities. The governor was instructed to select a new site for the colony's capital away from major navigable rivers and therefore safe from attack by Spanish warships. The Company believed Jamestown was poorly located and vulnerable to Spanish attack and had therefore decided to reduce it to a small garrison. Three Indian towns—one at the falls of the James River (possibly the village of Powhatan in present-day Richmond), and Ohonahorn and Ocanahowan to the south in what is now North Carolina—were to be occupied and developed as major new settlements instead. They would be the destination for the hundreds of settlers who were gathering in London and elsewhere waiting to board ships that would carry them to a new life in Virginia.[16]

As well as strengthening their political and financial powers, Company leaders acted to transform the entire scale of the Virginia enterprise. No longer seen as a private commercial venture, in the latter half of 1608 and early months of 1609 Sir Thomas Smythe and his advisors expanded Company efforts into a national undertaking of, as they saw it, immense consequence to England's honor, virtue, and future success. Their vision was articulated in the opening months of 1609 by Robert Johnson, an important London merchant and deputy treasurer of the Company, and represented a first major phase of reform that anticipated some of Sandys's initiatives introduced ten years later.

In an influential promotional tract entitled *Nova Britannia*, Johnson exclaimed that the land the English had "searched out, is a very good land" and "if the Lord love us, he will bring our people to it, and will give it us for a possession." He lavished fulsome praise on Virginia, describing an extensive country with a pleasant climate, well-watered valleys and plains, and hills and mountains where "hidden treasure, never yet searched" was yet to be discovered. Throughout the country, there were infinite varieties of game, fish, and fowl, as well as an abundance of all sorts of trees, covering the land in an immense woodland. He explained that the produce of the colony would supply a great variety of goods to the "great service" of England: timber, copper, and iron; vines to produce wine; mulberry trees for silk manufacture; hemp and flax for cordage and linen; pitch, tar, turpentine, and soap ashes for industries. Establishing manufactures in Virginia and transporting the country's natural produce to England would encourage the growth of a strong mercantile marine. At the same time, England would be able to put the idle and unwanted poor to profitable work in America, for both their own benefit and the country's. Eventually, England would become self-sufficient in raw materials and be able to supply manufactured goods as well as Virginia's produce to the rest of Europe.[17]

Johnson's approach was greatly influenced by an earlier promotional work authored by Thomas Hariot, polymath and advisor to Sir Walter Ralegh during the Roanoke voyages twenty years earlier. In 1588, Hariot had published *A Brief and True Report of the New Found Land of Virginia,* whose comprehensive description of the natural resources of the Roanoke region and lands to the south of the Chesapeake Bay read like a merchant's dream. *A Brief and True Report* remained the most authoritative and detailed account of an English colony in America, so it's no surprise that in the winter of 1608–1609, Hariot, one of the few men alive to have explored the North Carolina littoral, was called upon by Sir Thomas Smythe to join discussions about the future of the colony. He and another of Smythe's advisors, Richard Hakluyt the younger—a prolific writer and leading advocate of American ventures—were vigorous advocates for enlarging Virginia by connecting the Roanoke region to the James River valley.[18]

Accordingly, the Company petitioned the king to extend the colony's bounds two hundred miles north and south of the original settlement area stipulated in the 1606 charter, and inland from "sea to sea." King James granted their request, and as a result, the Virginia Company controlled an area along the Atlantic seaboard that extended from near modern-day Cape Fear, North Carolina, to the head of the Delaware Bay, close to where Philadelphia would be founded seventy years later. Westward, the colony extended to the Pacific Ocean.

Lastly, in a political and promotional masterstroke, Company leaders closely associated the colony's seemingly bright prospects with the transcendent vision of a Protestant crusade to convert Indian peoples to Christianity. In a series of sermons in London sponsored by the Company, preachers exhorted settlers to cross the ocean and spread the light of the true faith into the dark corners of a heathen and savage land, "even where Satan's throne is." What "comfort to those subjects who shall be a means of furthering of so happy a work," the Reverend Richard Crakanthorpe declared, "not only to see a New Britain in another world, but to have also those as yet heathen barbarians and brutish people . . . to learn the speech and language of Canaan?" The Reverend William Symonds was confident that Virginia would grow into a country "formidable to all the enemies of Christ, and be the praise of all that part of the world." Robert Johnson, aware that Spain had been hugely successful in spreading Catholicism among the Indian peoples of Spanish America, exhorted all well-affected subjects to adventure their purses or persons to support the new colony and "spread the kingdom of God, and the knowledge of the truth, among so many millions of men and women, Savage and blind, that never yet saw the true light shine before their eyes."

Conversion of the Indians would lead to a blossoming of the Church of England in a new land and the establishment of a Protestant empire in North America that would serve as a mighty bulwark against Spain's vast Catholic dominion in the south. "Thus shall we honor our God, our religion, our Nation," London preacher William Crashaw proclaimed grandly. Taking the true church to Virginia endowed settlers with a divine mission. The Company's council encouraged the undertaking by assuring investors and settlers that the "eyes of all Europe are looking upon our endeavors to spread the Gospel among the Heathen people of Virginia, [and] to plant our English nation there." Jamestown was to be England's first godly society in America.[19]

———•——

A DEFINING CHARACTERISTIC OF EARLY AMERICA WAS THE EX-traordinary diversity of peoples. Before arriving in Virginia, few English settlers had encountered Indians, but many would have heard about them from tales of "remote and unknown Countries," plays that popularized the image of the Indian, or godly works that emphasized the task of civilizing the

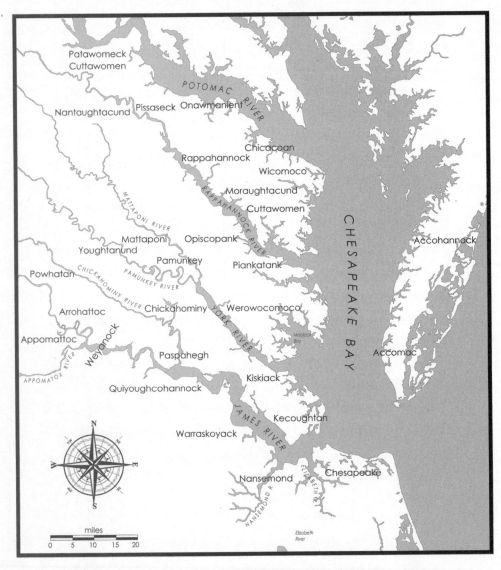

FIGURE 1—Indian peoples of Tsenacommacah (Virginia). Drawn by Jamie May.

"savages" and converting them to Anglicanism. Indians might be portrayed as exotic and wild, perhaps offering a glimpse of what ancient Britons had been like before they were conquered and civilized by the Romans. The task of creating an English settlement in Virginia similarly carried the sacred obligation of civilizing the Indians, eradicating savagery, and redeeming them from idolatry. Redemption became one of the central themes of the Company's colonizing plans, just as it was in the case of English efforts to civilize the "wild" Irish by settling plantations throughout Ireland under way at the same time.[20]

Other than men who had been involved in privateering voyages in the West Indies or fishing in the northern Atlantic, the majority of settlers had never seen Indians and were likely unsure about what to expect from them. The Virginia Company offered advice that suggested a guarded approach, friendly (or at least not antagonistic) but cautious, which reflected the English experience with Indian peoples during the short-lived Roanoke colonies twenty years earlier. Though they lived side by side, colonists established their own settlements along the James River, and Indian peoples lived separately according to their own laws and customs in communities on tribal lands ruled by local chiefs.

Tsenacommacah, the Indians' name for Virginia, was home to approximately fifteen thousand Powhatan people who lived in several hundred communities scattered across the land from south of the James River northward to the Potomac River and from the shores of the Atlantic to the gently rolling hills of the piedmont, where hostile Siouan-speaking peoples halted expansion farther west. In the 1570s, Wahunsonacock, great chief of the Powhatans, had inherited six districts located between the upper James and York Rivers that together with two or three more comprised the historic core of his territories. By the beginning of the seventeenth century, he had acquired more than two dozen additional chiefdoms, described by Captain John Smith as "either by force subdued unto him, or through fear yielded." The English had entered a land inhabited by one of the most powerful Indian chiefdoms of the mid-Atlantic.[21]

Wahunsonacock was acknowledged to be a remarkable leader. English accounts describe him in quasi-regal terms. A man of "grave and Majestic countenance," Captain Smith wrote, "as drove me into admiration to see such state [dignity] in a naked Savage." "All he knew," Smith added, were under his rule. William Strachey wondered how a "barbarous and uncivil" Indian chief devoid of the magnificent outer trappings of European royalty could yet express a form of such grandeur as to strike awe not only in his own people but also in the English. Opechancanough, his brother or kinsman, was described in similarly regal terms as "a brave Prince" of noble presence, "perfectly skilled in the Art of Governing." He was feared, eyewitnesses said, by peoples near and far who dreaded his name.

Yet, in practice, both Wahunsonacock and Opechancanough's powers were considerably more limited than the English believed. The chiefdom had been pieced together from the 1570s onward by wars, threats, marriage, and diplomacy, which involved granting concessions on the part of the two great chiefs to local rulers and allowing considerable autonomy to especially powerful peoples and to those who lived on the periphery. Far from being a centralized polity ruled by a tyrannical king, Tsenacommacah was a patchwork of differing jurisdictions and districts connected by a variety of relations based on force, kinship, or mutual benefit in varying combinations; diversity was its strength but also its greatest weakness.[22]

From the earliest encounters, English-Powhatan relations had been ambiguous. Violence or the threat of violence was ever present, but so too was a desire on both sides to learn about the other and, if conditions were favorable, to trade or perhaps gain an advantage. In late April 1607, on the very first day the settlers made landfall, an exploratory party was attacked by Indians on the southern shore of the Chesapeake Bay, leaving two of the English injured. By contrast, over the next few weeks while the English surveyed the James River, they were received warmly by many of the peoples along its banks. Then, toward the end of May shortly after establishing themselves on Jamestown Island, the English were besieged in a "furious Assault" by a couple of hundred warriors who nearly overwhelmed the new settlement before being beaten back by cannon fire from the ships anchored offshore. Two settlers and several warriors were killed and many injured. Ambivalence and uncertainty characterized English-Powhatan relations for several years, and despite regular meetings between the settlers' leaders and the two great chiefs, deep distrust persisted on both sides.[23]

IN THE SUMMER OF 1609, A LARGE FLEET COMMANDED BY veteran soldier Lieutenant Governor Sir Thomas Gates left

England to reestablish Virginia. Six principal ships and three smaller vessels carried approximately five hundred settlers, including as many as eighty women and children, making up one of the largest expeditions to leave English shores for North America. The presence of women and children represented a significant shift in Company policy, which signaled a new expectation that families, rather than single men, would be the basis of self-sustaining, orderly, and stable communities in the colony.

The voyage was largely uneventful until a month and a half after leaving the south coast of England when, on July 25, a massive hurricane turned day into night, scattered the fleet, and caused severe damage to many of the ships. Disastrously, the flagship *Sea Venture*, which carried Gates and the rest of the high-ranking leaders, was separated from the fleet and driven onto reefs surrounding the Atlantic island of Bermuda. The shipwrecked colonists were forced to take refuge on Bermuda for the next ten months until they completed the construction of two small vessels from the ruins of the *Sea Venture* that would successfully carry them across the ocean to Virginia. Meanwhile, the surviving storm-tossed vessels arrived at Jamestown in August, adding 350 battered and weary survivors to the 130 settlers already there.[24]

What followed was one of the most harrowing periods in the colony's history. Much of the food brought by the new arrivals had been spoiled in the crossing, and their remaining provisions, along with what was available at the fort, were quickly consumed. John Ratcliffe reported from Jamestown in early October that the settlers were in "exceeding much need" of food. In a revealing comment, he pointed out that the Indians produced only enough food for their families and had little to trade even if they were so inclined. As for the English, they did not have enough laborers to clear the land and plant crops on a large-enough scale to support the colony's new arrivals.[25]

Conditions among the English deteriorated rapidly. The region remained in the grip of a severe drought, the worst for half a millennium, which led to severe food shortages among the Powhatans as well as the colonists. Efforts by soldiers to take the Indians' meager supplies by force proved the last straw. When the ships that had arrived in the colony in August left two months later, the Powhatans rose up against the English to "murder and spoil all they could encounter." Captain John Martin, who commanded a small fort recently constructed on the Nansemond River, abandoned his post and returned to Jamestown. Shortly after Martin's departure, seventeen men at the garrison mutinied and stole a boat, saying they intended to trade with Indians, but were never heard of again. With supplies running out, another thirteen men sought to bargain for food with the local Nansemond people and were killed. The remainder of the garrison returned to Jamestown, where they were soon joined by men who had suffered heavy losses at a garrison near the falls of the James River. Within a couple of months, attacks by the Powhatans had resulted in the deaths or desertion of approximately 130 settlers.[26]

At the end of October 1609, some three hundred men, women, and children were trapped inside Jamestown's fort. Many of them were already suffering from malnutrition and sickness, and overcrowding and unsanitary conditions allowed pestilence to spread rapidly through the settlement.

Even on short rations, the president leader, George Percy, calculated they would not be able to support themselves for more than a few months, which would leave them entirely without food in midwinter. The Powhatans, well aware of the colonists' desperate circumstances, besieged the island, killed the settlers' livestock roaming in the woods, and waited for the settlers to perish. In desperation, starving settlers consumed the small amounts of fish they caught and also devoured their horses, dogs, cats, rats, and mice. When these ran out, they ate their boot leather, starched ruffs, and other trash. Some went out beyond the palisade into the woods to "feed upon Serpents and snakes and to dig the earth for wild and unknown Roots" where they were cut off and slain by Indians. Looking "ghastly and pale in every face," Percy recalled, "nothing was spared to maintain Life and to do those things which seem incredible, as to dig up dead corpses out of graves and to eat them, and some have Licked up the Blood which had fallen from their weak fellows." Some who died in their beds were eaten by those who took up their bodies; others were killed by Powhatan warriors trying to escape the horror within the fort. Traditional markers of English civility, what they considered distinguished them from "savages," degenerated. No story, William Strachey observed, "can remember unto us, more woes, anguishes, then these people [the English], thus governed have both suffered and pulled upon their own heads." (He evidently believed the settlers were partly to blame for their own misfortunes.) When relief finally arrived in May 1610, only sixty sickly English remained alive at Jamestown, so emaciated they looked like cadavers.[27]

War with the Powhatans was disastrous for the settlers and the Virginia Company alike. Hostilities, vicious and protracted, took the form of pitched battles, skirmishes, ambushes, sieges, and brutal murders, which over the next five years led to the deaths and maiming of hundreds of English settlers and Powhatan men, women, and children. Indian communities were destroyed and prime Indian farming lands ruined. War wrecked the Company's carefully laid plans for Virginia's rapid commercial development, ruined prospects for expansion to the south of the James River into the Roanoke region, and forced Gates and subsequently Lord De La Warr and Sir Thomas Dale to focus their energies on defeating the Indian enemy rather than on profitable enterprise and the building of stable, orderly communities.

During the summer of 1610 the English retaliated, determined to wreak havoc. Reinforced by the hundreds of settlers and soldiers who had recently arrived with Lord De La Warr, the English attacked Indian communities with a systematic ferocity the Powhatans had never before experienced. De La Warr and Gates adopted scorched earth tactics, reminiscent of recent wars against the Catholic Irish. Moving troops by ships along the James River valley, soldiers shot or put to the sword Indians of all ages and both sexes, despoiled their houses and temples, and cut down and carried away their corn and plantings. The cruelty perpetrated by both sides was shocking even to battle-hardened soldiers and warriors.[28]

The appalling violence ebbed and flowed for another three years. Lord De La Warr, taking most of his ablest men, established a fort upriver at the falls in the heartland of the Powhatans' chiefdom, where fierce fighting pinned down the

English during the winter. Chronic sickness forced De La Warr to return to England in the spring of 1611, but in May another seasoned veteran of the wars against the Irish and Spanish, Sir Thomas Dale, arrived with 300 men, bringing the total English population to approximately 750. Dale replaced Gates as the colony's leader and immediately set about rebuilding Jamestown, fortifying the garrisons at the mouth of the James River, and dispatching more than half the new English arrivals fifty miles upriver to the Indian town of Arrohattoc, where they laid out a spacious new settlement that Dale named Henrico in honor of his patron, Prince Henry, the heir to the throne. Following the Virginia Company's instructions, Henrico was to be the principal English settlement, "a convenient, strong, healthy, and sweet seat," secure from attack by Spanish warships, which the English rightly judged a persistent threat, and nearer to the mountains where precious minerals might be found. Dale was confident that gaining control of the James River from its mouth to the falls and establishing settlements at strategic locations along its banks would "so over master" the Powhatans that Chief Wahunsonacock would have little choice but to abandon his territories or come to terms with the English and agree to live in peace.[29]

The two chiefs were fully aware of English intentions. Years earlier Wahunsonacock had told Captain John Smith that the settlers had come not to trade but to possess his country. The arrival of hundreds of more colonists with De La Warr, Dale, and Gates together with the establishment of new English settlements, particularly at Henrico and its environs, confirmed the chief's assessment. For Wahunsonacock and his peoples, the war was no longer an effort to expel the intruders from their lands or contain and control them but had evolved into a struggle for the very survival of Tsenacommacah. Defeat might lead to the breakup of the chiefdom and the Powhatans' reduction to mere tributary status, subservient to the settlers.

For their part, English leaders in Virginia and London understood that the outcome of the war would strongly influence the success of their entire venture. The future of English America hung in the balance and, as Anglican clerics never tired of reminding Company leaders, so did English hopes of prevailing in their divinely appointed task of converting the Indians to Christianity and the Church of England. This "work [of conversion] is of God," the Reverend William Crashaw declared, "and will therefore stand." God was the settlers' friend and protector. If the English failed, it could only be their fault, a consequence of the settlers' corrupt and unworthy nature.[30]

When it eventually came, the arrival of peace was almost an anticlimax; no decisive battle marked the end of the war but rather a kidnapping that offered a convenient pretext for negotiations. In the spring of 1613, one of Wahunsonacock's favored daughters, Pocahontas, was abducted by a prominent English mariner and colonist, Captain Samuel Argall, trading along the Potomac River for corn. She was well known to the English from her many visits to James Fort before the outbreak of hostilities and for her friendship with Captain John Smith. Over the next year, her captivity at Jamestown was a vital bargaining chip in talks between Wahunsonacock and Dale to bring hostilities to an end, the English offering to return her in exchange for stolen weapons, English prisoners, and a "ship full of Corn." Perhaps to the English commander's surprise, the great chief eventually agreed to terms that were sufficient to satisfy both sides and to allow both to conclude an agreement without losing face. After years of killings, destruction of settlements, slaughter of livestock, and despoiling of crops, both sides, the English hoped, could look forward to living in harmony.[31]

———•———

IN EARLY APRIL 1614, POCAHONTAS, NOW CHRISTENED REbecca, wed gentleman-planter John Rolfe before the chancel rail of Jamestown's first church, sealing the new peace accord. But neither the English nor the Powhatans fully comprehended the union's implications. Wahunsonacock had grudgingly come to accept that his warriors were unable to rid his lands of the invaders in the near future, yet he had not capitulated and did not view his people as a conquered nation. The truce, as he saw it, was just as beneficial to the English as it was to him. Both sides were exhausted, and he may have interpreted the alliance brought about by his daughter's marriage as an agreement by the English to not expand their settlements any farther and to coexist on equal terms. Marriage alliances, after all, were a familiar aspect of Powhatan diplomacy in building relationships and forging alliances with neighboring peoples.

English leaders, especially Sir Thomas Dale, on the other hand, viewed the peace quite differently. The English had beaten back Powhatan attacks, consolidated their hold on the James River valley, and entered into independent alliances with several peoples of the Powhatan chiefdom, undermining the influence of the great chief. The conversion of Pocahontas and her subsequent marriage to an Englishman seemed to presage success in the great work of bringing the Powhatans to Christianity. The "knowledge and true worship of Jesus Christ," Rolfe wrote, would bring "1000s of poor, wretched, and misbelieving people: on whose faces a good Christian cannot look, without sorrow, pity, and commiseration" to the true faith. God's house could now be erected in a new country by a people divinely appointed to possess it.[32]

More tangibly, the Virginia Company anticipated the end of hostilities would promote long-hoped-for commercial success. Virginia's potential could not be doubted. "Let me tell you all at home this one thing, and I pray remember it," Dale wrote forcefully to Sir Thomas Smythe, "if you give over this country and lose it, you with your wisdoms will leap [at] such a gudgeon [false bait] as our state has not done the like since they lost the Kingdom of France . . . The more I range the country the more I admire it. I have seen the best countries in Europe: I protest to you before the Living God, put them all together, this country will be equivalent unto them if it be inhabited with good people." Besides a variety of natural commodities, industrial commodities such as pitch, tar, potashes, and charcoal were being produced, and some planters were beginning to cultivate new goods such as silk grass, hemp, and tobacco. John Rolfe had been experimenting with tobacco seeds brought from Bermuda (and possibly the Spanish West Indies) for a couple of years to create a strain of Virginia leaf palatable to English taste. Anyone could grow it, the influential planter Ralph Hamor wrote, and he judged a crop would provide sufficient profit for all the planters' needs with relatively little labor.[33]

But despite Company hopes, the colony's fortunes continued to languish. John Chamberlain, Jacobean London's busy correspondent and court observer, spoke for many dissatisfied investors when he observed that "I hear not of any other riches or matter of worth, but only some quantity of Sassafras, tobacco, pitch, and clapboard, things of no great value." No "present profit" was to be expected, he concluded. Approximately £30,000 had been spent on the colony since 1609, a vast sum for the time, but by the time Dale set off from Jamestown for England in the spring of 1616, accompanied by Pocahontas/Rebecca, John Rolfe, their baby son, Thomas, and an entourage of Powhatans, there had been very little return. The enormous effort and expense of outfitting the expeditions of Gates, De La Warr, and Dale, involving some two dozen ships carrying 1,300 soldiers and settlers between 1609 and 1611, together with the failure of various Company schemes to raise support and money in England, had left the Company's coffers bare.

During the war, the reputation of the colony had sunk so low in London that the Company had been forced to declare that anyone who returned from Jamestown and was discovered spreading "vile and slanderous reports" would be sent back to the colony immediately for punishment. Rumors told of settlers living in such extreme misery that many had abandoned civility and fled to the Indians. It was later claimed that settlers were "Constrained to serve the Colony as if they had been slaves, 7 or 8 years for their freedoms," and put to "as hard and servile labor as the basest Fellow that was brought out of Newgate." All of which was "contrary to the express Letter of the King in his most gracious Charter." The Company, as might be expected, took a very different view. In the midst of war and owing to the poor caliber of many of those recruited, Virginia's leaders considered they had had little alternative other than to enforce martial law. Dale, for example, had complained bitterly that of the men he had brought with him to the colony in 1611, the great majority were "so profane, so riotous, so full of mutiny and treasonable Intentions" that were it not for their names, it would be doubted they were Christians.[34]

The recruitment of new settlers had dried up and the settler population in Virginia dwindled to less than half of what it had been during its high point. Back in London in the summer of 1616, Dale argued that he had "left the colony in great prosperity and peace, contrary to many men's expectations." Peace had indeed been achieved, but to assert the colony enjoyed "great prosperity" was a wild exaggeration. A survey by John Rolfe of the same year revealed only 351 settlers living in the colony, scattered in five areas along the James River and one across the bay on the Eastern Shore. A small number, Rolfe remarked, "to advance so great a *Work*." Consequently, the most pressing need was the recruitment of "good and sufficient men": the highborn to command, soldiers to make discoveries and defend the colony, and farmers, craftsmen, and laborers to promote profitable enterprises. With such men Virginia would become self-reliant in provisions, valuable commodities might yet be found inland, and towns and shipping built. Many things, he concluded, "might come with ease to establish a firm and perfect Commonweal."

While the colony was secured for the time being against the Powhatans, Sir Thomas Smythe and other Company leaders in London were fully aware that if Virginia were to survive, they had to attract significantly more investors and settlers as quickly as possible.[35]

Two

The Great Reforms

We have thought good to . . . the settling there of
A laudable form of Government by Magistracy and
just Laws for the happy guiding and governing of
the people.

—*Virginia Company of London (1618)*

And these laws and ordinances are not to be
chested or hidden like a candle under a bushel, but
in form of a Magna Charta to be published to the
whole colony.

—*Anonymous, "R. F." (1618)*

BESIDES PROMOTING COMMERCE, COMPANIES INVOLVED
in empire building were also responsible for establishing governments overseas. The broad range of proclamations
and instructions issued by Virginia Company leaders during
the great reforms of 1619 were designed first and foremost

to create an effective form of government and civil society based on the idea of a commercial commonwealth—trade, prosperity, and Company profits would follow from good government. Of the developments that shaped this process, two stand out above all others: the establishment of private property and Company leaders' decision to curtail martial law and end the military regime they had sanctioned. Sir Edwin Sandys and other officials of the Company who supported him were convinced that the most effective means of attracting substantial investment in the colony and large numbers of immigrants was to offer tangible incentives in the form of property. The shift from a society based on Company control of the land to a society founded on individual ownership was momentous and necessarily required wholesale changes to the way the colony was governed. Safeguarding private property was of paramount importance since without security of ownership the Company would not be able to persuade settlers or investors to involve themselves in the venture. Private property, just laws, and good government were all of a piece.[1]

———

BY THE TERMS OF ITS CHARTERS, LAND WITHIN THE BOUNDS of the Company's grant was under the authority and at the disposal of the Company's leadership. The charters of 1609 and 1612 had given the Company formal control of a vast area that encompassed much of the mid-Atlantic coastal region as well as unexplored territories to the west. Indian occupation of lands was recognized, but their absolute right of possession was not. While English colonizers were prohibited from claiming American regions possessed by other Christian sovereigns, notably the Spanish and Portuguese, they had the moral and legal right to settle lands inhabited by "heathens" and "savages." Any number of justifications could be cited, from European laws that guaranteed the rights of Christians to trade wherever and with whom they wished to the "Law of God," which enjoined monarchs to conquer "barbarous" peoples for the advancement of God's word. From the very beginning of European colonization of America in the late fifteenth century, successive popes and monarchs had legitimized taking and inhabiting Indian lands.[2]

The different forms of landed property that might be adopted in the colony—small farms, large plantations, or corporate holdings—and exactly how individual or collective interests would be protected by law were vital considerations, the outcomes of which would have major implications not only for Virginia but all English colonies that followed. At first, no particular plan governed the introduction of private property other than expediency. The Virginia Company had sought initially to avoid conflict with local Indians by occupying only what they believed were vacant lands, but the onset of war in 1609 changed Jamestown's leaders' attitudes. Settlers quickly began taking up prime Indian lands along the James River valley.

Toward the end of the war Sir Thomas Dale had been forced to allow some of his men their own land as a means of encouraging increased food production. He had initially tried to compel them to work harder by adopting tough measures to supply the common store, but after several years it was clear the effort had failed. Most of them avoided work at all costs, actively hoping to bring about the collapse of the colony and their return home. With little personal incentive to produce more than the bare minimum, yields remained perilously low. "When our people were fed out of the common store," planter and publicist Ralph Hamor explained, "and labored jointly in the manuring of the ground, and planting corn, glad was that man that could slip from his labor, nay the most honest of them in a general business, would take so much faithful and true pains, in a week, as now he will do in a day."

Finally, Dale divided his men into companies and permitted some of them to raise crops of their own and tend livestock. Then he allotted smallholdings, three to twelve acres of cleared ground, to those "in the nature of Farmers" who had completed seven years' service to the Company and were granted their freedom. As long as they provided for their own households and agreed to serve in the local militia when required, they were permitted to work for themselves eleven months of the year; the twelfth month they were obliged to work for the Company in respect of the common good. They were also allowed to grow tobacco or other crops if they maintained two of the three acres under corn. In this way, the colony quickly became self-sufficient: three men, Hamor reported, producing as much as thirty had previously, and the settlers thereby not only able to support themselves but potentially to provision hundreds of new arrivals the Company was planning to send over. By the end of 1614, approximately ninety independent smallholdings had been created in the colony. Dale's new course was the first tentative acknowledgment by the Company that if settlers were permitted to work partly for their own profit, food production would increase significantly.[3]

Another innovation was to prove equally significant. Much of the population growth that occurred after the colony was relaunched in 1609 had taken place fifty miles upriver from Jamestown at new settlements established by Gates and Dale during the war. Seized from the Appomattocs in revenge for attacks on the English, Dale considered the especially fertile area at the mouth of the Appomattox River an ideal location for the cultivation of corn and development of various industries. Resolved "to possess and plant it," Dale named it the New Bermudas, or Bermuda Hundred, after the Atlantic islands where the English had been shipwrecked a few years before. In the heartland of the Powhatan chiefdom, the English fortified the area and scores of Company soldiers and laborers moved in. Sometime in 1614, he issued a "patent" (order) that incorporated the settlement and gave inhabitants certain unique rights and extensive common lands in return for their service over the next few years, after which they would be free. The precise terms of the patent no longer exist, but Dale clearly believed the potential of Bermuda Hundred was sufficiently promising that it was worth experimenting with a general grant of privileges to the community as a whole.[4]

The next step, encouraged by Sir Thomas Smythe and other leading Company officers, followed in the spring of 1616. Drawing upon the experience of the early introduction of private land ownership on the island of Bermuda—which as a commercial venture had proven far more successful than Virginia—a declaration was issued in London stating the Company's intent to allocate Virginia's extensive lands to settlers and investors both existing and prospective. The English, the Company proclaimed in a gross overstatement, were now "by the Natives liking and consent, in actual possession of a great part of the Country," and as a consequence were ready to proceed with a general distribution of land. In other words, whether they had once been settled by local peoples or not, investors and adventurers could feel secure in their possession under the terms of the general distribution and new laws that would shortly follow. Those who had been in the colony for at least seven years, together with investors who had previously purchased shares in the venture or planned to buy shares in the future, would receive 50 acres. Investors would get 50 acres for every share with the possibility of another 150 acres per share to come. Land would be made available along both sides of the James River and near established settlements, not in remote places, and property would be granted to individual owners and their heirs under the Company's authority. The division would be undertaken by "a new Governor with Commissioners and surveyors to be sent from hence" to assure every man received a fair allotment.[5]

For the English, land was the key to unlocking Virginia's potential. They hoped that extensive grants would attract investors' and merchants' interest in the colony both short and long term. The first of a series of large-scale land grants was made by the Company to important individual investors and private associations ("societies of adventurers") as an immediate measure to improve the Company's still languishing finances. Terms were vague and extremely generous, reflecting the Company's desperation for funds and more settlers and investors for the private development of lands. Captain Samuel Argall, appointed deputy governor in the winter of

1616–1617, and his financial backers were assigned 2,400 acres just west of Jamestown for the recruitment of two dozen colonists. A grant of similar size, fifteen miles farther upriver, was awarded to another former deputy governor, George Yeardley, in recognition of his services to the colony and as acknowledgment of a gift of land from the powerful Indian chief Opechancanough of the same year. Both grants were dwarfed by two others made to syndicates of powerful merchants: Smith's Hundred (named for the Company treasurer, Sir Thomas Smith) and Martin's Hundred. The first comprised between eighty thousand and one hundred thousand acres (125–150 square miles) along the north bank of the James River from the Chickahominy to the lands of the Weyanocks and was operated as a private joint stock venture that included among its principal investors a roll call of the Company's leading officers. Martin's Hundred, also a private joint stock enterprise a few miles downriver from Jamestown, was of similar size and was organized by a group of "ancient adventurers," the Society of Martin's Hundred, who had been long associated with the colony and who worked diligently to recruit hundreds of settlers to make the venture profitable.[6]

What is striking about these early "particular" (private) plantations is that their extensive privileges allowed them to be virtually independent of the Virginia Company. Each of them assumed the role of a local unit of administration equal in status to those already established by Dale's forts and hundreds. They ran their own affairs in England, raised funds, recruited settlers, and furnished themselves with ships and supplies and in return were permitted to produce whatever crops or commodities they wished and trade with whomever and wherever they wanted without any payment to the Company. Across the river from Smith's Hundred, for example, Captain John Martin, a survivor from Jamestown's earliest days, acquired an extraordinary grant. On his plantation, named Martin's Brandon, he governed "in as large and ample manner" as any lord in England. He was given the right of free trade throughout the Chesapeake Bay and along its rivers, including the privilege of holding "convenient markets" on his land that allowed him to enter into commercial relations with anyone he wished.

Commanders of other settlements were also granted great latitude. With the advice of senior members of their companies, they were allowed "to make Orders, Ordinances and Constitutions for the better ordering and directing of their Servants and business Provided they be not Repugnant to the Laws of England." These settlements were modeled on similar grants in Ireland where huge estates worked by tenants were awarded to individuals and powerful companies of merchants in return for their commitment to settle and improve the land. During a particularly low point in their fortunes, Company leaders believed that such liberal grants were necessary. Yet the ad hoc dispersal of governing authority to particular plantations threatened to undermine the entire basis of government in Virginia, creating the possibility that the colony might disintegrate into a score of quasi-autonomous fiefdoms.[7]

Nonetheless, it was precisely the privileges associated with particular plantations, along with the promise of large amounts of cheap land, that attracted investors who saw great potential in tobacco cultivation. The spectacular growth of tobacco production and resulting profits from markets in

London and elsewhere proved another key stimulus to sustained investment and immigration. Instead of a hardscrabble existence producing small amounts of goods of limited value for trade, even smallholders could make a handsome living from high-quality tobacco. In short, it was an ideal poor man's crop as long as demand was buoyant.

Introduced into England half a century before by mariners who had sailed to Spanish America as privateers, tobacco quickly became fashionable with London's elite during the 1580s and 1590s. Depending on its quality and condition, leaf imported (legally or otherwise) from Spanish colonies might sell for up to £2 or £4 per pound in London. Despite the expense, smoking spread rapidly from the gentry to the lower classes. According to Barnaby Rich, a contemporary critic of the "nicotian weed," there was not a groom so base who "comes into an Alehouse to call for his pot but he must have his pipe of Tobacco." Bermuda led the way, exporting nearly 20,000 pounds in 1617 worth £2,355 on the London market. By contrast, a mere 1,250 pounds were exported from Virginia in 1616 worth just £141; but in the following year, 9,000 pounds were shipped, and in 1618 almost 25,000 pounds valued at nearly £3,000.

Planter Ralph Hamor described with unrestrained enthusiasm "the valuable commodity Tobacco of such esteem in England . . . which every man may plant, and with the least part of his labor, tend and care will return him both clothes and other necessaries." In the summer of 1617, Deputy Governor Samuel Argall found Jamestown's marketplace and streets "and all other spare places planted with Tobacco." Elsewhere, planters were "dispersed all about" busily attending to their crops. The Company did not approve of the planters' reliance on tobacco, which it considered likely a short-lived fashion, and encouraged a diversified economy of crops and manufactures, but as more private plantations were established and profits from leaf remained buoyant, Company leaders could at least take satisfaction from the rapidly increasing numbers of settlers who were moving to the colony.[8]

The Company's willingness to allow individuals or groups of investors to own private property in the colony was a decisive turning point at the end of Jamestown's first decade. Company leaders were aware, however, that merely dispensing land grants, large or small, was insufficient. Without firm guarantees that their property rights and investments would be protected against arbitrary seizure or embezzlement, settlers, especially those of means, would not be tempted to move to the colony; the risk to themselves and their property would be too great. A fresh course was adopted, therefore, to give assurance that the rule of law would be applied as closely as possible to English traditions and precedent.

KING JAMES I WAS THE FOUNT OF LAW AND "AUTHORITY OF all things" in England and its dependencies. His royal prerogatives included the sovereign right to govern, conducting relations with foreign nations, regulating trade, and declaring war and peace. The king also enjoyed ordinary or limited prerogatives that were constrained by English custom and practice, such as property rights, existing parliamentary statutes, and the common law, known collectively as the "ancient constitution" as handed down from time out of mind. English monarchs were expected to abide by these laws and customs with the advice of their councilors and approbation of Parliament, a form of mixed rule that distinguished Christian kings from tyrants. Significantly, however, these limitations applied only in England, not to overseas colonies. Parliament and the common law had no jurisdiction in Virginia, although the principle of common law would be asserted in the colony after 1618. English lands beyond the seas, historian Ken MacMillan writes, were "ruled by the king alone rather than the king-in-parliament," an absolute right that would have profound consequences for the colony and ultimately all of British America.[9]

Monarchs were divinely appointed to oversee the well-being of their subjects. In *The Trew Law of Free Monarchies*, James compared his duty to his people to those of a loving father or of the night watchman to their charges, who must "foresee and prevent all dangers, that are likely to fall upon them and to maintain concord, wealth, and civility among them." The sacred ritual of coronation confirmed the vital bond and reciprocal duties that existed between the monarch and his subjects. "As the Father [because] of his fatherly duty is bound to care for the nourishing, education, and virtuous government of his children; even so is a king bound to care for all his subjects." *All* James's subjects included those living overseas in Europe and America. The king made this duty clear in the Virginia Company's first charter, declaring that

> all and every persons being our subjects which shall dwell
> and inhabit within every or any of the said several Colonies

and plantations and every of their children which shall happen to be born within the limits and precincts of the said several Colonies and plantations, shall have and enjoy all liberties Franchises and Immunities within any of our other dominions to all intents and Purposes, as if they had been abiding and born within this our Realm of England or any other of our said Dominions.

For the good of the people, James affirmed, the substance of laws should be as close as possible "to the Common Laws [of] England, and equity thereof." This clause was repeated nearly word for word in the charter of 1609 and in an abbreviated form in that of 1612.[10]

Yet kingly guarantees of subjects' rights did not contradict the Virginia Company's own extensive powers. Initially, only James had the right to make laws for the colony, but in 1609 he delegated authority to the Company's council in London to establish laws, magistracy, and forms of government that were "fit and necessary" for the colony. The rights of English settlers in Virginia were generally under the protection of the king, but such stipulations did not restrict the Company from employing a broad range of English laws and legal processes as conditions in the colony warranted. England was governed by many different varieties of law—statute, common law, ecclesiastical, manorial, and martial—and the Company could draw upon any of them as needed.

Conciliar government, for example, offered an important precedent that could be readily applied to settlements on the margins of the English Atlantic world. In the late fifteenth and sixteenth centuries, the threat of serious disorder or even rebellion on England's borders, far removed from the seat of government at Westminster, had persuaded Tudor monarchs to establish special courts to control marcher (lawless) lands. These conciliar courts, historian David Konig has commented, were "virtually beyond accountability," and wielded enormous powers locally, unchecked by common law procedures such as trial by jury. Ruling councils were similarly adopted by the Company to conduct its affairs in London and Virginia. Even more extreme, as in Ireland where the use of military commissions and martial law brought about years of bloodshed and scorched earth campaigns that had left broad swaths of the country wasted, so in Virginia similar tactics were adopted by successive military commanders in the war against the Powhatans. Authoritarian councils and martial law emerged as the dominant forms of government in Virginia down to 1619.[11]

THE WHOLESALE CHANGES THAT LED TO THE OVERHAUL OF the colony's laws and government probably coalesced sometime during 1616 following Dale's return to England. Complaints about the corruption of governors in Virginia such as Captain Samuel Argall and of Company leaders in London, who were more concerned with "their own immoderate gain" than the general welfare of ordinary planters, were sufficiently common by 1617 as to cause serious concern among supporters of the venture that the entire enterprise was at risk. Formulated by an uneasy alliance of Company magnates, Sir Thomas Smythe, alderman Robert Johnson, Sir Robert Rich, Sir Edwin Sandys, and Sir Henry Wriothesley, the Earl of Southampton, the plan came to fruition over the next couple of years.[12]

Sandys was the principal architect of the great reform program. Described by a contemporary as "our Solon and Licurgus" in reference to two legendary Greek lawmakers, he was uniquely qualified for the task. Born in 1561, his father and namesake was one of the most prominent clerics in the newly established Church of England, eventually rising to become the archbishop of York, the second-most powerful position in the Anglican hierarchy. Appropriate to his rank, the young Sandys profited from an impeccable education. At Corpus Christi College, Oxford, he was taught the virtues of civic and Christian humanism that drew upon the wisdom of ancient Greek and Roman philosophers and statesmen as applied to his own times by a host of prominent European intellectuals. At Oxford, he also formed an enduring friendship with the brilliant scholar Richard Hooker and later assisted him with the preparation and publication of what was to become Hooker's masterpiece, *Of the Laws of Ecclesiastical Polity*, a staunch defense of Anglican faith and practice against Puritan critics. Sandys's own desire to promote a moderate form of Anglicanism in the Church of England, likely derived from his father and Hooker's influence, was a vital influence on his ideas for reform in Virginia.[13]

Following the accession of James I in March 1603 and the king's contentious first session of Parliament the next year, Sandys suddenly burst upon the national scene. Putting his prodigious energy and intellect at the service of Parliament, he quickly established himself as a relentless critic of the king's political agenda and leader of the opposition in

FIGURE 2—Sir Edwin Sandys was treasurer of the Virginia Company and a leading member of the House of Commons throughout the reign of James I. He was the inspiration for the series of reforms that thoroughly overhauled the Company and the colony after 1619. Courtesy of Mr. Edward Sandys.

the House of Commons. He was involved in all the major confrontations with James and his ministers over the next twenty years, issues related to the king's repeated financial demands, challenges to the House of Commons' privileges, James's strong desire to bring about a constitutional union between England and Scotland (he styled himself king of Great Britain), and the extent of James's royal prerogative. Sandys spoke for the majority of the Commons when he opposed monopolies that gave court favorites exclusive privileges that restricted freedom of commerce for everyone else. It was "against the natural right and liberty of the subjects of England," he declared, "to restrain a [trade] into the hands of some few." He organized the opposition to the union with Scotland, which earned him the displeasure of the king for blocking a measure close to his heart. Within a few years, he emerged as one of the major spokesmen of the country's independent gentry by championing the "ancient constitution," and he voiced the Commons' concerns about their privileges and the rights of subjects being undermined—"Parliament is no Parliament, if not free."[14]

Sandys was, at the same time, becoming increasingly influential in the Virginia Company. Owing to his reputation as a fervent defender of free trade and his awareness of trade issues generally, he was sought out by merchants and gentry with significant overseas commercial interests and persuaded to join the king's council for Virginia in 1607. The translation of the Virginia enterprise into a national undertaking fueled by religious zeal and Christian humanist rhetoric doubtless appealed to Sandys. Over the next several years, the extent of his participation in the colony's affairs is unclear. He may have assisted with the drafting of the Company's 1609 charter and likely was one of the leading councilors involved in efforts to raise money throughout the country on behalf of the Company then and thereafter.

During the first half of the 1610s, Sandys had been content to leave the running of the Company to Sir Thomas Smythe and his associates. By the time he eventually took charge in all but name in 1618, however, he had come to the realization that simply responding to particular problems one by one would be insufficient to solve the colony's most serious challenges. Even if a series of discrete solutions had been possible, the effort would have fallen far short of his overall vision. What he and his supporters proposed was nothing less than the founding of a new type of society in Virginia built on good government, just laws, Protestant morality, and rewards for everyone who invested or settled in the colony. Contrast this with society in England where huge numbers of people lived in dire poverty without regular work and had no land or property of their own. The masterless men and women, vagrants, and idle poor who swarmed to the towns and cities bringing disorder and diseases were notorious for their dissolute ways. Few of Sandys's contemporaries understood the importance of what the Company under Sandys's leadership was about to attempt—the reformation of English society in the New World—just as few historians have comprehended the reform program's singular originality and scope.[15]

Sandys was ably supported by a number of notable courtiers, politicians, and merchants. The Earl of Southampton was a seasoned member of James's court, a privy councilor, and a major investor in the Virginia Company as well as other overseas ventures, although he is best remembered today as William Shakespeare's patron and possible lover. He remained a steadfast ally of Sandys throughout the period, even when Sandys fell out of favor with the king, and succeeded him as treasurer in 1620. John Ferrar and Nicholas Ferrar were equally faithful lieutenants of Sandys as well as the administrative workhorses of the Company. Sons of a wealthy London merchant who had made a fortune in the privateering war against Spain, they would both serve as deputy treasurer and were zealous supporters of the entire reform program, especially the commitment to convert the Powhatans to Christianity and to found a Christian commonwealth. These four men, together with Sir William, Lord Cavendish, and Sir John Danvers, both experienced parliamentarians, were the leading advocates for a commonwealth in Virginia that emphasized the rule of law and consent of the governed. They were the first founders of representative government in America.[16]

———•———

THE MAJOR REFORMS THAT TOOK PLACE IN 1619 WERE EM-braced in a series of commissions and instructions issued by the Company to the new governor, Sir George Yeardley. In mid-November 1618, he was ordered to establish a "laudable form of government by Magistracy and just Laws . . . for the happy guiding and governing of the people." Subsequently known as the "great Charter," the instructions were designed broadly to restrain arbitrary rule and to establish a government founded firmly on the rule of law. The immediate objective, however, was more modest and focused on a variety

of serious practical problems that required Yeardley's immediate attention. He was to raise provisions for the hundreds
of new colonists who would shortly arrive, lay out public
lands to support the colony's principal officers, announce the
long-awaited distribution of land to "ancient planters" (those
who had arrived in Virginia before April 1616), and apportion
land to newcomers and shareholders. The entire apparatus
for dispensing, confirming, and recording land grants was to
be thoroughly overhauled to prevent a repetition of abuses of
the previous two years when large land grants had been made
to individuals favored by former deputy governor Argall with
little reference to the Company. Yeardley was also instructed

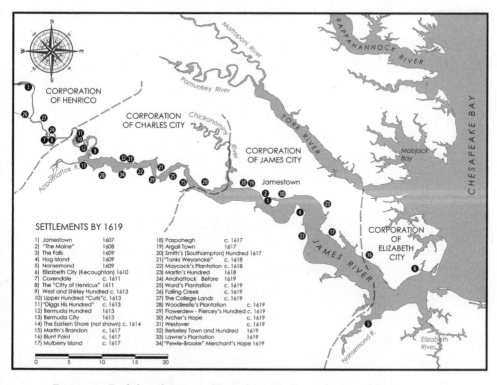

FIGURE 3—English settlements in Virginia in 1619. Drawn by Jamie May.

to confirm legitimate individual and Company land grants to underline the Company's determination to protect private property.[17]

Ensuring orderly settlement along the James River valley and establishing local government were closely related priorities. Yeardley acted quickly to organize dispersed settlements into four new jurisdictional units termed "Cities or Burroughs": Jamestown, Charles City, and Henrico upriver and Kecoughtan, later Elizabeth City, at the mouth of the James River.

As largely self-governing civic bodies, the boroughs would enable the establishment of law and order guided by directives handed down by the Company via the governor, council of state, and the General Assembly. Although the great charter is frustratingly vague about the form the boroughs' governing bodies would take, we can surmise that the Company had in mind that each would have a local council similar to those of incorporated (chartered) towns in England led by captains or chief officers. They were to be responsible, among other duties, for overseeing the public lands, encouraging the Company's economic plans, and maintaining lists of the living and the dead as well as marriages and christenings. Boroughs and particular plantations would have their own monthly courts for "all small and petty matters" and would be responsible for the enfranchisement of male landowners, tenants, and servants to allow them to vote for their local representatives to sit in the General Assembly. Existing and planned particular plantations were granted similar privileges but with provisions that severely limited the generous terms they had been formerly granted, which were now viewed as highly detrimental to the welfare of the colony. Yeardley was to ensure that these private plantations were part of "one body corporate and live under Equal and like Law and orders with the rest of the Colony." By this highly significant measure, the potentially corrosive drift of the colony's government toward multiple proprietary and independent jurisdictions was brought to an abrupt halt. There would now be one civic authority at Jamestown, governing over the four corporations and the particular plantations.[18]

Little indication is given in Yeardley's commissions and instructions of the broader thinking that informed the new direction taken by the Company. However, a letter of early December 1618 written by "R. F.," possibly Richard Ferrar, the youngest brother of John and Nicholas, provides a unique insight into Sandys's and his associates' far-reaching ambitions.

R. F.'s main purpose in penning his letter was to assure the recipient, also anonymous, that martial law and the largely unrestricted powers of the governor would be brought to an end and therefore that future investments in the colony would be safe. "[M]atters are no more to be carried [on] haphazardly [or arbitrarily] in a Marshalls court," he wrote, "or after the uncertain and unlimited humor of one man but there is now a council of estate erected to assist and advise the governor in all his courses." All disputes, whether civil or criminal, were to be judged and resolved according to "our laws and customs here in England," and the Company had devised many "excellent laws and Ordinances," designed specifically to meet the needs of the colony. These laws, R. F. underlined, do not "like the traditions of the Pharisees lay heavy burthens [taxes or impositions] upon the people, but contrariwise do bring them liberty and reward," and were to be expressly set down so that every person would know what they could trust and "what he or she may forever challenge as their right."

The care the Company accorded to settlers' rights was given further emphasis in one of R. F.'s most revealing passages, spelling out what the rule of law meant as applied to Virginia:

> Lastly they [the laws] set down what lands or immunities every person is presently to enjoy, according to their merit and quality, and what duties they are tied to, besides many other excellent particulars too long here to write, a copy whereof I will provide you against your coming up to London the next term. And these laws and ordinances are not to be chested or hidden like a candle under a bushel, *but in form of a Magna Charta* [my italics] to be published to the whole colony, to the end every particular person though never so mean, may both for his own right challenge it and in case he be at any time wronged, though by the best of the country, he may have law to allege for his speedy remedy.

It was a remarkable promise that decisively addressed the wrongs of the past and set a bold course for the future. The rights and responsibilities of settlers were to be explicit, and all, from the lowest to the highest, would have the same standing before the law. As in the case "of a Magna Charta," the new laws and ordinances would be published throughout the colony to make sure everyone knew their rights and would be able to appeal for justice should they have cause.[19]

TWO OTHER MAJOR INNOVATIONS OF 1619 THAT WOULD HAVE enduring significance were the establishment of the council of state and a General Assembly. A governor's council was not new; it had first been created in 1609 to support Lord De La Warr's administration but was merely an advisory body and councilors served at his pleasure, and De La Warr had the authority to appoint and dismiss them as he wished. Members of the new council of state, by contrast, were appointed by the Company to govern in partnership with the governor, the latter being first among equals. Decisions were taken by a majority vote, and if a tie resulted, the governor would cast the deciding vote. Councilors were expected to assist the governor in encouraging settlers to maintain "Justice and Christian Conversation among themselves" and advance the "honor and service of almighty God" by seeking ways to promote the Anglican faith among Indian peoples. Together with the governor, they comprised the colony's superior court, named variously the Quarter or General Court.

The significance of the General Court, legal historian Paul Halliday points out, has been overshadowed by the General Assembly but was just as important, if not more so, in establishing new laws and precedent. Owing to the volume of business, monthly courts as well as quarterly sessions were held to oversee the application of the colony's laws as the council created them and to ensure the efficient upkeep of borough and particular plantations' vital records that would be sent to the Company on a regular basis. In regard to the former, the governor and his councilors serving as judges in the General Court borrowed freely from a wide variety of

English jurisprudence. Given its broad range of judicial, legislative, and executive functions, it is hardly surprising that the council became the backbone of successive colonial administrations, a powerful and enduring institution by which daily supervision of Virginia's affairs was maintained and promoted. Yet the concentration of power in the hands of a minority of wealthy planter-merchants, together with the lack of oversight from English central courts, could encourage the exercise of "naked self-interest" on the part of councilors in formulating a new "customary law" for Virginia, especially in regard to processes governing land distribution and terms of servant and slave labor.[20]

The second of the two "Supreme Councils" was the General Assembly. R. F. described it as "a general council" that was to convene annually or more frequently if circumstances required it. For some Company leaders, the term *council* may have been closer to the form and function they initially had in mind, corresponding to the governing courts in London where shareholders could have a say in the Company's affairs and vote on important issues; none of the leaders wished to promote "popular government" in Virginia or weaken their control over the colony. Even so, there was an obvious distinction between the Company's courts, in effect meetings of stockholders, and the General Assembly, which was an elected body that represented the settlers. By endowing the people with their own governing assembly, the Company further strengthened the colony's emerging commonwealth and also its ties to the sovereign authority in England. "The highly symbolic creation of a Virginia parliament," Alexander Haskell comments, "established the *corpus mysticum* in which the king's own sovereign will was theoretically bound" and was an explicit appeal to principles of England's "ancient constitution" in the colony. Just as in the mother country the king-in-parliament was the ultimate expression of sovereignty, so in Virginia the creation of a parliament-like representative body confirmed the colony's conformity with England's traditional balance of powers between monarchy, aristocracy, and democracy.[21]

The assembly was unquestionably a representative body. In late June 1619, Sir George Yeardley sent writs to the colony's corporations, hundreds, and private plantations ordering the selection of two "sufficient" men from each jurisdiction to be decided by male freeholders and tenants by a "plurality of voices." Called *burgesses,* in acknowledgment of their role as representatives of the newly founded boroughs, they were to join the governor and his council in a single body at Jamestown. Following the maxim that "every man will more willingly obey laws to which he hath yielded his consent," planters would henceforth be able to participate in government and promote measures for their own and the general good. Settlers, the leadership believed, could not object to Company policies if they were given an opportunity to consider them by way of their representatives' deliberations in the assembly.

The beginning of self-government in the form of the General Assembly was one of the most important political events to take place in British America before the Revolution, and yet its founding role in this country's democratic experiment is almost completely overlooked.[22] Convened on Friday, July 30, 1619, the assembly met in the heat and humidity of a typical Virginia summer. Thirty men gathered in the newly built church at Jamestown: Governor Yeardley, his four councilors—Samuel Maycock, Captain Nathaniel Powell, John Rolfe, and the secretary of the colony, John Pory—and twenty-two burgesses representing the four corporations and seven private plantations. Yeardley acted in the capacity of president, overseeing deliberations and exercising the powers of veto, adjournment, and dissolution. He probably selected Pory for the office of speaker before the assembly convened and the appointment was confirmed before proceedings got under way. How Pory came to be styled speaker is uncertain. He may have proposed the title himself to distinguish his role from his more general duties as the colony's secretary, although his responsibilities in the assembly were almost entirely clerical. Without doubt, his adopted title of speaker was derived from the House of Commons in which Pory had sat as a member for Bridgwater, Somerset, between 1605 and 1611. The assemblymen adopted English parliamentary procedures from the start, determined not be perceived in London as a mere local council on the fringes of the English-speaking world.[23]

Before business commenced, acknowledging that "men's affairs do little prosper where God's service is neglected," the assembly gathered in prayer led by the Reverend Richard Bucke, minister of Jamestown, then they moved to the nave where they were called upon one by one to swear an oath of allegiance to the king. Afterward, they formally entered "the assembly" and took their seats. The governor took his place in the center of the chancel, his councilors on either side of him, and beyond them the burgesses sat in the choir.

Figure 4—The first General Assembly convened in Jamestown's wooden church on July 30, 1619. The painting shows governor Sir George Yeardley and members of his council seated in the chancel with the Reverend Richard Bucke on his right and the sergeant at arms, Thomas Pierse, on his left. Secretary John Pory and clerk of the assembly John Twine are seated at the table. The first row of the burgesses can just be seen on the far left of the painting. Sidney King, courtesy of Preservation Virginia.

In a clear signal of the gravity with which the assembly took its responsibilities, after reading aloud the burgesses' names, Pory objected to the inclusion of two of its members, Captain John Ward and Lieutenant John Gibbs of Ward's plantation, on the grounds that Ward had not received permission from the Virginia Company to settle his plantation.

Captain Ward and Gibbs were required to remove themselves while the matter was deliberated. Due consideration
being given to Ward's personal investment in the colony, the
value of his trade in bringing provisions to the colony, and,
tellingly, Yeardley's instructions that stipulated two burgesses
were to be admitted for every plantation "without restraint or
exception," the two men were given the opportunity to take
their seats on condition that Ward registered his land with
the Company before the next assembly, to which he agreed.
Accordingly, the assembly gave its approval by general voice,
and Ward and Gibbs were permitted "to make up their number and to sit among them."[24]

Captain John Martin's two burgesses were not so fortunate. Yeardley himself challenged their right to be seated on
the basis that a clause in the Martin's Brandon plantation
patent exempted those living there "from that equality and
uniformity of laws and orders which the great charter says
are to extend over the whole Colony." Captain Martin's patent gave him broad powers to "govern and command all such
person or persons as at this time he shall carry over with him,
or that shall be sent him hereafter, free from any command of
the Colony."

Yeardley's public challenge in front of the entire assembly was likely premeditated, the first salvo in what would
turn out to be a lengthy process by the Company to curb the
terms of Martin's grant. Yeardley argued that by virtue of his
patent, Martin, his deputies, and people were not bound by
any laws passed by the assembly for the good of the colony,
and they "might deride the whole company [assembly] and
choose whether they would obey the same or no." If this was

so, then Martin's patent would in effect be "of a higher condition, and of greater force then any act of the General Assembly"; a state of affairs that could not be tolerated. Pory's
report of the proceedings noted that at this point the "Court"
(a reminder that the assembly functioned as a court as well
as a deliberative and lawmaking body) ordered that Martin's
deputies should withdraw until such time as Martin made
a personal appearance before them. If Martin appeared,
however, he would not be permitted to argue his case; the
decision had already been made, probably well before the assembly met. If Martin was willing to give up the offending
clause, his two burgesses would be admitted, but if not, Pory
recorded in remarkably uncompromising language, the two
representatives would be "utterly excluded, as being spies,
rather than loyal Burgesses."

Yeardley, with the Company's blessing, had asserted the
primacy of the rule of law over all settlers in the colony. Martin, if he insisted on maintaining the terms of his original
grant, would be considered outside the community, incapable of representation because he refused to consent to decisions taken on behalf of the community. He was in effect
given a stark choice: acknowledge the authority of the assembly or be debarred.

The governor, however, was not content to leave it there.
To do so would present another risk. If Martin opted to adhere to the letter of his grant and interpret his plantation as
an independent entity outside the jurisdiction of the governor, council, or assembly, his independence might jeopardize
the welfare of settlers throughout the colony as a whole. In
what appears as a second staged set piece, a complaint was

brought against Martin for his role in an incident that took place in the Chesapeake Bay involving a number of Indians. Martin had sent a shallop to trade for corn under the command of Ensign James Harrison, which had encountered a canoe coming out of a creek. The Indians had refused to trade, and Harrison had ordered his men to board the canoe and take the corn by force, measuring out the corn with a basket carried for that purpose and giving the Indians copper beads "and other trucking stuff" (small trade goods) in return. The story was confirmed by Thomas Davis, ironically one of the burgesses of Martin's Brandon recently expelled, and by word from Opechancanough to the governor saying that the Indians had appealed to him.

In response, the assembly ordered Martin to appear before them to answer the accusation and to give security that "his people" would not commit any further such outrages. Again, the reason was made clear: "because such outrages as this might breed danger and loss of life to others of the Colony which should have leave to trade in the bay hereafter, and for prevention of like violence against the Indians in time to come." In sum, Martin and his men could not do as they pleased. The interpretation secured by Yeardley from the assembly further restricted Martin's freedoms by attaching the limitation to his grant that any actions he or his men undertook could not jeopardize other settlers or Indian peoples. This decision had been rendered not by executive fiat but in open debate in the assembly; its broad representative basis gave sanction to the legitimacy of laws passed for the common good.

The measures taken against Captain Martin were in many ways the result of a growing dissatisfaction among major officeholders within the Company. Sir Edwin Sandys and his supporters were frustrated by the lack of accountability and transparency of the Company's leaders, led by Sir Thomas Smythe, who had been in charge of the colony since its beginning. Sandys was appalled by the financial losses of the previous decade and the highly preferential treatment that influential private investors such as Martin had enjoyed during Smythe's tenure. Little wonder that a significant component of the reforms adopted in 1618 and 1619 took the form of efforts to reverse such ill-advised decisions of prior years. If Martin's privileges could be challenged successfully, then other grandees with similar generous grants would also fall into line.

The principle was driven home a couple of days later on August 2 when Captain Martin appeared at the bar of the assembly to answer the questions put to him. Regarding the first, whether he would voluntarily give up the special privileges contained in his patent, he replied he would not. The assembly then resolved that the burgesses for Martin's Brandon should not be seated. In answer to the second question, whether he would agree to give security to the governor for the good behavior of his men toward Indian peoples when trading in the bay, he confirmed he would. At that, returning to the first issue, the assembly and speaker agreed that they should seek guidance from the Company and council in London about the offending clause in Martin's patent, and in particular how they were to reconcile the preferential treatment enjoyed by Martin with the principle expressed toward the conclusion of the great charter that all grants should be made equally so that "partiality . . . may be avoided." The assembly humbly beseeched the Company to consider and remove any such hindrances to the equality of laws and orders extending throughout the colony that might "divert out of the true course the free and public current of Justice."

By employing the assembly to define the limits of Martin's rights, Yeardley posted an unambiguous message: that whatever the circumstances before 1619, grandees like Martin were now expected to follow "the general form of government as all others did." In hindsight, July 30 and August 2 turned out to be two of the most important days of Yeardley's entire governorship; he had laid down the principle of the rule of law and secured the support of the assembly to enforce it.[25]

Martin's case involving Ensign Harrison and the confrontation with Indians in the Chesapeake Bay also raised another significant issue: Whose law? Following the death of Wahunsonacock, Opitchapam (also known as Itoyatin) had formally succeeded as the great chief, but his kinsman Opechancanough had assumed the role de facto even when Wahunsonacock was still alive, and it was to him that the Indians wronged by Harrison turned for help. Opechancanough sent a message to Governor Yeardley saying that the Indians had appealed to him to "procure them justice," and Yeardley had duly obliged by bringing Martin to judgment before the assembly. The incident and the manner by which the governor and chief dealt with it reveal a clear understanding of discreet jurisdictions and practices. Rule of law, as far as the English were concerned, applied only to those areas settled by the English and legitimized by the Company— what became known later as "English ground in America." Settlers were well aware that the Indian peoples had their own laws and codes of behavior that governed their actions, social relations, and communities. Where gray areas existed, such as serious transgressions that occurred in places outside the direct jurisdiction of either the English or the Powhatans, or when one people wronged the other, then the governor and the great chief were obliged to act together, dealing with the offenders according to their own laws as suited the circumstances.[26]

In comparison to the drama of the assembly's assertion of the rule of law, much of the other business of the meeting took a more sedate tone. On July 30, following a briefing that detailed the purposes of the assembly, Pory read aloud the Company's commissions that established the council of state and the General Assembly and then the great charter, or "commission of privileges," together with the orders and laws sent by the Company with Yeardley. Adopting a parliamentary procedure, he divided members into two committees of eight to undertake a review of the great charter and laws, explaining in a later report that the assembly's desire to examine the charter and laws was not out of any disrespect for the Virginia Company's diligence in perfecting the measures "but only in case we should find anything not perfectly squaring with the state of this Colony or any law which did press or bind too hard, that we might by way of humble petition, seek to have it redressed, especially," Pory added weightily, "because this Great Charter is to bind us and our heirs forever."

Four principal tasks were put before the assemblymen: they were to review the charter, laws, and privileges; to recommend which of the instructions granted to Sir George and two previous governors, Lord De La Warr and Captain Argall, might be conveniently drawn up into laws; to consider private issues brought before the assembly; and finally, to determine what petitions should be drafted and sent to the Company.

The following day, recommendations of the assembly were framed into a series of petitions to be presented to the treasurer, council, and Company in England. As might have been anticipated, many of the proposed revisions addressed safeguarding the rights of "ancient planters." The assemblymen suggested changes related to improving the use and administration of Company lands, sending more tenants and workmen, and facilitating the efficient collection of planters' rents. They also suggested changing "the savage name" of Kecoughtan to Elizabeth City. Given "these doubtful times between us and the Indians," the assembly proposed that the Company's requirement of ten miles between particular plantations (to avoid boundary disputes) was too great and advised that in the interests of strength and security they should be drawn closer together.[27]

The assembly then proceeded to consider the instructions from the Company that been directed to Yeardley and two previous governors. Pory turned once again to the two committees for recommendations about how best to convert them into laws, requiring the first to study the general instructions and the second particular instructions. Since the next day was a Sunday, the committees were asked to report to the assembly on Monday, August 2. Taken together, their recommendations covered the entire range of the colony's affairs: commercial and economic arrangements for the colony as a whole—setting the price of tobacco, regulating prices and accounts of the Company store and trade, restricting the trading privileges of particular plantations, and regulating trading voyages in the bay.

Further regulations were passed requiring the enforcement of contracts with tradesmen, tenants, and servants, and the production of a range of crops such as corn, hemp, silk, flax, vines, and mulberry trees was encouraged or required. In addition, laws were recommended to prohibit idleness, gaming, drunkenness, and "excess in apparel." Moral offenses—failure to attend divine service upon the Sabbath, inveterate swearing, and "incontinency" such as whoredom or "dishonest company keeping with women"—were to be punished by ministers and churchwardens, as was the practice in England. Settlers were advised also on relations with the Powhatans: maintaining the peace and promoting "the Conversion of the Indians to Christian Religion." Strict laws were passed banning settlers from providing firearms or other weapons to the Indians upon pain of being declared a traitor to the colony and hanged if proven guilty.

The final business of the assembly, acting as a court, was to consider grievances brought by individual or groups of settlers. The inhabitants of Argall's Town petitioned to be released from £650 owed to Captains Argall and William Powell, the latter one of the burgesses of James City, for three thousand acres of land and the building of houses that the petitioners believed should have been paid for by Argall. The same William Powell accused one of his servants, Thomas

Garnet, of malicious behavior in refusing to work, abusing his master and mistress, drunkenness, theft, and treachery in seeking to discredit Powell in the eyes of the governor and council. Garnet was sentenced to have his ears nailed to the town's pillory for the next three days and to be publicly whipped each day. Punishment for the neglect of his work was referred to the colony's council of state. John Rolfe then brought forward a complaint against Captain Martin claiming that Martin had behaved toward him in an "unseemly" and unfair manner and had accused him of "certain things" for which he was not to blame. Martin had also been disparaging about the government, which in Rolfe's opinion was the "most temperate and just that ever was in this country." Martin, it seems, had spoken his mind to Rolfe about his treatment by the assembly the previous day. The case was also referred to the council.

Martin was not the only one to cast aspersions on Yeardley's new government. The final case brought before the assembly for judgment was potentially far more serious. Robert Poole was an ancient planter who had arrived in Virginia with his father and brother in 1611. He had learned Algonquian and become one of the colony's interpreters. In that capacity, he had been present at Opechancanough's "court" when another interpreter, Captain Henry Spelman, had allegedly spoken "irreverently and maliciously" about the governor. Spelman denied much of what Poole recounted but confessed that he had told Opechancanough that within a year another governor would be sent to the colony "greater than this that now is in place." By this and other reports, the assembly concluded, Spelman had "alienated the mind of Opechancanough from this present governor, and brought him in much disesteem, both with Opechancanough and the Indians, and the whole Colony in danger of their slippery designs." Belittling the governor to the great chief of the Powhatans alone could have been viewed as treasonous and therefore sufficient to warrant the death penalty, but the assembly took a lenient view, aware that only one witness had brought the allegations and perhaps in acknowledgment of Spelman's long experience as an Indian interpreter. He was stripped of his rank of captain and bound for seven years to serve the colony as an interpreter for the governor, a sentence he did not accept gracefully. Pory reported that Spelman "as one that had in him more of the Savage then of the Christian, muttered certain words to himself neither showing remorse for his offenses, nor yet any thankfulness to the assembly for their so favorable censure."[28]

Spelman's case, and to some degree Martin's, were echoes of the growing fissures within the Virginia Company's leadership that found their way into the assembly's deliberations. Sir Thomas Smythe had been indignant of his treatment by the Sandys group, having his accounts inspected and his integrity implicitly questioned in council meetings from 1616 onward. Although he had decided to voluntarily resign from the leadership of the Company, he had done so only under pressure from Sandys and his associates and felt that his own strenuous efforts to support the Company during the difficult times of the previous decade had been given insufficient credit. He was scathing about Sir George Yeardley's elevation to a knighthood and believed Yeardley was wholly unworthy of the honor. Compared to Lord De La Warr, a nobleman of impeccable lineage and repute, Smythe pointed to Yeardley's modest middle-class origins and his humble background as a soldier. The contemporary correspondent John Chamberlain described Yeardley as "a mean fellow" who after his knighthood paraded up and down the streets of London "in extraordinary bravery [ostentation], with fourteen or fifteen fair liveries [servants] after him." Smythe's lack of confidence in him together with initial hostility from leading men at Jamestown formerly close to Argall very nearly persuaded Yeardley to step down during his first few months in the colony.[29]

Yet in many respects personal rivalries in London and Jamestown were symptoms of a deeper problem. Sandys and his supporters embraced the rule of law as the sine qua non of the thorough-going reformation of society that would follow; one that involved the evolution of corporate structures and accompanying civic virtues under the umbrella of an inclusive Christian commonwealth. But it was not a view shared by other powerful leaders of the Company such as Smythe or Sir Robert Rich, the newly minted Earl of Warwick, who considered the plan utterly impractical. Smythe favored a trading venture that maximized profits for the Company from goods produced in the colony and commodities sent from England in exchange. As long as settlers were productive and the colony stable, he was not especially concerned about the form society took. For the Earl of Warwick, a militant Puritan and passionate adversary of the Spanish, American colonies offered an ideal opportunity to raid Spanish possessions and shipping from English-controlled islands such as Bermuda or mainland colonies such as Virginia. He supported colonization as much for the creation of privateering bases as enduring settlements.[30]

On August 4, Yeardley called an abrupt halt to the assembly's proceedings, citing the oppressive heat (one burgess, Walter Shelley, had already died during the meeting). He was likely pleased with the outcome even if the assembly was able to sit for only six days. Aided by the unflagging labors of John Pory, he had established a commitment to just laws and the orderly management of the colony's affairs. Free male settlers had followed the governor's instructions to elect their representatives from the corporations and private plantations, and the assembly had avoided any major conflicts between the governor and his council on the one hand and the burgesses on the other. They had sat together as one body and worked together to confirm and expand upon the laws propounded by the Company. With the exception of the Martin and Spelman cases, the business of the assembly had aroused little controversy among its members. The assembly concluded its work with the plea that it should be permitted to enforce the laws agreed upon until such time as the Company was able to review them and that the Company would consider implementing their promise as soon as convenient to permit the assembly "to allow or disallow of their orders of Court [Company], as his Majesty has given them power to allow or to reject our laws," a clear indication that the assembly wished to expand its powers. Yeardley then prorogued the assembly until March 1 of the following year.[31]

HIGHLY GRATIFIED BY NEWS OF THE ASSEMBLY'S ACCOMPLISH-
ments, the Company published a glowing description of the
colony in June 1620 that declared "the Colony begins now to
have the face and fashion of an orderly State, and such as is
likely to grow and prosper." As a capstone, Company leaders
committed themselves to compiling a book of standing laws
and orders that would be regularly updated to include new
legislation as well as a second book that would "reduce into
a compendious and orderly form in writing, the Laws of *England* proper for the use" of colonists. This would be first sub-
mitted to the king for his review and approval, "it being not fit
that his Majesty's Subjects should be governed by any other
Laws, then such as receive the influence of their life from
him," a reminder that the colony's existence was grounded
firmly upon the sovereign's grace and authority.

The first assembly did not establish a fully fledged form
of common law in the colony; the institutions that underpinned the common law in England, such as the petty courts
and Quarter Sessions of English counties, simply did not exist in Virginia. Nonetheless, the great charter and new laws
passed by the assembly brought the colony into much greater
conformity with legal practice in the mother country. Neither
did the General Assembly initiate a recognizably modern democracy (which would have been unthinkable at this time),
but it most certainly heralded a broadly representative form
of government based on an extraordinarily wide male fran-
chise and the consent of the governed.[32]

The reforms of 1619 were by any measure an extraordinary achievement. Within eighteen months, the arbitrary government and harsh punishments that had stigmatized years of

military rule had been left behind, widespread private property established, and the colony's laws and local government thoroughly overhauled. The complex layers of jurisdictions, courts, and laws that had evolved across half a millennium in England had been reduced to a simple set of formulas that were (for the most part) transparent to colonists. Yet despite these conspicuous successes, the future of the colony continued to be uncertain. Serious divisions had emerged within the Company's leadership, James I remained an unreliable ally, and Spain continued to contest the very legitimacy of the colony. Doubts had been raised indirectly in the assembly about Yeardley's fitness for office, and fears were voiced that his government might be too mild for those settlers "whom unwanted [unlooked for] liberty has made insolent and not to know themselves," or their place. Members of the assembly urged the Company to accept their revised laws in part to enable them to maintain control over ordinary planters who had tasted the heady fruits of self-government and who would be bitterly disappointed if their efforts came to nothing. In the peculiar conditions of England's first enduring colony, fashioning a satisfactory balance of powers and rights between the sovereign, governing classes, and the people would prove the most intractable problem colonial officials and settlers would face. The introduction of the great charter and General Assembly represented only a beginning.[33]

Three

First Africans

He brought not anything but 20. and odd Negroes,
which the Governor and Cape Merchant bought
for victuals (whereof he was in great need as he
pretended) at the best and easiest rates they could.
   —*John Rolfe (1620)*

Others not Christians in the Service of the English—
Indians in the service of several planters—04
Negroes in the service of several planters—32
   —*General Muster of Virginia (1620)*

A T ABOUT THE SAME TIME SIR GEORGE YEARDLEY WAS
preparing for the first meeting of the General Assembly,
two heavily armed English privateers lay windward of a Portuguese slave ship in the Gulf of Mexico. The privateers were
the *Treasurer,* owned by Sir Robert Rich, the Earl of Warwick, and captained by Daniel Elfrith, and the *White Lion,*

commanded by Cornishman John Jope. Their meeting may have been by chance, but such associations were common; English privateers often joined forces to cruise the waters of the Caribbean in search of prizes. The slave ship *St. John the Baptist,* commanded by Captain Manuel Mendes da Cunha, had departed Luanda, the capital of Portuguese Angola, earlier that summer carrying approximately 350 African captives bound for Veracruz. As was common with slave ships, she was grossly overcrowded, which—together with a shortage of supplies and drinking water—resulted in appalling conditions on board and the deaths of approximately a third of the Africans en route. In late July or early August, the *White Lion* and *Treasurer* closed in on their prey off the Yucatan coast and engaged in a fierce battle that left all three ships damaged. Jope and Elfrith took approximately fifty-five to sixty Africans as booty and left the battered Portuguese slaver to her fate, setting their course for Virginia where they anticipated taking on provisions and selling the Africans.[1]

Piracy was practically the only means by which the English could acquire or trade African slaves in this period. Spanish officials claimed all of the New World as their own and refused to recognize the legitimacy of foreign colonies or allow foreign merchants to traffic in America. For their part, English sponsors of privateering voyages denied Spanish territorial claims and disputed their right to exclude them from sailing the high seas and trading wherever they wished. Warwick, for example, had sent ships from Bermuda and Virginia over the course of several years to rove in the West Indies in search of treasure or trade. He was only the most recent of a long line of Englishmen stretching back more than half a century to the days of John Hawkins, Francis Drake, and Sir Walter Ralegh who had profited enormously from pillaging Spanish ships and American settlements. Since the mid-sixteenth century, mariners, together with the English lords and merchants who sponsored them, were well aware of the huge numbers of Africans taken forcibly as enslaved laborers to work in the cane fields, on the wharves of bustling ports, or in silver mines of Spanish America. Termed *pieces* by Portuguese traders who had been trafficking along the west coast of Africa since the mid-fifteenth century, English mariners also viewed sub-Saharan Africans as slaves and had few qualms about treating them as a valuable form of plunder.[2]

The *White Lion* was the first of the privateers to arrive in Virginia. "About the latter end of August," John Rolfe reported to Sir Edwin Sandys,

> a Dutch man of War of the burden of 160 tons arrived at Point Comfort, the Commander's name Capt. Jope, his Pilot for the West Indies one Mr. Marmaduke, an Englishman. They met with the *Treasurer* in the West Indies, and determined to hold consort ship hitherward, but in their passage lost one the other. He brought not anything but 20. and odd Negroes, which the Governor and Cape Merchant bought for victuals (whereof he was in great need as he pretended) at the best and easiest rates they could.

The "Dutch man of War" referred to by Rolfe was the *White Lion,* sailing under a letter of marque from Vlissingen (Flushing) in the Netherlands that gave Captain Jope permission to attack and rob Spanish ships and possessions. Spanish authorities dismissed the legitimacy of such letters—they considered privateers no better than pirates—but letters of marque were recognized by several European states hostile to Spain as a means of promoting attacks on Spanish shipping. Jope's papers from Vlissingen may account for Rolfe identifying the *White Lion* as Dutch, or he may have had his own reasons to obscure the ship's true name and English origins. In any event, Rolfe is clear that Sir George Yeardley and the Company's cape merchant, Abraham Piersey, traveled downriver to meet the ship at Point Comfort, near Kecoughtan, which suggests they knew about the Africans on board. It is no coincidence that a few years later the two of them were recorded in a census as owning the majority of the captives.[3]

The "20. and odd" were the first documented Africans to arrive on the mainland of English North America. Shortly after, the *Treasurer* anchored off Point Comfort but did not stay long. Again, Rolfe provided an account of what happened:

Three or 4 days after the *Treasurer* arrived. At his arrival he sent word presently to the governor to know his pleasure, who wrote to him, and did request myself, Lieutenant Pearce [Pierce], and Mr. Ewens to go down to him, to desire him to come up to James City. But before we got down he had set sail and was gone out of the Bay. The occasion hereof happened by the unfriendly dealing of the Inhabitants of Kecoughtan, for he was in great want of victuals, wherewith they would not relieve him or his Company upon any terms.

The real reason why Captain Elfrith left so abruptly, as Rolfe well knew, was because Governor Yeardley had received instructions from Sir Edwin Sandys in London to detain the ship and question Elfrith about his involvement in acts of piracy in the Spanish Indies sponsored by his patron, the Earl of Warwick. Sandys's determination to prevent privateers using Virginia as a base from which to mount raids on the Spanish West Indies reveals a serious rift in the Virginia Company's leadership. He disagreed profoundly with Warwick about the role English colonies should play in the New World. Sandys's plans centered on the creation of a settler society in Virginia that would benefit from forward-looking governmental, religious, and economic policies; Warwick favored establishing societies such as Bermuda that would profit from commerce and privateering. Had Sandys subscribed to Warwick's view, far more Africans would have likely arrived in Virginia in these years.

Despite his rapid departure from Point Comfort, however, circumstantial evidence points to Elfrith selling or exchanging some of the Africans before leaving port. Just as Yeardley and Piersey had bought most of the Africans from Jope a week or so earlier, William Pierce and Captain Ewens (Evans), sent downriver from Jamestown by the governor to meet the *Treasurer,* also later had a couple of Africans in their households. It seems clear that more Africans arrived in the colony in early September 1619 than the twenty or so reported by Rolfe, possibly including a woman named Angela who in the mid-1620s was living in Pierce's household.[4]

After leaving the Chesapeake Bay, Elfrith set his course for Bermuda, where he would meet with a friendlier reception from officials aligned with the Earl of Warwick than he had received in Virginia, and traded twenty-nine Africans in return for provisions. There, the Africans were held under lock and key before being sold or put to work by Governor Nathaniel Butler on lands belonging to the Bermuda Company. In poor condition, the *Treasurer* remained in port and did not put to sea until February 1620, when she returned to Virginia with a few English passengers and about half a dozen Africans on board. After arriving in the colony and disposing of her passengers, the ship—rotten and unseaworthy—sank (or was scuttled) in a creek off the James River. These Africans, together with "the 20. and odd" and any others purchased from the *Treasurer* previously in September, made up the thirty-two "Negroes" listed in a colony-wide census the following month.[5]

NEW EVIDENCE HAS RECENTLY COME TO LIGHT THAT OFFERS a clearer understanding of the origin of the first Africans before they were forced to board the *St. John the Baptist*. They were not already enslaved workers who had been living in the Spanish Caribbean, as some historians had previously surmised, but rather came from West Central Africa, most likely from the Christian Kingdom of Kongo and the neighboring province of Ndongo. We now know also that they had been captured by the Portuguese during a period of intense warfare and arrived in the colony as slaves.[6]

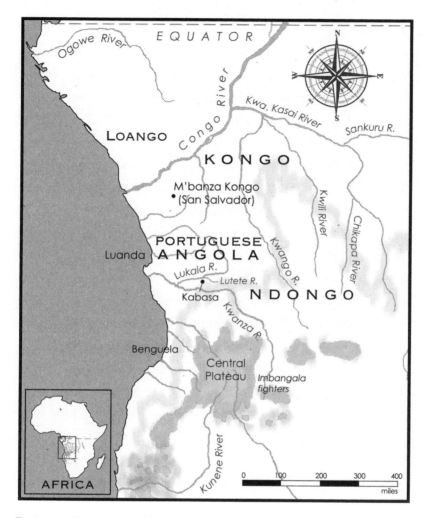

FIGURE 5—West Central Africa, 1619. Drawn by Jamie May.

In the early seventeenth century, West Central Africa was a highly diverse region politically and culturally that stretched approximately five hundred miles along the Atlantic coast from the Kingdom of Loango and Congo River in the north to Benguela and the Kunene River Valley in the south. Inland, extending several hundred miles, the region embraced broad coastal lowlands, fertile river valleys, and massive highlands in the interior rising to over four thousand feet in places. Kongo, a large centralized kingdom, dominated the region. Its core was the densely inhabited lands along the Congo River valley and highlands in the interior around the capital, but during the fifteenth and early sixteenth centuries, its borders expanded considerably to embrace smaller states to the east and along the coast as far south as the island port of Luanda. Across the same period, other powerful kingdoms emerged also, such as Loango northward beyond the Congo River bordering the coast, Benguela far to the south, and Ngola (from which the name *Angola* is derived) that included the rising power of Ndongo in the highlands.

Portuguese traders first arrived on Kongo's coast in the 1480s, sparking a remarkable and lengthy period of cultural exchange. Kongo was a well-established and powerful kingdom, and its rulers actively encouraged close relations with Portugal on equal terms in pursuit of mutually beneficial commerce and access to European technology and knowledge. Within a generation, the Kongolese had espoused their own distinctive form of Catholicism, constructed churches, established schools to encourage literacy among the elite, and entered into diplomatic dealings with the Portuguese. Lesser states such as Ndongo and provinces to the south were inclined to be more cautious, fearing subjection and conquest by the Europeans, but nevertheless favored alliances with the Portuguese to buttress their military strength and independence.[7]

One common objective of paramount importance shared by Portuguese and African traders alike throughout West Central Africa was the opportunity to profit from the immensely lucrative slave trade. The slave trade drew the Portuguese into ever-closer relations with African rulers all along the west coast, and for their part, Africans were drawn more and more into the Portuguese orbit of Atlantic commerce. The capture and sale of human beings was not introduced by Europeans—it was embedded in African culture and consequently had a long history—but the alliance with Portuguese merchants greatly expanded and extended the slave trade, bringing riches to ruling kings and merchants alike. In the early sixteenth century, Kongo was exporting two thousand slaves annually, primarily to southern Europe and São Tomé, Portugal's Atlantic island off the equatorial coast of Central Africa, where the rapid growth of sugar production relied on enslaved labor. By 1600, the number of enslaved workers sent from Angola to the Americas and elsewhere annually had more than doubled. Little wonder that to promote their own interests in the trade and to advance military alliances, the rulers of Ndongo, Benguela, and Loango each established their own relationships with the Portuguese. These partnerships were advantageous at first but would ultimately prove disastrous.[8]

For close to a century, relations between Portuguese settlements and African kingdoms in the region, notably Kongo, were based on reciprocal benefits. But in 1571, Sebastian I, king of Portugal, abruptly switched policy and commanded his military forces in Angola to carve out a discrete

Portuguese colony from Ndongo and bordering areas to the south that would be ruled directly by the crown. The new territory would become known as Portuguese Angola. King Sebastian justified this dramatic change in direction by his sincere wish to promote the "Holy Faith and Holy Evangelization," although profiting further from the slave trade was also likely on his mind. Brutal military campaigns over the next twenty years gravely undermined the Ndongo kingdom and paved the way for the subsequent ruinous wars of the seventeenth century.[9]

The immediate background to the capture of the men and women who ended up enslaved in Virginia was the appointment of Luis Mendes de Vasconçelos as governor of Angola in 1617. After conventional European tactics failed to achieve military victory, he enlisted companies of Imbangala, called Jagas, ruthless mercenaries who banded together in their thousands to plunder one area after another. Originating in the central highlands of Angola in the last quarter of the sixteenth century, they spread terror and misery throughout the region by their indiscriminate killing, rape, and cannibalistic rituals. Following incursions by Imbangala fighters, whole provinces were left devastated. Fields and valuable palm tree groves were ruined, livestock killed, villages plundered, and people murdered or enslaved. Portuguese clerics and missionaries looked on with shock. Instead of shunning the Jagas, Bishop Manuel Bautista Soares only complained to Spain's Philip III in 1619 that Governor Mendes had forged alliances with them, killing and "capturing innumerable innocent people, not only against the law of God but also against the expressed regulations of your Majesty." During Mendes's decisive campaigns of 1618–1619 in Ndongo, Portuguese and Imbangala forces completely overwhelmed Ndongo's defenses and quickly captured the capital, Kabasa. Both the city and the region's rich agricultural lands were plundered mercilessly. So many people were slaughtered, a contemporary wrote, that the rivers became spoiled and huge numbers of people were enslaved "without cause."

Most of those captured by the Portuguese were from large towns and heavily populated rural communities in the royal district around Kabasa between the Lukala and Lutete Rivers. Mendes's "Angolan conquista" was likely the origin of many of the enslaved men and women who ended up in Virginia and Bermuda. If so, historian John Thornton suggests, captives from Kabasa and surrounding areas would have shared a strong sense of their own cultural identity. They spoke a common language, Kimbundu ("ambundu"), came from an area where they felt strong allegiance to the king and his court, held common religious or spiritual beliefs, and had survived the same hardships of war and capture. It is possible also that some of the enslaved who eventually ended up in English America came from areas closer to Luanda or from a region east of the Kongolese capital, São Salvador, where Portuguese forces and the Imbangala wreaked havoc in 1618 and 1619. This kind of chaos was advantageous to the Portuguese, who were able to enslave victims caught up in the wars and at the same time consolidate their hold on the region.[10]

Enduring terrible conditions, captives were tied together in long lines and forced to trek hundreds of miles from the interior to the Atlantic coast and Luanda. The sheer number of new captives overwhelmed port authorities in 1618 and 1619, and thousands had to be held in slave pens that surrounded the town or kept on beaches waiting to be put on board the ships. This was generally the moment when priests would teach the rudimentary principles of Christianity to those not already Catholics. But it is hard to imagine that religious instruction offered much comfort to enslaved men and women who viewed the impending horror of the voyage as a form of prolonged death committed by Portuguese "witches" who might eat them or take them to the "land of the dead" (the Americas). Some died of starvation and sheer fatigue before boarding, and many others perished on the ships waiting to leave port or during the dreadful months of the crossing. Alonso de Sandoval, who wrote about the experiences of the enslaved in this period, observed that captives were chained together when boarding to prevent them from escaping or throwing themselves over the side. At sea, they were packed chained in long rows head to foot below deck "where they saw neither sun nor moon" apart from when they were allowed on deck periodically in small groups for fresh air. Slave ships were frequently grossly overcrowded and did not carry adequate provisions and drinking water for the journey.

An account by a former slave, Olaudah Equiano, taken from West Africa (Nigeria) in the mid-eighteenth century provides a graphic illustration of the experience endured by the millions of Africans forced to take the Middle Passage:

The stench of the hold while we were on the coast was so intolerably loathsome that it was dangerous to remain there for any time . . . but now that the whole ship's cargo was confined together it became absolutely pestilential. The closeness of the place and the heat of the climate, added to the number in the ship, which was so crowded that each had scarcely room to turn himself, almost suffocated us. This produced copious perspirations, so that the air soon became unfit for respiration from a variety of loathsome smells, and brought on a sickness among the slaves, of which many died . . . This wretched situation was again aggravated by the galling of the chains, now become insupportable, and the filth of the necessary tubs [toilets], into which the children often fell and were almost suffocated. The shrieks of the women and the groans of the dying rendered the whole a scene of horror almost inconceivable.

Equiano described a dismal litany of beatings, acts of casual cruelty, and deaths of Africans throughout the voyage. In 1619, thirty-six slave ships left Luanda for Brazil and Spanish America, one of which was the *St. John the Baptist*. During a passage of eleven to twelve weeks, the death rate on slave ships was typically between a fifth and a third of the captives. Tragically, the loss of 120 of 350 slaves on Captain Cunha's ship by the time she reached Veracruz was by no means exceptional, and more Angolans likely succumbed to disease or exhaustion soon after arrival.

By the time the first Africans arrived in Virginia, half a million slaves had already been shipped across the Atlantic to work in Spanish America and Brazil, the majority taken as captives in the vicious wars spawned by the Portuguese in Angola. Hispanic attitudes toward Africans, especially those from sub-Saharan regions, and their development of an Iberian Atlantic slave trading system would play a formative role in shaping English approaches to enslaving Africans from Virginia to Barbados.[11]

SEVENTEEN WOMEN AND FIFTEEN MEN FROM NDONGO OR Kongo (hereafter referred to as Angolans) lived in Virginia in early 1620. They were described, together with four Powhatans, as simply "Others not Christians in the Service of the English" and "Negroes in the service of several planters," with no further details. Four years later, only twenty-one Angolans were recorded, half of whom were residents at Flowerdew Hundred, a large plantation owned by Abraham Piersey on the south side of the James River a dozen miles from Jamestown. The following year, another muster provides more details. Twenty-three Angolans were listed: seven at Piersey's plantation, made up of four men, two women, and a baby, all unnamed and described as "Negroes"; at Jamestown eight were listed as living in Sir George Yeardley's household, again all unnamed, five "Negro Women" and three "Negro Men." Angela, the "Negro Woman [who arrived] in the *Treasurer*," lived in the house of William Pierce. Nearby, "Edward" worked on Richard Kingsmill's plantation, and downriver at Warraskoyack in the Puritan Edward Bennett's household, two Africans remained—"Antonio a Negro," who was reported as arriving in the *James* in 1621, and "Mary," who came on the *Margaret and John* in 1622. At Elizabeth City, Anthony and Isabella had a child named "William" after their master Captain William Tucker, who was baptized at

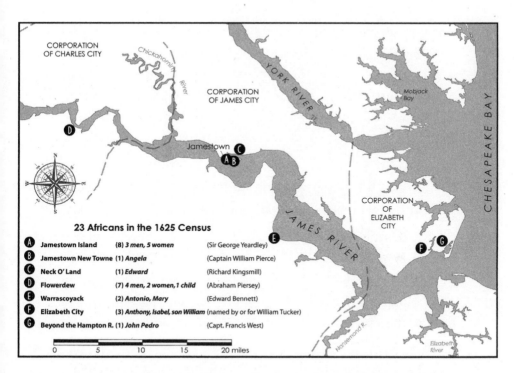

<FIGURE 6—Locations of first Africans in Virginia, 1624-1625. Drawn by Jamie May.

the small church near the plantation. Finally, also living in Elizabeth City was an African, possibly an Angolan, named John Pedro who was described as thirty years old and having arrived on the *Swan* in 1623. He lived in the household of Captain Francis West on the Company's Land, in Elizabeth City, close to the mouth of the James River.[12]

Several points stand out in these lists of the enslaved. In 1620, thirty-two Angolans were recorded in the colony, all from the *St. John the Baptist,* representing approximately 3.5 percent of the total settler population. However, five years later, only twenty-three were listed, less than 2 percent of the population, of which at least three were new arrivals and two had been born in the colony. Clearly, the arrival of the first group of Africans did not lead to a surge of slaves into the colony. Second, if the figures are reliable, it is likely that as many as fourteen had died by 1625, approaching half of the initial group. Virginia experienced exceptionally high mortality rates, white and black alike, during this period, owing to the poor health of many newcomers following the Atlantic crossing, the spread of contagious diseases brought from England, and the massive Indian attack of 1622, which alone accounted for the deaths of approximately 350 settlers. Having been forcibly taken from their own war-torn lands, by a malign twist of fate the Angolans found themselves in another country ravaged by war and famine. The emotional and psychological impact of the loss of their compatriots and of finding themselves once again in the midst of conflict is hard to imagine.

The census also tells us that from the outset ownership of Africans was dominated by wealthy settlers who controlled large plantations, held important official positions, and consequently acquired the majority of the captives and with a few exceptions held on to them. Most of the enslaved Angolans lived in households that included between four and ten other slaves. Governor Yeardley and Abraham Piersey owned the majority listed in 1624 and 1625, and the remainder were purchased by other high officeholders, burgesses, and wealthy merchants such as Pierce, Bennett, and Tucker, a trend that would continue thereafter. Even at this early stage, Africans were considered exceptionally valuable, more so than servants or tenants. "These Slaves," Governor Nathaniel Butler of Bermuda wrote in January 1621, referring to the arrival of fourteen Africans on the island the previous year, "are the most proper and cheap instruments for this plantation that can be." Few in Virginia would have disagreed.[13]

The individual experiences of the Angolans would have varied enormously depending on their masters or overseers, where they resided, and the particular nature of their work. Richard Ligon's description of Barbados a couple of decades later in relation to planters' treatment of white servants is just as applicable to enslaved Africans in Virginia. How servants fared, he wrote, rested on whether "the master is merciful or cruel; those that are merciful, treat their servants well, both in their meat [food], drink, and lodging, and give them such work, as is not unfit for Christians to do. But if the masters be cruel, the servants have very wearisome and miserable lives."

Africans were involved in all aspects of plantation work: raising tobacco and corn, tending cattle and other livestock, looking after the kitchen garden, and fixing fences and out-houses. For those who had lived in rural communities in Kongo or Ndongo, aspects of their new work in Virginia, such as looking after cattle, may have been similar to the work they did in their homelands, but those who had come from cities or had formerly worked in skilled trades likely found them-selves reduced to common laborers unless they were able to adapt their skills to their masters' demands. Unlike white maidservants who did not usually work "in the ground," Afri-can women were routinely put to heavy labor and frequently labored alongside men in the fields as well as doing arduous domestic chores such as pounding corn. To encourage pro-ductivity and cooperation, in rare instances some were given the opportunity to work a small plot of land for themselves for profit and thereby eventually purchase their freedom or that of their children from their owner. But the great majority of Africans in the colony were treated as "perpetual" slaves.

Most Africans resided in the main dwelling house along with the planter's family and white servants, typically in a loft, in a cellar, or wherever they could find space. In a couple of cases, where they lived in large groups, they may have cooked and slept in the planter's outbuildings close to the dwelling house. For those residing on Yeardley, Piersey, Bennett, and Captain Tucker's plantations, there would have been plenty of opportunity to spend time with other Africans and possibly too for couples to live together and have children, such as in the case of Anthony and Isabella at Tucker's plantation. In contrast, for Angela, Edward, and John Pedro, the sole Africans in their respective households, living in Virginia may have initially been a lonely experience. Periodic visits to neighboring plantations, if permitted, would have had to suffice to keep them in touch with their compatriots. Living without the immediate company of other Africans may have encouraged or forced them to integrate more quickly with their white families and neighbors.

Considering the majority of Angolans resided in households that included three or more other Africans, they may have been able to keep alive at least some of their cultural traditions, such as languages, regional customs, and spiritual beliefs. Possibly they spoke to each other in Kimbundu—or if from Kongo, in the related Bantu language of that kingdom, Kikongo. Those from Kongo may have shared their form of Catholicism. In some areas of Kongo where trade with Europeans was common, they also adopted to varying degrees the

Portuguese language, names, foodways, and manners. Those from Ndongo, on the other hand, likely retained religious beliefs that connected them in a continuous dialogue to their ancestors and spirits who inhabited the other world. It is possible some retained beliefs in "night flying," during which the person's spirit wandered freely at night and might occasionally return across the ocean to Angola.[14]

THE QUESTION OF WHETHER AFRICANS WERE ENSLAVED when they first arrived in Virginia or were treated similarly to white servants, who made up the bulk of the colony's labor force down to the 1670s, has generated a great deal of controversy among historians. Did slavery and racial prejudice gradually evolve in Virginia during the half century following the arrival of the Angolans, or did de facto enslavement of Africans begin in 1619?[15]

Advocates in favor of the gradual emergence of slavery from forms of initial black servitude have emphasized that Virginia initially lacked any laws clearly defining and providing legal sanction for slavery. Laws in Virginia that unquestionably indicate lifelong service for all African laborers, not just for those who had run away from their owners, did not enter the statute books until the 1660s and 1670s. In addition, some historians point to the evidence of nomenclature: none of the Africans who arrived in the *White Lion* or the *Treasurer,* or who entered the colony later in the 1620s or after, were termed *slaves.* In fact, rather than being identified as slaves, they were listed in the muster of 1625 alongside white servants. Even by 1649, John Ferrar would write that "there are in *Virginia* about fifteen thousand *English,* and of *Negroes* brought thither three hundred good servants."[16]

Perhaps the most telling evidence employed by those who support the theory of the evolution of slavery is the remarkable story of those Africans who against all odds escaped bondage and established themselves as free planters. On the Eastern Shore of Virginia in the 1660s and 1670s, for example, thirteen (ten men and three women) were listed as free householders, nearly a fifth of all the Africans living there. The best known is Anthony Johnson, possibly the same Angolan man as "Antonio" who was listed on Edward Bennett's plantation in 1625. If so, it appears he married "Mary a Negro Woman" who had lived on the same plantation from 1623. Fifteen to twenty years later, and still enslaved, they moved with their children in the late 1630s or early 1640s to a plantation in Northampton County on the Eastern Shore of Virginia. Over the next couple of decades, the Johnsons achieved their freedom and acquired substantial property, including enslaved Africans. In the mid-1660s, Anthony, Mary, and their extended family moved farther north to Somerset County, on the Eastern Shore of Maryland, where Anthony died shortly after. The possibility that Anthony Johnson was one of the first Africans taken from the *St. John the Baptist* is given credence by Johnson's son, John, naming a plantation he bought some years later *Angola*.[17]

Those Africans who were able to free themselves and their families in this period were extraordinary, yet their experiences contrast starkly with the lives of the vast majority of Africans brought to America, including the first Angolans. As already noted, the English inhabited an Atlantic world where the enslavement of Africans by Europeans was unremarkable. Lagos, Portugal, was Europe's first African slave trade port and had prospered greatly since the mid-1440s thanks to the profits. Even before trade to America began, thousands of slaves passed through the town's slave market on their way to Lisbon and Seville. On the arrival of hundreds of slaves in Lagos in 1444, Prince Henry the Navigator (1394–1460), brother of the Portuguese king, commented that he "had no other pleasure than in thinking that these lost souls would now be saved." Papal bulls issued by the Catholic Church sanctioned the enslavement of sub-Saharan Africans and legitimized the trade as part of their holy mission to convert the heathen, precisely the same reasoning employed to justify the Spanish conquest of America and enslavement of Indian peoples. "In asserting a religious justification for slavery," historian James Sweet remarks, "the Portuguese and Spanish avoided subjecting the practice to debate." From their point of view, slavery was a small price for Africans to pay in return for their immortal souls.[18]

It is true that indigenous forms of slavery had not existed in England for centuries. Serfdom and villenage, feudal labor systems whereby men and women were bound through descent to particular lordships and manors, persisted but impacted only a small and rapidly decreasing minority of people. The wide-ranging economic changes that swept across much of the lowland countryside in the late fifteenth and sixteenth centuries were unconducive to the persistence of servile labor ("bond men"). In many cases, labor requirements were commuted to particular fees and annual payments. Yet if slavery had long since departed their own shores, English people were aware that a great variety of forms of non-freedom had and still existed throughout the world, such as various types of apprenticeships or service by contract, penal servitude, tales of Christians taken by Muslim pirates and forced to become galley slaves, or in the Bible, which was full of references to the enslavement of peoples. Increasingly, too, the English were becoming aware of the vast numbers of African slaves being shipped to America and parts of Europe. Although it was with pride that the English considered themselves a "uniquely free" people, they lived in a world where the mass enslavement of Africans was resurgent.

English people's attitudes toward the relatively few Africans living in England in this period are unclear. Free and enslaved Africans resided in cities and major ports such as London, Plymouth, and Bristol and worked in a wide range of occupations among the lower and middling ranks of society, although some were highly accomplished and educated in specific occupations. Small numbers also inhabited towns and parishes throughout the realm where they seemingly lived alongside their neighbors with no obvious sign of white prejudice. Only at the end of the sixteenth century, possibly as a result of an influx of "Blackamoors"—people of color usually from North Africa—into London, was any alarm expressed about the number of black residents in Britain, and even in this case it appears the government was far more concerned about a possible threat to public order than were English people.

By contrast, depictions of sub-Saharan Africans in travelers' accounts or popular plays and pageants tended to be extremely negative. They were "a people of beastly living, without a God, law, religion, or common wealth," wrote Captain John Lok following his voyage to Guinea in 1554, adding descriptions of monstrous black-skinned peoples that were barely human if human at all. Other writers described Africans as wild and savage peoples, some of whom were cannibals "accustomed to man's flesh" or were as "Libidinous as Apes." Having translated an account of Africa by the sixteenth-century Spanish Moroccan "Moor" Leo Africanus, John Pory was likely the most knowledgeable man about Africans in Virginia and may have agreed with Africanus's assessment of Africans as "being utterly destitute of the use of reason, of dexterity of wit, and of all arts." If English people showed little inclination to discriminate against Africans in their own communities, nevertheless Europeans' general view of Africa and Africans, especially south of the Sahara, was bleak.[19]

The coerced transportation of Africans to America was a major component of the Atlantic commercial world from its beginning, a key driver of the Atlantic system itself. Enslaved Africans were treated as commodities, as a peculiar type of property. John Hawkins, one of the first English traffickers of slaves from Africa to the West Indies, for example, commented that "*Negroes* were very good merchandise in *Hispaniola,* and that store of *Negroes* might easily be had upon the coast of *Guinea.*" English mariners and merchants involved in the Atlantic slave trade recognized the complexity of relationships with Africans along the coasts of West and Central West Africa, which frequently involved dealing with sophisticated African rulers or merchants to acquire captives for shipment, and took for granted African traders' designation of black captives as slaves. In the slave markets of Africa, Portugal, and

Spain, as in Atlantic and American colonies, African captives' classification as chattel slaves whether by Europeans or African merchants determined their fate and that of their offspring in perpetuity. Such was the chilling effect of the transatlantic trade in African men, women, and children.[20]

The absence of legislation formally legalizing slavery in early Virginia does not indicate that the terms by which the first Africans were employed were similar to those of white indentured servants. Specific laws defining slavery in England's emerging global empire were considered superfluous in the face of long custom and wide usage that accepted the practice. "Slavery," Jonathan Bush writes, "simply evolved in practice, as a custom, and then received statutory recognition." The rule of law introduced by Sandys and Yeardley to protect English rights did not apply to Africans, as a matter of course.

Apart from expense and availability, nothing prevented settlers from acquiring African slaves from merchants who sometimes brought them to the colony or from claiming absolute ownership on the basis of their assumed property rights. To argue, as does the historian Edmund Morgan, that Africans in Virginia were treated in much the same way as white servants or that English planters were content to absorb them into "a New World community on the English model" is simply unconvincing, as is the opinion put forward by another historian that examples of black experiences similar to the Johnsons' are to be found throughout the early Chesapeake. If the Eastern Shore of Virginia and Maryland was briefly a haven for a small number of freed blacks such as the Johnsons, very little evidence exists of Africans being freed elsewhere in the colony at any time during the century. A few arrived from England with indentures, and in one exceptional case, a mulatto woman—born of a white father and married to an Englishman—eventually won her freedom following a lengthy period of service and a remarkable legal battle. But that a few Africans came to Virginia as servants, Lorena Walsh emphasizes, "has for too long confused the issue of the fate of the great majority."[21]

The condition of Africans, including the first Angolans, was undoubtedly slavery. On the arrival of the *White Lion* at Point Comfort, John Rolfe reported, "Governor [Yeardley] and Cape Merchant [Piersey] *bought*" (my italics) the Angolans for victuals. The transactional character of the encounter is evident. No mention is made of the length or terms of service, only the terse remark that the Africans were purchased.

Six years later, in a significant case that was the first of its kind to come before the General Court, the governor and his council considered what should be done with an African man named "Brase" brought to the colony by Captain Nathaniel Jones. Cruising in the West Indies in early 1625, Jones and his men captured a Spanish frigate and from the small ship took a Portuguese pilot as well as two men, described simply as "a Negro and a Frenchman," both of whom wished to go with them. Jones had originally intended to make for England, but bad weather damaged their ship and forced them instead to put into Virginia. There, in a disastrous turn of events for the African, the court took upon itself the disposal of the three men. Initially, Brase was sent to work at the plantation of Sir George Yeardley on Jamestown Island, but not long after the court ordered that he "shall *belong*" (my italics) to the governor, Sir Francis Wyatt. To underline the governor's title to the African the court added that the decision could not be challenged by an earlier arrangement, or "sale," by Captain Jones to another planter, or any "challenge by the ships' company." The judgment, legal scholar Paul Halliday argues, is the first evidence of an English court "disposing of an African's labor for nonpunitive reasons," which, he continues, "would have enormous consequences for Brase and for all the Africans who came after him to Virginia." When Brase had chosen willingly to accompany the English privateers, he had thought they were going to England where he might have hoped to be free; instead, he ended up on Wyatt's plantation as a slave.[22]

No subsequent commentary about the condition of the Angolans or Brase survives, but there is strong circumstantial evidence for their continued enslavement. In the fall of 1627, when Sir George Yeardley wrote his will, he left his wife, Temperance, "the rest of my whole estate consisting of goods, debts, servants, Negars, cattle, or any other thing or things, commodities or profits whatsoever." Since very few Africans are documented arriving after 1620 and before 1628, it is highly probable that Yeardley's workers were the same Angolans he had purchased from the *White Lion* eight years earlier. A quarter of a century later, his eldest son, Argoll, still owned two of them, Andolo and Maria, and in 1653 sold two daughters of the couple. Less certain, but possible, is a connection between the Angolans originally acquired by Abraham Piersey in 1619 and some of the "forty *Negro* servants" owned thirty years later by Captain Samuel Mathews. Mathews had married Piersey's widow and became one of the wealthiest planters in the colony by mid-century, and it's likely that Piersey's slaves would have passed first to his wife and then to her new husband. Mathews's plantation, Denbigh, became a model of industry producing a variety of crops and manufactures that occupied his servants and enslaved African workers.[23]

Additional indirect evidence of the early existence of slavery in the colony can be gleaned from other sources: the probate inventories (lists of movable goods) and wills of planters. A study by John Coombs reveals that more than four-fifths of white indentured servants through to 1676 had the number of years remaining of their service mentioned in their masters' inventories, compared to less than 1 percent of black laborers. The absence of terms of service and the much higher valuations placed on Africans strongly suggests they served for life, unlike poor whites who served fixed-term contracts. Similarly, only one black child out of thirty-three listed in inventories down to December 1662 had his years of service recorded; the rest did not, which implies they had inherited their enslaved status from their parents.[24]

The number of Africans in Virginia grew slowly during the first fifty years: a handful arrived in the early 1620s, followed by a large group plundered from an "Angola" ship in 1628, and then a few here and there over the next several decades. In Lower Norfolk County, on the south side of the James River, thirty-three Africans arrived between 1638 and 1650, including four men and one woman sold in 1649 to Captain Francis Yeardley, youngest son of Sir George, to serve "forever." Throughout the colony, no more than about five to six hundred arrived down to mid-century.

Elsewhere in the English Atlantic, however, settlers acquired enslaved Africans with alacrity. On Bermuda, where the first African in English America arrived in 1616, Governor Butler remarked that "Negroes . . . [were] a most necessary commodity for these islands" for the production of tobacco. Scores of Africans taken from Spanish ships in the West Indies arrived over the next few years. Settlers, Michael Jarvis writes, clearly viewed Bermuda's Africans "as subordinates whose labor was subject to white appropriation . . . Legally, black servile status was assumed from the outset." Planters on Barbados followed suit in the 1630s and quickly passed a law that stated "Negroes and Indians that came here to be sold [that is, were brought to the island] should serve for life unless a contract was before made to the contrary." When the sugar revolution took hold in the 1640s, Barbados was described as a "flourishing Island" where in a single year planters purchased "no less than a thousand Negroes." On Providence Island, a Puritan settlement sponsored by the Earl of Warwick in the West Indies in the 1630s, the Company reported that hundreds of "Negroes" were being "procured at cheap rates" and kept "perpetually" as servants. In practical terms, this means that by the mid-seventeenth century, the three essential components of Virginia's and British America's evolving plantation system were in place: a commercial crop, large landholdings concentrated in the hands of wealthy elites, and, increasingly, an enslaved labor force.[25]

———◦———

RACIAL PREJUDICE DEVELOPED SIMULTANEOUSLY WITH SLAVery. The most obvious early evidence is the ubiquitous use by settlers of the Spanish term *Negro* or *Negar* as the sole descriptor of African slaves. The term itself had become virtually synonymous with enslaved sub-Saharan Africans by the sixteenth century. Whereas Virginia's colony-wide censuses of the mid-1620s identified almost all English settlers by their first and last names, Africans were rarely recorded by name. In the 1624 census, for example, eleven Angolans owned by Abraham Piersey were recorded only as "Negors" or "Negors woman" and "Negors men." At Jamestown, three were listed, including "Angela" and two unnamed "Negro" women. Elsewhere, seven Angolans were documented only with given names.[26]

Early laws regulating Africans' and whites' behavior were overtly discriminatory. Officials were forced to clarify their attitudes toward Africans for the first time in 1630 when a white settler, Hugh Davis, was convicted of "abusing himself to the dishonor of God and shame of Christians by defiling his body in lying with a Negro." According to the authorities, he had sullied himself and disgraced his community by "mixing his Christian body with a heathen one." To emphasize the point, he was sentenced to be "soundly whipped, before an assembly of Negroes and others" on the next Sabbath day. The court's judgment reveals that not only did English settlers set themselves apart by skin color but that they were keenly aware of the fundamental distinction of religion—they were Christians whereas they perceived the Africans as heathens.[27]

During the next several decades, examples of institutionalized racial discrimination became increasingly common. In 1640, an act passed to encourage the security of the colony stipulated that "All persons except Negroes" should be provided with arms and ammunition. A series of legislative measures systematically discriminated against African women. Planters were obliged to pay taxes on African women over the age of sixteen and their descendants but not on white women, signifying that female Africans were routinely employed to work in the fields—the tax was indicative of the value they were assumed to bring to their owner. A highly significant act passed by the General Assembly in 1662 decreed the status of African or African American children should in the future follow the condition of the mother. In other words, if an Englishman fathered a child with an enslaved African, the child would be accorded the status of a slave. This legislation, historian Kathleen Brown writes, was "a bold attempt to naturalize the condition of slavery by making it heritable and embedding it in a concept of race." No precedent existed in English law for such a measure.

Another important piece of legislation five years later closed any remaining glimmer of hope of freedom for Africans and their children. Henceforth, "the conferring of baptism," the assembly ruled, "does not alter the condition of the person [that is, slave] as to his bondage or freedom." This, it was explained, would allow slave owners of good Christian conscience to promote the conversion of the African children in their possession without fear of having their property rights challenged in court. When burgesses in the General Assembly passed a law in 1669 declaring that the casual killing of a slave during corporal punishment would not be accounted a felony, they based their ruling on the assumption that no one would intentionally destroy their own property.[28]

How settler prejudice translated into daily life in count-less small-scale encounters is less certain. Laws and practice clearly distinguished between white and black experience and the debasement of Africans' social and legal status inten-sified as increasing numbers began arriving after 1660. For the English, like other Europeans, individual property rights trumped all other considerations. Nevertheless, in the first four decades at least, given the relatively small numbers of Africans living on plantations scattered along the James River valley, relations among the enslaved and white servants may have been quite relaxed. Subject to similar working condi-tions, they found themselves sharing much in common. "Ra-cial prejudice," writes historian Philip Morgan, "was not yet strong enough to stop cooperation between the two. Not only did many black slaves and white servants work alongside one another, but they ate, caroused, smoked, ran away, stole, and made love together." However, while relations between poor whites and African or African American slaves could be flexi-ble according to particular circumstances, the immutable dif-ference between them, slavery, was not.[29]

THE FIRST AFRICANS TO ARRIVE IN MAINLAND ENGLISH AMER-ica survived capture in the bloody wars in Ndongo and Kongo, the exhausting march to the sea, starvation and sickness, the horror of the crossing during which many of their compatri-ots perished, and a fierce attack by two English privateers on the high seas. Yet escape from the *St. John the Baptist* and a future laboring in the fields, ports, or mines of Spanish Amer-ica did not allow the majority to escape the fate of slavery.

Instead, they ended up as enslaved workers on tobacco plantations in Virginia. They were the first of approximately four
hundred thousand enslaved men, women, and children
forcibly transported to British mainland America and then
the United States across two and a half centuries. Their remarkable fortitude and courage, and the rich variety of their
African backgrounds and cultural heritage, began to change
the social and cultural landscape of America from their first
arrival.[30]

What happened to one of the first Angolans, Angela, after her fleeting mention in records of the mid-1620s is unknown. She lived in the house of Captain William Pierce
in New Towne, Jamestown, rapidly developing as an area of
wealthy and well-connected residents. The house was one
of the finest in the colony, surrounded by three to four acres
where the Pierces planted garden crops and orchard trees.
It may have been an experimental garden where a variety of
plants promoted by the Virginia Company or brought from
the West Indies were cultivated. Angela probably toiled
alongside the mistress of the household—William's wife,
Joan—and a young maidservant, Ester Ederife, working in
the garden, around the house and yard, and perhaps in the
tobacco storehouse nearby. If she had come from an area
of Angola where a sizable population of Portuguese settlers
lived, she may have already been familiar with some European fruits and crops such as pears, peaches, and onions as
well as New World crops such as corn and tobacco.

Possibly she, like some other Angolans who arrived in
early Virginia, was a Catholic from Kongo, or she might have
been baptized by Portuguese priests in a meaningless ritual

in the traumatic days prior to taking ship from Luanda. Conversion had no bearing on her condition as a slave, however. Whether she was Catholic or she continued to adhere to her own Central African beliefs mattered little to the English, who recognized neither. No evidence suggests she attended Jamestown's small wooden church, but if she converted to Anglicanism, she may have occasionally attended divine service, standing with the Pierce family close to where the first General Assembly had met to establish representative government and the rule of law for the English a few weeks before she arrived in the colony.[31]

Four

Commonwealth

Nothing [is] so difficult as to establish a common wealth so far remote from men and means.

—*John Smith (1612)*

Every commonweal, as says Aristotle, . . . is a company, and every company is ordained to do some good, and most chiefly to obtain the most principal and most excellent good of others.

—*Henry Manship (1619)*

I N AN ENTHUSIASTIC REPORT DELIVERED TO THE COMPANY on November 15, 1620, Sir Edwin Sandys proclaimed that "the Commonwealth and State of the ~~Country~~ [*sic*] Colony in Virginia began generally to prosper." Aided by John Ferrar and Nicholas Ferrar and supported by the Earl of Southampton, Sandys looked to fashion a society that promoted an abiding commitment to Anglican ritual and God's word, just laws, equitable government, and an economy based on a wide variety of crops and industries, trade, and public works that would benefit the Company and the multitudes of settlers who would shortly flock to the colony. Essential also was the godly task of converting the entire Powhatan people to Protestantism, a "noble Action for the planting of *Virginia, with Christian Religion*" as the English saw it, thereby bringing tens of thousands of Indians to the Church of England and advancing their eventual integration into settler society.[1]

The establishment of a New World commonwealth was at the heart of Sandys's plans for the colony. It combined in a single framework the many political, social, and economic changes that Company leaders believed were indispensable to the creation of a well-governed society. Their approach, both in conception and in their determined efforts to implement it, represented an extraordinarily ambitious view of the potential of American colonies. The shape of English America in terms of good government, just laws, economic well-being, and friendly relations between settlers and Indians would rest upon the success or failure of their far-reaching ideas.

———

SANDYS AND OTHER COMPANY LEADERS WERE WELL VERSED in the major political theories of the day, and hence commonwealth was a familiar concept to them. Although its meaning had taken on different emphases from the late fifteenth to the early seventeenth centuries, at its core it remained the same: an expression of the critical relationship between a healthy body politic on the one hand and the people's welfare on the other. Inspired by the church's teachings, civic humanism, and the sweeping changes rapidly transforming the country, a rich and passionate debate had developed about the ideal balance between private enterprise and the common good. "A public weal is a body living," the humanist scholar Sir Thomas Elyot wrote, "made of sundry estates and degrees of people, which is disposed by the order of equity and governed by the rule of moderation and reason." Concerned above all with the maintenance of law and order, he outlined the proper roles each estate should play if the "public weal" was to thrive. A well-ordered commonwealth depended on everyone knowing and accepting their place within a finely grained hierarchy of households and achieving a harmonious balance of interests. Emphasizing the people's well-being, Thomas Starkey described a "true common weal" as nothing less than "the prosperous and most perfect state of a multitude assembled together in any country, city, or town governed virtuously in civil life according to the nature and dignity of man."[2]

Contemporary thinkers were unanimous in praising the blessings of England's constitutional commonwealth. Inspired by the teachings of classical thinkers such as Aristotle, Polybius, and Cicero, two of the most influential statesmen of the age, Sir John Fortescue and Sir Thomas Smith, gave primacy to the rule of law and Parliament as the twin foundations of the English constitution. As early as the 1470s, in one of the first statements of its kind, Fortescue wrote approvingly that English monarchs could not alter the law without the consent of their subjects or burden them with unjust impositions. The king was appointed by God "to protect his subjects in their lives, properties, and laws; for this very end and purpose he has the delegation of power from the people; and he has no just claim to any other power but this." By consenting to laws passed in Parliament, which represented the entire kingdom, the people were secured in their property and thereby enjoyed a higher standard of living than their counterparts in continental Europe, governed for the most part by absolute sovereigns who cared little for their people's rights or well-being. The peculiar genius of the English, Fortescue believed, lay in creating a series of mutually reinforcing relationships that brought together monarchy, government, and the people in the form of a res publica (commonwealth) that profited everyone. In this way, the people were able to prosper from the natural resources and commodities of the land and from trade. In turn, their affluence and happiness profited the monarchy and encouraged social stability.

Elaborating upon Fortescue's interpretation a century later, Sir Thomas Smith gave further definition to England's mixed constitution. In *De Republica Anglorum,* he maintained that although the monarchy was the most powerful part of the realm's body politic, the other two components— aristocracy and the people—also had an important role in governing, notably by their participation in the greatest of the sovereign's councils, Parliament. Parliament, Smith wrote, was the "most high and absolute power of the realm of England" where the people were "collected together and united by common accord." The sovereign and representatives of all the estates of the kingdom, from highest to the lowest, sat together to deliberate on laws and to consider "what is good and necessary for the common wealth." In one of his most famous remarks, he emphasized that Parliament gave expression to "the whole universal and general consent and authority as well of the prince as of the nobility and commons, which is as much to say of the whole head and body of the realm of England." By means of consensus in Parliament, described as the "whole realms deed," no man could justly complain if he disagreed with decisions taken "but must accommodate himself to find it good and obey it." Consent of the people, directly or indirectly, was essential to representative government.

Yet if England's mixed constitution depended on a judicious balance of rights and responsibilities between the rulers and the ruled, it was characterized by considerable ambivalence. English political thought evolved simultaneously in two opposing directions during the sixteenth century: the monarch provided a symbol of unity within the realm, but Parliament gave voice to the commonwealth, the people, which, according to the historian Glenn Burgess, had a "life of its own" and represented a multiplicity of opinion. Just how harmony and balance was achieved among the different spheres of government and between the government and the people was not explained at any length, for example. And what redress was available to the government or the people should England's constitutional well-being be compromised or lost was equally uncertain.[3]

The question was especially urgent given the social disruption caused by the far-reaching religious, political, and economic changes taking place during this period. Widespread enclosures of common lands, vitally important to small farmers and tenants for grazing their livestock or for cultivation, disrupted age-old practices; enormous transfers of property during the English Reformation stripped the Catholic Church of its properties and put them into the hands of the gentry and aristocracy; and rapid population growth and rising inflation led to a spectacular rise in the numbers of impoverished men and women out of work and on the tramp. Traditional society, it was said, was "far out of joint."

Writers trying to make sense of the turmoil penned fierce critiques of the unrestrained greed of the wealthy at the expense of the poor. "When I consider and weigh in my mind all these commonwealths which nowadays anywhere do flourish," the principal character of Sir Thomas More's popular satirical work *Utopia,* Hythlodaeus, remarked, "God help me, I can perceive nothing but a certain conspiracy of rich men, procuring their own commodities under the name and title of the common wealth." The idle rich bled the common people dry, reducing them to lives of unceasing toil just to eke out a bare existence. At the height of the social and economic crisis of the 1530s and 1540s, Protestant moralists such as Thomas Becon, Henry Brinkelow, Robert Crowley, and Hugh Latimer, known collectively as the "commonwealthsmen," wrote scathingly about the wealthy who lived without fear of God or conscience and who "would have all in their own hands," leaving nothing for others. They were "the very caterpillars of the commonweal," consuming all in their lust for more worldly possessions. "Overmuch regard of private and particular wealth," Thomas Starkey cautioned, "ever destroys the common[weal]."[4]

Such critiques also highlighted the importance and moral worth of work. "Let every man, of whatsoever craft or occupation he be of," the preacher William Tyndale declared, "refer his craft and occupation unto the commonwealth, and serve his brethren as he would do Christ himself." Work sustained people, undergirded order and hierarchy by emphasizing the importance of divinely appointed vocation, and fostered advantageous relationships between the people based on the principles of honest labor and just dealings. "Remember that we are members of one body," Tyndale continued, "and ought to minister one to another generously." Sir Thomas Smith agreed that people should help support those less fortunate than themselves but recognized that to inspire the better off to provide support for the poor, the government had to devise policies that simultaneously promoted self-interest as well as the common good. Men, he argued in *A Discourse of the Commonweal of England* (written for private circulation in 1549 but not published until 1581), "should be provoked to good deeds by rewards." Allowing people to benefit from their labor would lead to greater productivity and thereby profit the individual and the community.

The commonwealthsmen, of whom Smith was one, thus looked for solutions that encouraged responsible and virtuous gentry leaders to take care of the poor in their localities and at the same time arouse a strong sense of Christian stewardship and charity within the people. Their admonitions were infused with the righteous zeal of the Reformed religion that involved, as the historian Keith Wrightson has remarked, nothing less than "the remoralising" of society. On the whole, most reformers responded conservatively and nostalgically to the extreme economic dislocation that engulfed them, looking back to an idealized age of plenty in order to restore an earlier age of social harmony. But what if the wide-ranging changes taking place across the country were irreversible? What if there were too many people looking for work but not enough work to go around? What then?[5]

From this perspective, it is hardly a coincidence that promoters of English colonization schemes in Ireland and America came to prominence in government and mercantile circles following the social upheavals of the mid-sixteenth century. Commerce and colonization were linked to state policy in respect to foreign relations, propagating the new Anglican Church, and addressing domestic problems. Advocates of western planting argued vigorously that English settlements in America would relieve poverty and underemployment while promoting trade and manufactures at home. Christopher Carleill recounted that during the wars in the Netherlands, he had witnessed firsthand how men who had formerly "been very evil and idle livers" had proved most industrious against the armies of Philip II of Spain. Employment in the colonies would serve a similar purpose.

Richard Hakluyt the younger, the foremost writer in favor of American colonization of the day, observed that despite all the statutes devised by Elizabeth I's government to punish "idle vagabonds," the country continued to be overrun by "multitudes" of able-bodied poor and unemployed, an "altogether unprofitable" drain on the country. "[Y]ea, many thousands are within this Realm, which having no way to be set on work be either mutinous and seek alteration in the state, or at least very burdensome to the common wealth, and often fall to pilfering and thieving and other lewdness, whereby all the prisons of the land are daily pestered and stuffed full of them, where either they pitifully pine away, or else at length are miserably hanged." In the colonies, he wrote, they could be found work to their own and the nation's advantage. Petty thieves and vagabonds who "for trifles may otherwise be devoured by the gallows" could save themselves by laboring in America. Later writers such as Gerard de Malynes and Francis Trigge continued to comment on the close relationship between dire poverty and lack of work in early seventeenth-century England.[6]

The settlement of English colonies, then, had a dual role—it was a means of addressing intractable social problems at home and an opportunity to extend the realm overseas. Although the Virginia Company was a private commercial enterprise, it was supported by the Crown and carried the king's sovereignty to America. Such an arrangement was expedient for James I, who could take advantage of the potential benefits of colonization but deny Virginia was a state-sponsored undertaking when put under pressure by a succession of Spanish ambassadors to intervene and prevent settlement. More generally, overseas expansion was a primary means by which ambitious nation-states asserted their power and pursued "greatness"—a theme in contemporary political literature—as English statesmen and adventurers such as Sir Walter Ralegh and his half brother Sir Humphrey Gilbert were well aware. Their efforts to establish colonies in the 1580s were influenced significantly by the strategic imperative to counter the existential threat posed by Philip II of Spain's global empire to England and to confront the Spanish American empire by establishing an English empire in the north.

Sir Edwin Sandys was similarly attracted by the pursuit of greatness in a colonial setting but viewed it instead through the lens of commerce and the creation of a New World commonwealth, a "perfected" English society in America. As well as trade, Sandys strenuously advocated a colony devoted to the "publique," a commonwealth that would benefit all those that ventured themselves or their money and which represented an improvement on English society, principally in respect to the well-being, moral as well as economic, of the people.[7]

FUNDAMENTAL TO A FLOURISHING COMMONWEALTH WAS HIerarchy and good order. Sixteenth-century commentators were agreed that the happiness of the people rested squarely on the quality of their governors' judgment and virtue. The effective exercise of authority by rulers depended on rank, ability, and character. They "which be superior in condition or property should also have preeminence in administration" because a gentleman's virtue was commonly mixed "with more sufferance, more affability, and mildness." Ordinary working people or those of base lineage, it was held, lacked the capacity for learning or a level of reason that allowed them to rule and therefore could only occupy the lowly stations that God had ordained for them. Starkey observed that the people benefited from "laws well administered by good officers and wise rulers, by whom they be governed and kept in politic order." For this reason, the Company received proposals from a couple of its members in July 1619 and the following year to establish a nobility in Virginia made up of earls, viscounts, barons, and baronets that would underline the colony's conformity with English society as well as "faith and fidelity to the Crown." The scheme came to nothing, but the desire to attract men of "extraordinary quality and good condition" remained. Impartial and moderate rule by leaders was not only a practical requirement but also a moral one, the London preacher Robert Gray emphasized. "There must be a special care in the Magistrate," he wrote,

> how to carry himself in his place and order: for herein consists the very main matter of the success of this business [the founding of a commonwealth]. As therefore the Magistrate has the eminence of dignity conferred upon him by his Prince, so must he furnish himself with eminence of virtue: for he shall the better contain others within the bounds and limits of honesty and godliness, if he first be able to contain himself . . . A Magistrate therefore must have a good conscience towards God, and he must also have a loving affection towards those over whom he has the government.

Such precepts reflected a conventional emphasis on hierarchy and obedience that went back time out of mind and highlighted expectations about the reciprocal duties of rulers and the ruled. A leader who failed to maintain order failed not only in his responsibilities to the people under his charge but also to God.[8]

Company officers could feel confident in the "quality" of those who supported the enterprise in London: the list of lords, knights, and merchant princes involved in the management of the Virginia enterprise or who had signed up as investors reads like a who's who of the time and represented

an emphatic endorsement of the project by men of high political and social standing. It was important, therefore, that
the governor of Virginia should be of similar rank. Hence the
Company was highly gratified by Lord De La Warr's decision
to sail for Jamestown with his wife and retinue to resume
his position as captain general and lord governor of Virginia
in 1618. Apart from the ill health that had dogged him over
the years, there could be little doubt about his suitability for
the position or that his presence would confer luster to the
new form of government they planned to introduce. During
his absence of seven years, the leadership of the colony had
rested on the shoulders of knights and captains, for the most
part able men but not lords. Consequently, De La Warr's
death at sea in the summer of 1618 was a serious setback
for the Company that required a speedy resolution. The man
chosen for the role, Captain George Yeardley, had arrived in
the colony with Sir Thomas Gates in 1610 and had proven to
be a dedicated commander, briefly serving as acting governor
before returning to England in late 1617. Yet while Yeardley
was from a respectable middling background, he was not remotely of high rank.

The solution that emerged in the fall of 1618 illustrates
the paramount importance attached by the Company to social hierarchy and status. At the end of November, several
senior members of the Company's council, including Lord
Doncaster, a gentleman of the king's bedchamber and member of the privy council, joined James I at Newmarket and
spoke on behalf of their recently chosen governor. Yeardley
was ordered to attend to learn what service he could render
the king. Shortly after arriving in the king's presence, James

commanded Yeardley to a "withdrawing chamber, where with the sword of estate he dubbed him knight," after which he joined James at a church service and then with the king's entourage for dinner. The king spoke to Yeardley for a full hour and a half about many aspects of the colony, after which he remarked to the bishop of Durham, "My Lord this is the first day that ever I began heartily to love Virginia, and from this day forward I will ever protect and defend it." A promise, as it turned out, he did not keep.

Returning to London a few days later, Yeardley met with several of the great officers of state and peers of the realm who also conferred their blessings on him and his endeavor. The anonymous letter writer R. F. concluded "that I may justly say, that no governor nor other officer that ever were sent to Virginia, departed the land with so great encouragement from his Majesty and the great ones, or with so general notice and hopeful expectation of all men, as this gentleman we have now employed." Yeardley had been elevated to the highest level of society and carried with him to Virginia the king's approval as well as the backing of many of his most important clerics and ministers of state. No better endorsement of the new governor and the Company's plans could have been hoped for.[9]

As WELL AS EFFECTIVE AND VIRTUOUS RULERS, SANDYS'S conception of a well-run commonwealth was founded on involving the people in their own public affairs. As a member of the House of Commons, he had enthusiastically advocated consulting with his constituents before adopting a final position in Parliament. He fully acknowledged the divine right of sovereigns to govern but also believed passionately in the constitutional right of the people to have a means of expressing their opinion. Consent bred concord, "the strongest and loveliest bond of security in every Commonwealth, being always accompanied by Justice and Equity," the great Roman orator and statesman Marcus Tullius Cicero remarked in one of his most famous statements.

In this vein, Sandys and his supporters considered a representative body located at Jamestown absolutely essential; otherwise, settlers would have insuperable difficulties making their voices heard at the colony level or before the Company in London. The newly established General Assembly offered a collective means by which settlers could seek remedies for perceived injustices, general or particular, react to laws devised by the Company, and propose legislation of their own based on their familiarity with conditions in the colony. In fact, a few years later, such was the encouragement given by these measures that members of the assembly declared the people followed their labors with "singular alacrity" and Virginia flourished as never before. Sandys and his followers understood that to persuade settlers to adopt the Company's vision of a new reformed society, a broadly representative body in the colony was indispensable. In that realization, the principle of representative government in America was born.[10]

At the local level, towns and corporations would carry the main burden of implementing commonwealth principles. "[N]othing does sooner cause civility in any country," Edmund Spenser had commented in 1596, "than many market towns, by reason that the people repairing often thither for their needs, will daily see and learn civil manners of the better sort . . . there does nothing more enrich any country or realm than many towns." Spenser was writing of Ireland where efforts to establish towns were strongly supported by English and Scottish undertakers (sponsors and colonizers), but the comment was equally applicable to America.

From the beginning, Virginia's backers anticipated the colony would quickly develop an urban network extending from Jamestown along the James River valley. Robert Johnson, deputy to the treasurer Sir Thomas Smythe, wrote in 1609 that in addition to Jamestown, the Company planned to settle "six or seven plantations more, all upon, or near our main river, as capital towns, twenty miles each from other, and every plantation shall manure and husband the lands and grounds lying near unto it, and allotted for the circuit thereof." Initially established as garrisons, the Company favored the creation of towns for the same reason their counterparts sponsored towns in Ireland and the Spanish founded cities and ports in their New World colonies: urban settlements would evolve their own local governments, courts would be established to redress of grievances, and the creation of regular markets would encourage prosperity, all thereby promoting order and stability. During the early years of Sandys's reforms, so much emphasis was given to the foundation of towns by the colony's investors that the prospects of Virginia as a whole were measured in terms of urban growth. The Company believed that a "flourishing Church, and a rich Commonwealth" depended on towns.[11]

Towns' charters conferred valuable privileges on their

inhabitants. Corporate rights endowed townspeople with freedoms that protected their trades and craft practices that in turn promoted their collective and individual wealth. Company leaders, like prominent merchants and statesmen elsewhere in Europe, were town and city dwellers "steeped" in a "corporate civic humanist tradition." Multiplied hundreds of times over, the wealth of prosperous towns collectively added up to the wealth of nations. Giovanni Botero, an influential intellectual and scholar, had no doubt when he wrote in his *On the Causes of the Greatness of the City* of 1588 and his *Reason of State* of the following year that the preeminence of states and princes rested on the fortunes of their cities, calculated by population, trade, and industry rather than purely by the size of their territories or strength of their armies. For Sandys, who was familiar with Botero's writings, the creation of towns and eventually cities in Virginia was essential not only in the immediate term of encouraging civility and prosperity but also to the longer-term vision of a continental-sized English North America founded on transoceanic commerce.[12]

Virginia's four "ancient general Burroughs" would not have looked like towns to most English observers, however. They covered enormous areas: Henrico, Charles City, James City, and Kecoughtan (Elizabeth City) extended west to east from the falls of the James River to its mouth at the entrance of the Chesapeake Bay and beyond to the Atlantic coast, a distance of more than one hundred miles as the crow flies. Each corporation was made up of hundreds of thousands of acres spanning both sides of the James. The handful of wooden towns (there was little brick or stone) that existed in anything more than name were small and rudimentary affairs, typically laid out in a few streets with a church, a couple of storehouses, and several dozen dwelling houses, "built homelike," the whole protected by palisades. They formed tiny urban cores of the corporations, the latter made up of plantations, large and small, Company and common lands, and huge areas of uncleared land, marsh, and woods scattered along the rivers. Despite these humble beginnings, Sandys and Company leaders were confident that their "city commonwealths" would develop as the essential building blocks of the new, reformed society about to arise.[13]

THE CREATION OF TOWNS AND CORPORATIONS WAS NECESsary to provide local governing structures for the thousands of settlers who would shortly arrive. Mass migration was essential for Virginia to prosper. Twelve hundred settlers had been sent in 1619, and a similar number had left or were about to leave England in the following year. Most of them, the Company claimed, were hardworking men "born and bred up to labor and industry." Men and boys from all parts of the realm were sent to work the land as servants, tenants, or freeholders, and artisans and tradesmen were recruited to provide important services. After entering into an agreement with London authorities, the Company was able to transport to Virginia hundreds of poor children who would serve as field-workers and domestic servants and who would otherwise have pestered the streets and public places of the city. The arrangement was considered an especially pious and reputable undertaking that both relieved London of the unwanted poor who drained municipal coffers while at the same time provided needed workers for the colony. City authorities organized the rounding up of vagrant children for transportation and threatened those who did not want to go with imprisonment. Robert Gray had warned Company leaders a decade earlier of the social dangers of overpopulation in the mother country. Poverty and unemployment inevitably led to social unrest, food shortages, "and sundry sorts of calamities." By contrast, as the Company was quick to point out, opportunities for productive work in Virginia would both profit the poor and supply England with the valuable commodities needed at home.[14]

Company leaders sought to recruit the best artisans in Europe to establish profitable manufactures in the colony. Skilled Frenchmen were hired from Languedoc and La Rochelle to oversee the "planting and dressing of vines," silk production, and development of saltworks. (One of them, John Bonoeil, had written *A Treatise on the Art of Making Silk* for James I.) Poles, or "Polackers," from "Eastern parts," probably the Baltic region and Northeast Europe, were recruited to produce potash, pitch, and tar; Germans were recruited from the Rhine to make wine and from Hamburg to set up lumber mills and shipbuilding; and Italians were sent to Jamestown to produce beads "for trade in the Country with the Natives" and to make glass "of all sorts." Sandys's and the Company's commonwealth was to be peopled by skilled workers, industrious planters, virtuous women, the redeemed poor, and Christianized Indians.[15]

Persuading women from respectable backgrounds to settle in the colony was especially important. The assembly had

petitioned the Company in 1619 to recruit more women settlers, stating "that in a new plantation it is not known whether
man or woman be more necessary." Sandys and his followers
were of the same mind and undertook measures to address
the shortage of virtuous and hardworking women. A "Plantation can never flourish until families be planted," the Company confessed. "Wives and Children fix the people on the
Soil." A special fund was raised to pay the costs of passage,
clothing, and provisions for "young, handsome, and honestly
educated Maids," who in Virginia would be "disposed in Marriage to the most honest and industrious Planters." Approximately 150 young women were sent to Virginia during 1620
and 1621 to be wives to planters who could afford to start
their own families. Among them was Lettice King, whose
brother was "an Attorney at the Law" and cousin a knight.
From Newbury, Berkshire, she had been "in divers [many]
good services" from which she came recommended. Cicely
Bray of Gloucestershire, twenty-five, was related to Sir Edwin Sandys. Katherine Finch was in service with her brother
Mr. Erasmus Finch, the king's "Crossbow maker," and was
recommended by two other brothers, all living in the Strand,
London. Alice Burgess, twenty-eight, a maid from Linton,
Cambridgeshire, was an orphan who had been in service to a
goldsmith and then a silk weaver near Whitechapel Church in
London. She was described as "skillful in any Country work"
and could "brew, bake, and make Malt etc." The Company's
effort to recruit reputable young women to marry planters was
among the most ambitious of their social initiatives and one
of the clearest indications of their desire to create a stable,
well-ordered society based on virtuous families.[16]

To give further encouragement to new colonists as well as the settlers already in Virginia about future prospects, Company leaders granted two extraordinary boons. Recognizing free settlers' investment, whether by service or stock, Sandys and his associates authorized that everyone would receive land for themselves and their heirs. Settlers who had arrived before spring 1616, who were termed "ancient planters," were to receive one hundred acres for their own adventure and if they were investors another one hundred acres for every share purchased. Those who had arrived after April 1616 and paid their own passage would receive fifty acres for themselves and an additional fifty for every person they transported. The latter arrangement, which became known as the headright system, was for the rest of the century the primary means by which laborers were recruited and sent to the colony. Secondly, following "the laudable Example of the most famous Commonwealths both past and present," the Company pledged to relieve settlers of the corporations of all taxes and public costs "forever."

Keeping in mind that the enormous areas of land attached to each of the four corporations were only made possible by the convenient fiction that the Powhatans had freely given up their territory, Company leaders in London could afford to be generous. Confident therefore that huge tracts of land would be available for private as well as public use for many decades to come, the Company commanded Sir George Yeardley to set aside public lands "for the maintenance and support as well of [the] Magistracy and officers as of other public charges." Three thousand acres of "good land," to be called the "Company's Land," was to be allotted within each of the four corporations and would be worked by tenants transported to the colony at the Company's expense. Tenants would receive half the return from their labor, and the other half would be reserved for the Company. Before remitting the Company's share to London, the expenses of the colony's officials and other Company costs would be paid. In addition, another 1,500 acres were assigned to each corporation as common land for "the Support and Entertainment" of magistrates, and local officers as well as "other charges to the said Cities and Burroughs respectively belonging." Finally, the governor would receive 3,000 acres for his own support, the land to be laid out a few miles from Jamestown. Particular plantations were to remain separate from the Company's corporations, but if their sponsors cooperated by obeying the new government in Jamestown, they would also receive 1,500 acres of common land.[17]

THE LEADERS OF THE FOUR CORPORATIONS AIDED BY COM-
pany officials were to implement plans for the diversified economy that Sandys and others in London demanded. James I had urged Yeardley on the eve of his departure for Jamestown to pay particular attention to silk production, which he thought "would prove a sufficient recompense for all o[u]r labors," and showed great interest in many other natural commodities and manufactures that the colony might produce. The "precious liquor" of vines, the king reckoned, "would not only prove merchantable" but would attract "good company to come and live there."[18]

A promotional pamphlet of June 1620 gave full voice to

the Company's enthusiasm for the type of economy they believed would dramatically improve the colony's fortunes. For
at least thirty years, writers had claimed that Virginia was capable of producing many of the goods that had been imported
into England from Europe and Asia for centuries. Now that
they had the political and governmental structures to allow
the blossoming of the diversified economy, regular trade with
Britain could be established. To underline the point, the
pamphlet writer spelled out the particular commodities available in the colony and which old-world countries had traditionally imported such goods into England:

> We rest in great assurance, that this Country, as it is seated
> near the midst of the world, between the extremities of
> heat and cold; So it also participates of the benefits of
> both, and is capable (being assisted with skill and indus-
> try) of the richest commodities of most parts of the Earth.
> The rich Furs, Caviar, and Cordage which we draw from
> *Russia* with so great difficulty are to be had in *Virginia,*
> and the parts adjoining, with ease and plenty. The Masts,
> Planks, and Boards, the Pitch and Tar, the Pot-ashes and
> Soap ashes, the Hemp and Flax, (being the materials of
> Linen,) which now we fetch from *Norway, Denmark, Po-*
> *land,* and *Germany,* are there to be had in abundance and
> great perfection. The *Iron,* which has so wasted our *En-*
> *glish* Woods, that itself in short time must decay together
> with them, is to be had in *Virginia* (where wasting of
> Woods is a benefit) for all good conditions answerable to
> the best in the world. The Wines, Fruit, and Salt of *France*
> and *Spain;* The Silks of *Persia* and *Italy,* will be found also

in *Virginia,* and in no kind of worth inferior. We omit here a multitude of other natural Commodities, dispersed up and down the various parts of the world: of Woods, Roots, and Berries, for excellent Dyes: of Plants and other Drugs, for Physical service: Of sweet Woods, Oils, and Gums, for pleasure and other use: Of Cotton wool, and Sugar-Canes: all which may there also be had in abundance, with an infinity of other more.

Company leaders hoped that by producing at least some of these commodities on Company lands in each corporation and reaping the healthy profits that would follow they might also tempt settlers to produce them on private lands. To this end, they passed legislation that required settlers to plant mulberry trees, vines, and silk grass for the next few years as well as trials with hemp, flax, and aniseeds the following growing season. In subsequent years, reports mentioned the cultivation of fig trees, pomegranates, cotton wool, sugarcane, indigo, and potatoes, all part of the effort by Company and colony leaders (the council, assembly, and local corporations) to persuade planters to abandon their reliance on tobacco in favor of a range of crops and manufactures that would lead to a strong economy and a sturdy class of independent farmers and craftsmen.[19]

Land reforms, including individual allocations to planters and economic initiatives, were intended to promote a durable commonwealth. Company-sponsored common lands offered further incentives. While only slight evidence exists about how the 1,500 common acres located in each corporation were used, whether in the form of communal grazing for cattle and hogs or as smallholdings, there can be little doubt that the symbolism of common land would have been obvious to settlers, especially those from rural regions of England. Many of the settlers' parents and grandparents had lived through the mid-sixteenth century when across the country landlords attempted to encroach upon tenants' common lands or enclose them altogether. From the 1530s onward, the English countryside was peppered with demonstrations by small farmers and poor industrial workers against challenges to their customary rights. The "earth is the poor man's as well as the rich," Henry Brinkelow thundered. Whereas the true gentry were "fathers of the country [and], maintainers of the poor," Thomas Becon wrote, corrupt and avaricious landlords were by contrast "no gentlemen" but "extortioners" who had reduced the common people to ruin and beggary.

Sandys's Virginia offered an opportunity to escape the vicious cycle of overpopulation and unemployment that had stunted the lives of English poor and lower-middling working people for a century. Huge tracts of land taken from the Powhatans were available for cultivation, and hence there was plenty of work for everyone who ventured the Atlantic crossing, whatever their social condition. The destitute boys and girls with "no places of abode or friends" swept up from the streets of London would find a new life along the James River employed "in some Industrious pursuit." Land and work would give them and all immigrants a livelihood, a place in society, and even to some degree respectability.[20]

VIRGINIA WAS TO BE A GODLY SOCIETY. THE CHURCH OF England had arrived with the first settlers who held their services initially under sailcloth suspended between trees. Early in 1608, the colony's first church was built at Jamestown in the middle of the fort as a clear statement of the presence of the Anglican Church in English America and was followed a few years later by three more churches at Henrico, Charles City, and Kecoughtan. With Sandys's energetic support, the Company promoted further construction: a new church was built at Jamestown in 1617–1618 to replace the earlier structure that had fallen into disrepair, and churches or places of assembly were built at several private plantations including Smith's Hundred, Berkeley Hundred, and possibly Wolstenholme Town. James I had told Governor Yeardley at their meeting at Newmarket that the colony's churches were to be recognizable as such, not built "like Theaters or Cockpits . . . but in a decent form, and in imitation of the churches in England."

The Christianizing of the landscape by the construction of churches and places of worship was vitally important to the Company's emphasis on establishing a "reformed" society in which Anglicanism and piety guided the everyday lives of colonists. At Berkeley Hundred, a group of Gloucestershire settlers were enjoined to gather daily for prayer and meals and to hold the day of their arrival as a special day of thanksgiving. The Sabbath was to be kept "in holy and religious order" and used for preaching and teaching and manual labor; "vain sports and scandalous recreations" were banned. To attract "learned and painful [conscientious] Ministers," each corporation and private plantation was to allocate one hundred acres as glebe land for maintenance and in addition provide a very handsome living of £200 yearly. Ministers and churchwardens were to be responsible for keeping watch for "all ungodly disorders," described by the General Assembly as idleness, gaming, swearing, drunkenness, and whoredom. They were to set an example in morals and to avoid factions and "Novelties," which tended "only to the disturbance of peace and unity."[21]

Ministers were expected also to emphasize the vital importance of community and *bonum publica* (public good) in everyday life. In churches throughout England, by way of communion, sermons, psalms, and homilies, the laity was exhorted to come together to bear witness to the natural bonds of human fellowship, underpinned by the mutual love and charity for which Christ had died on the cross. Following the first great commandment to "love the Lord thy God," Jesus explained that the second commandment was to "love thy neighbor as thyself." The homily on *Christian Love and Charity* (1547) reiterated the commandment and amplified Christ's message: "Thus of true charity, Christ taught that every man is bound to love GOD above all things, and to love every man, friend and foe." Christian charity in daily life meant helping the poor, sick, helpless, and even enemies in distress. Participation of the laity in church services, maintaining the church and churchyard, and celebrating holy rituals throughout the year were vital expressions of the ties that bound local communities together. The teachings of the church offered moral guidance to the community, helped individuals understand their place within it and within the social hierarchy at large, and provided compelling lessons about how to live as good Christians, lessons that held special meaning to men and women living on a distant shore of the English world, surrounded by a heathen population.[22]

From the Company's point of view, Christian charity, community, and caring for neighbors translated above all to the great work of converting the Powhatans to Anglicanism, a keystone of Sir Edwin's plans. A decade earlier, the Company had sponsored a series of sermons that recast the relaunching of the colony by Sir Thomas Smythe following its near collapse as a divinely appointed national undertaking. The "plain necessity of this present action for Virginia," William Crashaw proclaimed in 1610, "the principal ends thereof being the plantation of a Church of English Christians there, and consequently the conversion of the heathen from the devil to God." As a chosen people, English preachers and settlers had been given a sacred mission: to cross the ocean and spread the light of the true faith into the dark corners of a heathen and savage land, "even where Satan's throne is." Robert Johnson, aware of the huge expansion of Catholicism among Indian peoples of Spanish America, exhorted all well-affected subjects to adventure their purses or persons to support the new colony and "spread the kingdom of God, and the knowledge of the truth, among so many millions of men and women, Savage and blind, that never yet saw the true light shine before their eyes."[23]

Despite the glorious providential rhetoric and exhortations from the Company for support from investors and godly settlers, the effort collapsed amid the vicious fighting of the Powhatan war of 1609–1613. Following the end of hostilities, the conversion of Pocahontas and her subsequent marriage

to John Rolfe gave the Company renewed hope, briefly kin-
dling the possibility that the daughter of the great chief Wahunsonacock would involve herself in the conversion of her
people. Her death at Gravesend, England, at the beginning
of the voyage back to Virginia in the spring of 1617 dealt another grievous blow to the Company's ambitions. Yet disappointing as earlier efforts had been, Sandys and his associates
were determined to revive widespread support for conversion
of the Powhatans; their vision of a Christian commonwealth
depended on it. "We hold," Sandys's former mentor the great
Anglican theologian Richard Hooker had written, that "there
is not any man of the *Church* of *England,* but the same man
is also a member of the *commonwealth,* nor any man a member of the *commonwealth* which is not also of the *Church*
of *England.*" A shared faith was necessary to create a single
community.[24]

Sir Edwin Sandys was an intensely religious man. Ironically in this regard, for all his political differences with James I,
in his passion for religious reconciliation in Europe he shared
much in common with the king. James I was viewed by Protestant thinkers in Europe as a "reconciler" of faiths, a monarch who might promote "the concord of the Church with
common consent." The church, James was convinced, encouraged "moral behavior, peace in the commonwealth, and
true learning." Most important, achieving stability and peace
in Europe depended on bringing about reconciliation among
the major religious factions. Sandys was of the same opinion.
In midlife he had written a comprehensive account of the
religious landscape of western Europe following two years
of traveling on the continent. The manuscript, *A Relation*

of the State of Religion . . . in the severall states of those west-
erne parts of the worlde (1599), surveyed the impact of the
massive religious upheavals of the sixteenth century, the Reformation and Counter-Reformation. Civil wars in France
between Catholics and Protestants (Huguenots) and the revolt of Dutch provinces against Spanish rule had torn western Europe apart, devastating once-flourishing cities and
provinces.[25]

What could be done to end the carnage? Sandys believed
the solution lay with "worthy princes" who following a middle
course would bring about "unity over all Christendom, if it
may be." He favored a moderate church and believed that
Anglicanism came closest to a model for compromise. The
key phrase, however, was "if it may be," because he did not
consider political conditions in Europe remotely conducive
to religious unity. He, like many other religious humanists,
may have fervently hoped that the Christian church would
eventually reunify, but he did not think it possible as long
as Catholic Spanish monarchs backed Rome as the only
true church. Unless Spain's global dominance was significantly reduced or their support for the papacy withdrawn,
the bloody conflict between Protestant and Catholic states
would continue. This being the case, the best that could be
achieved was to encourage a peaceful coexistence grounded
on religious toleration among those states not at war.[26]

With religious conflict breaking out in Europe in 1618
once again, the appeal of converting the Powhatans and
founding a new Protestant Christian order in Virginia was
irresistible to Sandys and his supporters. They understood
the wider implications. Reconciliation and peace among

Protestant faiths in Europe, espoused by the king, would be complemented by English efforts to bring Anglicanism to the Indians of North America. If the Company succeeded in bringing the Powhatans into the Church of England, it would be but a short step to converting them en masse to civility and Englishness. Five years earlier, Sir Thomas Dale had overseen an important ceremony with leaders of the Chickahominies, a large and powerful people in the heart of Powhatan's territories, during which they had pledged to recognize James I as their king and to take the name of "Englishmen." As far as Dale was concerned, because of the Indians' willingness to be called English and pay an annual tribute, they had put themselves under James's protection and were therefore his vassals, even if they viewed the relationship quite differently. Before Sandys's and the Company's efforts of 1619–1622, the arrangement was the closest colonists had come to adopting the Indians as English, albeit as vassals rather than subjects. But even that success was short-lived; there had been no further progress with other peoples and a few years later the Chickahominies repudiated the agreement and took Opechancanough as their king.[27]

Sandys's predisposition to compromise and his pragmatism in public matters inclined him and his principal advisor, John Ferrar, to adopt a cautious approach in trying again to bring the Powhatans into the church. To this end, the Company urged settlers:

> both present and to come, may be faithfully brought up in the true knowledge and service of Almighty God, and so learn to frame their lives and conversations, . . . [that] by

their good example, to allure the Heathen people to sub-
mit themselves to the Scepter of God's most righteous and
blessed Kingdom, and so finally join with them in the true
Christian profession.

Such was the intention in theory, but in practice Company
and colony leaders placed their faith in first converting Indian children who in turn would convert their parents, their
kin, and the larger population. Each borough, city, and particular plantation, the General Assembly ordered, was to take
"a certain number of the natives' children to be educated"
and the most promising boys would be "fitted for the College
intended for them that from thence they may be sent to that
work of conversion." James I had already expressed his enthusiasm for the project by ordering charitable collections to
be taken throughout the country by the Church of England
in 1616 and 1617. Monies would be used to establish a college, which would be built in Henrico together with (eventually) a university on ten thousand acres, allocated by the
Company, for teaching Powhatan children.[28]

The king supported the Company's pious efforts, which
corresponded to his own broader ambitions in Europe. At
Newmarket, he had expressed to Governor Yeardley his enthusiasm for the college and the prospect of Indian children
"as laborers into gods harvest," converting those of "their own
nation to the Christian faith." The letter writer R. F. observed
that in discussions about spreading religion "his Majesty, like
a true nursing father of god's church, expressed marvelous
great zeal and affection." In England, support for the Company's religious initiative continued to grow. An anonymous

message left on Sandys's chair at a court meeting wished him good luck "in the name of the Lord, who is daily magnified by the experiment of your Zeal and Piety in giving beginning to the foundation of the College in Virginia the sacred work so due to Heaven and so Longed for one [on] earth." Together with the letter, several items of valuable church plate were donated, adding to the thousands of pounds collected over the previous five years for the building of churches and schools as well as the college at Henrico.[29]

Company plans were given further impetus by the arrival of Mr. George Thorpe from Berkeley, Gloucestershire, in the spring of 1620. Formerly a member of Parliament and gentleman of the king's privy chamber, Thorpe was a major investor in Berkeley Hundred and the Company and was well known to Sandys. Owing to his status and the respect he commanded, he was put in charge of the college lands as one of the governor's deputies and added to the colony's council of state. Passionate about the mission to bring Christianity to the Powhatans, he was critical of settlers' hostile attitude toward the Indians and advised Sandys and the Company to offer gifts such as clothing and household goods to show their "love and hearty affection." The way to convert the Indians and win them over to English ways, Thorpe believed, lay in improving their material conditions.

His advice was written into instructions by the Company and issued to the new governor, Sir Francis Wyatt, in July 1621. Governor Wyatt was to take special care that "no injury or oppression" be perpetrated by the English against the Indians "whereby the present peace may be disturbed and ancient quarrels (now buried) might be revived." He was instructed also to draw the better disposed of the Powhatans into a closer relationship with the English and to reward them accordingly. These converts would be a "great strength" to the English as missionaries for the "more general Conversion of the Heathen people which we so much desire." Meanwhile, George Thorpe had established a warm relationship with the great chief Opechancanough and was rewarded in the early spring of 1622 with the extraordinary news that the chief and his people were ready to abandon their heathen ways and embrace the Anglican faith. At last, the "perfecting of this happy work," the English believed appeared to be in reach.[30]

———•+•———

IN THE EARLY 1570S, SIR THOMAS SMITH AND HIS SON AND namesake described the many advantages of founding settlements in Ireland in a promotional pamphlet intended to attract support for the venture. English *coloni* (settlers) would cultivate a sparsely populated land, build towns, stimulate commerce, and establish "law, justice, and good order." The English were unlikely to fall into the barbarous practices of the Irish, Smith wrote, because farming and settled communities would ensure they maintained their virtue. "How say you now," Sir Thomas asked exuberantly, "have I not set forth to you another Eutopia?"[31]

Half a century later, Sandys's view of Utopia in Virginia shared much in common with Smith's, especially regarding the effort to create a prosperous, just, and civil society. Although the Company was critical of settlers' overdependence on tobacco, a buoyant market in London and handsome profits gave great encouragement to merchants and planters alike. From 1619 to 1621, 3,570 settlers had been sent to the colony in forty-two ships, English laws and representative government had been established, and local communities supporting diverse crops and manufactures were expanding all along the James River. To promote education, the Company was committed to the construction of a free school named for the East India Company, which had contributed funds to instruct settlers' children in "the principles of religion Civility of life and humane learning." John Ferrar commented that the undertaking was of the "highest consequence unto the Plantations . . . whereof both Church and commonwealth take their original foundation and happy estate." Money was raised for the purchase of books for the school and to assist with the tutoring of Indian children. Above all, Sandys and his supporters eagerly awaited the conversion of the Powhatans. Over time, Indians and godly and hardworking English settlers would unite and live under the benevolent care of the Anglican Church. Virginia, a "New Jerusalem," would be the first Protestant commonwealth in America.[32]

Five

Tumult and Liberty

Our first work is expulsion of the Savages to gain
free range of the country.

—*Governor Sir Francis Wyatt (1622)*

Extreme liberty being worse than extreme Tyranny,
as it first appeared by the troubles in Rome after
Nero's death.

—*Captain John Bargrave (1622)*

I N A LONG LETTER SENT TO THE COMPANY IN JANUARY 1622,
the new governor, Sir Francis Wyatt, described the colony's well-being and prosperity. Wyatt had recently convened
a General Assembly at Jamestown in which measures were
passed to advance the planting of a "great store" of vines and
mulberry trees "in all places" throughout the colony and to
have planters cultivate English grains and pulses as well as
Indian corn. If the Company were to give encouragement

to planters to grow more corn for their own sufficiency and to provide for the multitudes who would shortly arrive from England, the governor believed far less tobacco would be planted and corn would soon replace tobacco as the colony's principal crop. He reported that an ironworks had been constructed upriver beyond Henrico, a windmill on Yeardley's property at Flowerdew, and that George Sandys, Sir Edwin's younger brother and the newly appointed treasurer on behalf of the Company in the colony, was building a watermill on his estate near Jamestown. Industries were being established and thousands of newcomers had arrived in good health over the previous few years and had been well received by those already settled in the colony. Most pleasing of all, the English lived "in very great amity and confidence with the natives." Wyatt and his council were confident that the two Powhatan chiefs, Opechancanough and Itoyatin, wished to further strengthen relations with the colonists.

Delighted by the news, in April, Company leaders commissioned a sermon of thanksgiving to be delivered by Patrick Copland under the title "Virginia's God be Thanked." Unknown to them, however, a few weeks earlier, the colony had suffered the first of a series of disasters that would ultimately bring about the Company's demise and the subsequent emergence of a society radically different from the Christian commonwealth envisaged by Sir Edwin Sandys and his supporters.[1]

ON FRIDAY, MARCH 22, 1622, IN A MASSIVE AND HIGHLY skilled attack led by the war chief Opechancanough, approximately 350 English men, women, and children were killed in their homes or at work about their plantations. Company official Edward Waterhouse wrote in a bitter account that elite warriors of the Powhatans and Pamunkeys, supported by other local Indians and hundreds of mercenary allies, had known exactly where to find the settlers "in regard of their daily familiarity, and resort to us for trading and other negotiations, which the more willingly by us continued and cherished for the desire we had of effecting that great masterpiece of works, their conversion." All along the James River valley, from far upriver at the ironworks recently established at Falling Creek to the populous settlements of Henrico and Charles City, and as far downriver as Elizabeth City and Warraskoyack, English settlers were killed in brutal hand-to-hand fighting, overwhelmed by wave after wave of Indian warriors. Crops, livestock, and dwellings were destroyed and churches burned to the ground. The massacre, described by the English as "contrary to all laws of God and men, of Nature and Nations," was to the Powhatans long-awaited revenge for the devastation of their towns, theft of their hunting grounds, and occupation of their lands by settlers; it was an utter repudiation of everything the English stood for, including their Protestant God.[2]

In stark contrast to his first report, Governor Wyatt's next letter to the Company described in somber terms the catastrophe that had befallen the colony:

It has pleased God for our manifold sins to lay a most lamentable Affliction upon this Plantation, by the treachery of the Indians, who on the 22th of March last, attempted in most places, under the Color of unsuspected amity, in some by Surprise, to have cut us off all and to have Swept us away at once throughout the whole land.

Owing to God's mercy many English had been saved, "but yet they [the Indians] prevailed so far, that they have massacred in all parts above three hundred men women and Children."[3] Incredulous at the news, which arrived in London in July, the Company and English observers laid the blame squarely on settlers' complacency and dissolute living. The reason why they "were so easily subject to the surprise of those naked people," the letter writer John Chamberlain observed, was their "own supine negligence" whereby they had lived "as careless . . . as if they had been in England." In his opinion, the disgrace and shame of the successful Indian attack was as bad as the losses sustained, "for no other nation would have been so grossly overtaken." Company leaders were outraged, accusing the settlers of failing to heed clear warnings of an attack in a time of known danger. What had happened could only be interpreted as a sign of God's dissatisfaction. The drunkenness and excessive ways of settlers were notorious, and it seemed obvious to observers in England that their neglect of divine worship had inevitably brought down the righteous anger of Almighty God. To avoid further retribution, the Company demanded they seek forgiveness and conform to His "most just and holy laws." Only with His protection and blessing could they secure themselves from more attacks and rebuild the colony.[4]

Between a quarter and a third of the English settlers died that fateful day; it was one of the most devastating attacks to befall colonists in any part of the British Empire over the next several centuries. William Capps, an "ancient planter" of Elizabeth City, spoke for many traumatized survivors when he wrote: "God forgive me I think the last massacre killed all our Country, besides them they killed, they burst the heart of all the rest." The enormity of what had befallen the colonists can be judged by the widespread fear that gripped them in the aftermath. The "land is ruined and spoiled," a young servant Richard Frethorne lamented, and "we live in fear of the Enemy every hour." He resided at Martin's Hundred where he reported eighty of his countrymen had been killed, reducing the plantation to such a weak state that they would not be able to defend themselves should the Indians come again "for we lie even in their teeth." Continuing attacks led the governor to order planters to vacate outlying plantations and find safety in larger communities and fortified settlements. As they withdrew, Opechancanough's warriors were able to carry out the next stage of the plan, the wholesale destruction of settlers' property, which the great chief hoped would ultimately compel the English to abandon the enterprise and Virginia. Before "two Moons," Opechancanough assured his people, not a single colonist would be left in all their "Countries."[5]

THE COMPANY HAD NO INTENTION OF LEAVING VIRGINIA, however. Owing to the continuing high price of tobacco in London and the possibility of reaching an agreement with James I guaranteeing a monopoly on the importation of tobacco from the colony, private investors continued to support the venture. Even after such a disaster, long-term prospects appeared promising. Hundreds of settlers were recruited to replace those who had been lost, "for, in the multitude of people is the strength of a Kingdom," and schemes were put in place to organize a regular supply of young men from England's shires. The Company ordered the four corporations and the particular plantations to be repeopled when safe from further attacks, and the manufacture of iron, trials of silk, and production of wines and other crops were to be resumed as soon as possible. Every good "Patriot" knew, Edward Waterhouse commented, that the founding of Virginia reflected glory upon the king and nation and was vital to the spreading of "Christian Religion" and to the enlargement, strength, and fortunes of James's dominions. To abandon Virginia would be unconscionable. It would be "a Sin against the dead," the Company stated, to give up the enterprise for which "so many of our Brethren have lost their lives."[6]

As news of the massacre spread throughout England, an outpouring of racially charged language called for extreme measures and merciless reprisals. The attack had been a massive violation of natural law, contemporaries wrote, by which the Powhatans had lost all rights to their land and civilized treatment. Edward Waterhouse's influential apologia written on behalf of the Company was subtitled *A Relation of the Barbarous Massacre in the time of peace and League treacherously executed by the Native Infidels upon the English*. The word *massacre* carried a special meaning for the English, recalling atrocities perpetrated by Catholics against Protestants such as the St. Bartholomew's Day Massacre in France of 1572, during which thousands of Huguenots (French Protestants)

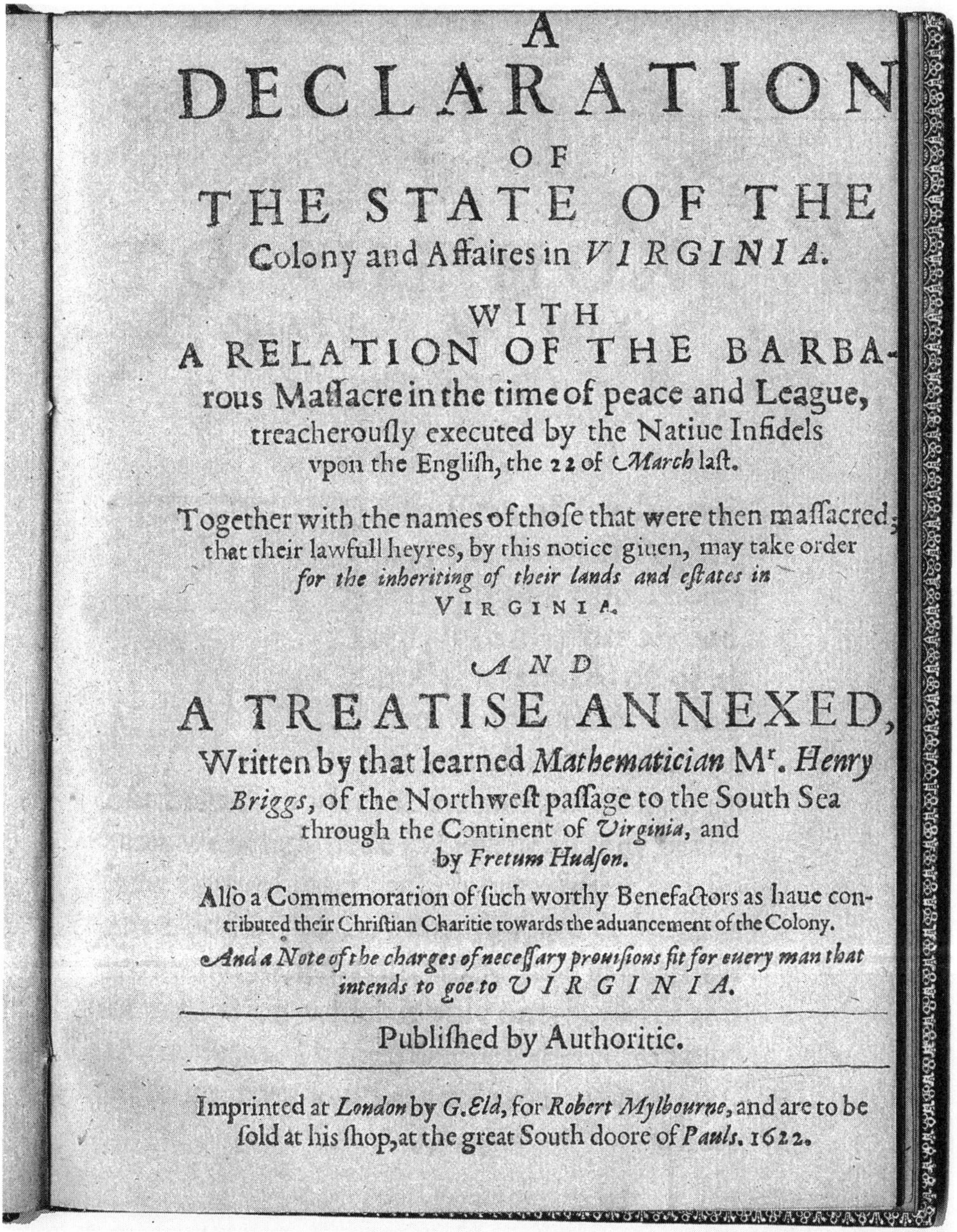

A
DECLARATION
OF
THE STATE OF THE
Colony and Affaires in *VIRGINIA*.

WITH
A RELATION OF THE BARBA-
rous Maſſacre in the time of peace and League,
treacherouſly executed by the Natiue Infidels
vpon the Engliſh, the 22 of *March* laſt.

Together with the names of thoſe that were then maſſacred;
that their lawfull heyres, by this notice giuen, may take order
for the inheriting of their lands and eſtates in
V I R G I N I A.

AND
A TREATISE ANNEXED,
Written by that learned *Mathematician* M^r. *Henry*
Briggs, of the Northweſt paſſage to the South Sea
through the Continent of *Virginia*, and
by *Fretum Hudſon*.

Alſo a Commemoration of ſuch worthy Benefactors as haue contributed their Chriſtian Charitie towards the aduancement of the Colony.

And a Note of the charges of neceſſary prouiſions fit for euery man that
intends to goe to V I R G I N I A.

Publiſhed by Authoritie.

Imprinted at *London* by G. *Eld*, for *Robert Mylbourne*, and are to be
ſold at his ſhop, at the great South doore of *Pauls*. 1622.

FIGURE 7—Title page of Edward Waterhouse's *Declaration* of 1622. Permission of
the Virginia Museum of History and Culture.

were murdered, or the "Spanish Fury" in the Netherlands a few years later when mutinous troops went on a killing spree in Antwerp, one of the most important cities in western Europe. Since the founding of Jamestown, settlers' leaders had feared above all the possibility of Spanish forces finding their way to the Chesapeake Bay, destroying the colony, and cutting the throats of the colonists, just as they had killed hundreds of French Huguenots from Fort Caroline half a century earlier on the bloody sands of Matanzas Inlet near St. Augustine, Florida. Such horrific cold-blooded killings had sent shock waves throughout Europe. The Reverend Joseph Mede, a millennialist who believed the end of times was fast approaching when Jesus Christ's thousand-year reign would begin, had no doubt that God was on the side of the English. Just as a maleficent god was responsible for "the massacres now in France, and in other parts of Christendom," the massacre in Virginia was encouraged by the Powhatan's "wicked God Ochee [Okeus]." But "our God, the God of Gods," he exclaimed, will "confound them quickly."[7]

Waterhouse expressed the bitterness and frustration of the English public on learning their countrymen in Virginia had been undone by the Powhatans. His *Relation* embraced conventional attitudes toward American Indians that had long been widespread in Europe. European superiority was unquestioned, adopting, as philosopher and historian Tzvetan Todorov puts it, a combination of "authoritarianism and condescension." In literature and images of the period, Indian peoples were typically portrayed either as inhuman or barely human, godless cannibals, or conversely as childlike, loving, gentle, and "void of all guile . . . such as lived after the manner of the golden age." By their actions, the Powhatans proved they were of the treacherous and barbaric sort. Waterhouse's account brims with pejorative terms such as *unnatural, pagan, bestial, perfidious, false-hearted, inconstant, wicked,* and *miserable*. Colonists, he wrote, had been unwise to place their trust in the Powhatans but had done so only with the best intentions. They had sought the Powhatans' conversion "by peaceable and fair means," seldom was a sword or musket drawn against them; they had been welcome at English tables or to shelter in settlers' homes. In return, the English had been rewarded with treachery and cruel murder. Trust was *"the mother of Deceit."*[8]

Yet to Waterhouse's mind there was one tangible benefit of the disaster. Settlers' efforts to occupy and profit from the land would no longer be inhibited by their responsibility to convert and civilize the Powhatans. "Our hands, which before were tied with gentleness and fair usage," he wrote, "are now set at liberty by the treacherous violence of the Savages, not untying the Knot, but cutting it: So that we, who hitherto have had possession of no more ground than their waste, and our purchase at a valuable consideration . . . may now by right of War, and law of Nations, invade the Country, and destroy them." In chilling prose, he set out what amounted to a justification of mass slaughter and forced removal that would serve as a blueprint for European colonizers over the centuries to come:

> Because the way of conquering them is much more
> easy than of civilizing them by fair means, for they are
> a rude, barbarous, and naked people, scattered in small

companies, which are helps to Victory, but hindrances to Civility: Besides that, a conquest may be of many, and at once; but civility is in particular, and slow, the effect of long time, and great industry. Moreover, victory of them may be gained many ways; by force, by surprise, by famine, . . . by pursuing and chasing them with our horses, and blood-Hounds to draw after them, and Mastiffs to seize them, which mistake this naked, tanned, deformed Savages, for no other than wild beasts, and are so fierce and fell upon them, that they fear them worse than their old Devil which they worship, supposing them to be a new and worse kind of Devils then their own. By these and sundry other ways, as by driving them (when they fly) upon their enemies, who are round about them, and by animating and abetting their enemies against them, may their ruin or subjection be soon effected.

Such techniques had been effective for the Spanish in the West Indies and South America and would be equally effective for the English. Though they were initially highly critical of the Spaniards' brutal treatment and exploitation of indigenous peoples and had sought to distinguish their own compassionate approach to the Indians of Virginia, the English now cited the conquistadors' bloody methods with approval.[9]

Waterhouse was not alone in his views. An epic poem by Christopher Brooke, a prominent supporter of the Company and parliamentarian known to Sandys, provides another example of the racially charged language that circulated after the massacre:

For, but consider what those Creatures are,
(I cannot call them men) no Character
Of God in them: Souls drown'd
in flesh and blood;
Rooted in Evil, and oppos'd to Good;
Errors of Nature, of inhumane Birth,
The very dregs, garbage, and spawn of Earth;
Who ne're (I think) were mention'd
with those creatures
Adam gave names to in their several natures
But such as coming of a latter Brood,
(Not sav'd in th'Ark) but since
the general Flood
Sprung up like vermin of an earthly slime.

"Father'd by Satan, and the sons of hell," the Indians had forfeited knowing "Th' Eternal God," joining the Anglican Church, and adopting English ways that would have brought them peace and prosperity. Jean Bonoiel, the French expert on silk production and viticulture, spoke for the Earl of Southampton and other Company leaders in repudiating the Indians as devoid of culture, industry, or arts. They were ignorant, idle, and brutish. As a consequence, he considered that "there is a *natural kind of right* [my italics] in you, that are bred noble, learned, wise, and virtuous, to direct them aright, to govern and to command them."[10]

The massacre had demonstrated beyond doubt that the Powhatans could not be redeemed and converted to Christianity and English ways. For Sir Edwin Sandys and the Ferrars, it must have been a bitter realization. Lost to them once and for all was the hope of a Christian commonwealth in the New World that would unite English and Indian peoples in spreading the Anglican faith across the continent, creating a Protestant bulwark in North America to counter Catholic Spain in the south. It was left to George Sandys, who arrived in Jamestown shortly before the massacre, to come to the inevitable conclusion. Government, he wrote, was the principal "bond of society" allowing every man to suppress vice and advance virtue that were "the two main columns of a Commonwealth, without which it can have no support." Man was "a political and sociable creature, [Indians] therefore are to be numbered among the beasts who renounce society, whereby they are destitute of laws, the ordination of civility." By this standard, there was no longer any place for Indian peoples in the English colony.[11]

JUSTIFICATIONS FOR TAKING POSSESSION OF INDIAN LANDS IN America had been a central theme of English colonial discourse for half a century before Jamestown. Promoters of overseas expansion such as Sir George Peckham, writing in the early 1580s, explained that by the law of nations Christians had the right to enter the lands of "infidels" for trade and live there if they wished. Since "the nativity of Christ, mighty and puissant [powerful] Emperors and Kings have performed the like," he emphasized, "I say to plant, possess, and subdue." Such views formed the basis of European claims to Indians' lands founded on the principles of just wars, the right to trade freely, and the holy work of converting the heathen to Christianity. Following the establishment of the Jamestown colony, the Company believed that redeeming and civilizing the Indians fully justified their right to settle in the Powhatans' country. "Our intrusion into their possession [land] shall tend to their great good," Robert Johnson declared, "yet not to supplant and root them out, but to bring them from their base condition to a far better." However, should the Indians resist conversion, the colonists could lawfully make war on them providing the ultimate objective was to reclaim them from barbarous and sinful ways.[12]

Commencing the bloody work of conquest, the Company ordered Governor Wyatt to launch a "perpetual" war against the Powhatans without peace or truce. He was to deploy tactics adopted by Lord De La Warr, Gates, and Dale earlier, dispatching companies of soldiers to destroy the Indians by "burning their Towns, demolishing their Temples, destroying their Canoes, plucking up their [fish] weirs, carrying away their Corn, and depriving them of whatsoever may yield them succor or relief." Usual rules of engagement did not apply. Nothing was unjust, Wyatt and his commanders told the Virginia Company, if it led to the Indians' ruin. Children were to be spared in the hope that eventually they might be brought to Christianity, but the rest of the "bloody miscreants" were to be put to the sword or removed, as "they intended against us."[13] Implicit in the phrase *perpetual war* was a strategy of total war, "for the glory of God, and love toward our brethren (whose blood, no doubt, cries to heaven for vengeance)," Wyatt proclaimed.

As occurred in the fighting of a decade earlier, the English were given license to kill Indian men and women or to starve them into submission. References to raids and the killing of Indian peoples from this period read as almost routine events in the colony's reports. Sir George Yeardley's men, for example, ranging the shore of the Weyanock people upriver from his plantation at Flowerdew, found only the Indians' old houses, which they burned. In another report, Captain William Powell out on patrol met three Indians by chance "whose heads he cut off." By the Indians' own admission, the council in Virginia wrote, "we [the English] have slain more of them this year, than have been slain before since the beginning of the Colony."[14]

Dehumanizing and demonizing the Powhatans fully justified the use of extreme violence. The adoption of new and efficient forms of artillery, firearms, weaponry, and light armor had proceeded rapidly in Europe across the late fifteenth and sixteenth centuries. The king showed his support for the colonists by granting them a princely gift of arms, armor, and powder from the royal armory in the Tower of London that was to be delivered to the Company forthwith. Weapons and equipment included 300 matchlock muskets, 700 calivers (a light form of musket), 300 pistols, 1,000 halberds, 540 coats and shirts of mail, 2,000 helmets, and 400 war bows with 800 sheaves of arrows, all of which were to be distributed to the settlers as Wyatt and his councilors thought fit. Many of the men who arrived in the colony during the first war with the Powhatans had served in the Netherlands and Ireland and would have been familiar with such weapons.

Halberds and bills, polearms typically six to eight feet long, were designed variously with vicious hooks, spikes, and axes and were employed to spear and hack the enemy; swords were used to sever heads and limbs, and short swords and daggers could be used to slash and thrust, causing massive internal bleeding and trauma. Musket balls were capable of smashing through cartilage and bone, causing terrible injuries that were usually fatal, killing by shock or infection if not by immediate blood loss. Firearms could be used singly or in enfilade fire to devastating effect. Small ships such as pinnaces or shallops were capable of carrying swivel guns, aptly named *murderers*, loaded with small shot to pepper settlements along the shores or groups of warriors. While Powhatan war bows were formidable weapons capable of delivering fatal arrow shots or debilitating wounds, their stone arrowheads could not penetrate armor.[15]

When conventional methods did not suffice, other stratagems were employed. In the spring of 1623, an emissary from Itoyatin visited Sir Francis Wyatt with a message from the chief saying that "blood enough had already been shed on both sides, that many of his People were starved, by our [the English] taking Away their Corn and burning their houses" and that they wished to return to their former lands. He offered to deliver to the English captives taken in the fighting and also his brother, Opechancanough, "the Author of the Massacre," dead or alive. The offer was not considered genuine, but the governor and his council saw an opportunity to take advantage of the overture. Captain William Tucker was sent to the Pamunkey River with a dozen soldiers to conclude a peace with a large gathering of Indian chiefs and warriors. Following a number of speeches, Tucker passed round bottles of sack (fortified wine) to drink to the end of hostilities and the new peace. Tucker and his interpreter tasted the wine to show no treachery was intended, but drank from a different bottle while the Indians, including Itoyatin and other "great men," were given poisoned wine. How many died is uncertain, but many suddenly became sick, giving Tucker and his men the opportunity to open fire, killing approximately fifty. As trophies, or perhaps to claim the bounty for killing Opechancanough, Tucker returned to Jamestown with pieces of the Indians' heads.

Such a deceitful attack on European adversaries would have been unthinkable, but no criticism of the mass poisoning of Indians was voiced in either Virginia or London. Governor Wyatt sent a letter to the Company reporting that by a "successful stratagem" his men had not only rescued English captives but had also "cut off some kings and divers of the greatest Commanders of the Enemy, among whom we are assured Opachankano is one, it being impossible for him to escape." The Company and colonists alike were mistaken in believing Opechancanough was dead, however, as well as in their assumption that the Indians had been dealt a decisive blow. Sporadic hostilities would continue for the next eight years.[16]

A major outcome of the first Powhatan war of 1609–1613 had been the settlers' push into the heartland of Powhatan territory and establishment of settlements on the best lands along the James River valley as far upriver as Henrico. The "multitudes" of English taking up lands after 1618, a direct outcome of the Company's reforms, was the principal reason why the Powhatans had resolved to resist the invasion of their territories. Following the massacre and the Indians' failure to expel the English, settlers were determined to take possession of a far larger region than they had previously controlled, which embraced both the James and York River basins and potentially beyond to the Potomac. The assembly discussed building a palisade across the peninsula from Martin's Hundred to Kiskiak and from the James River to the York River to keep the Indians out; a safe haven "much bigger than the Summer Isles [Bermuda]," Captain John Smith remarked, that would serve as a vast cattle range and be capable of supporting ten thousand settlers.

Increasingly, Company and settler policy focused not only on security but on making the land exclusively English. By "this last butchery," the Reverend Samuel Purchas wrote of the massacre, the Indians had proved to be "more brutish than the beasts they hunt, more wild and unmanly than that unmanned [underpopulated] wild Country, which they range rather than inhabit." As "Borderers and Out-laws of Humanity," he continued, they had forfeited any rights to the land, and once rid of them, a bountiful Virginia enriched by European plants and animals and populated solely by English settlers would in time become "another England in America."[17]

As well as being expelled from their traditional lands, Indian peoples were also enslaved. The Company discussed raising a colony-wide levy to support the war against the Powhatans, advising that captives could be used as "slaves" to pay soldiers and defray the costs. Captain John Martin, the old planter, argued against simply slaughtering the Powhatans, saying that they were "more apt for work than yet our English are." He suggested using them to help produce silk, grow hemp and flax, act as guides for expeditions into neighboring "Countries," and "row in Galleys and frigates." William Capps assured John Ferrar that he could bring in "3 or

4 score [Indian] slaves to work about a fort or other servile work," adding ominously, "but before I deliver them up I will make them sing new Toes, old Toes, no Toes at all, because they shall not outrun me," meaning he would cut off Indian captives' toes to prevent them from running away.

Further evidence of the Company's interest in enslaving the Powhatans occurred a few years later when William Claiborne, surveyor and a member of the governor's council, announced that he had devised a contraption for the "safekeeping" of Indians. The council was sufficiently impressed by Claiborne's invention to grant him an Indian for the "better experience and trial" of it (no description was given of how the contraption worked). In any event, however it was achieved, Virginia was the first mainland English colony to enslave Indian peoples. Settlers had already adopted slavery following the arrival of the first Africans, and Indians would now suffer the same fate.[18]

Indian slavery never became a major institution in the colony, although following another large-scale attack in 1644 as well as hostilities in the mid-1670s, spates of enslavement ensued. Indian warriors taken prisoner during fighting were either sent to the West Indies or enslaved in the colony; only children under the age of twelve were allowed to remain in English homes, a distant echo of the Company's plans to convert them to Christianity. A new great chief, Necotowance, assented to the status of a "tributary," or subject, of the English king in 1646, and the chiefdom effectively broke up. Tsenacommacah was no more, only Virginia, and the Powhatans became a "declining minority" on the margins of their former lands. Some adopted English ways, abandoning their peoples altogether, while others were determined to retain their own traditional cultures and continued where they could to live largely separate from the English. By the end of the century, their numbers had dwindled to less than a few thousand dispersed across the region.[19]

The collapse of an inclusive Christian commonwealth was ultimately to prove ruinous for Sandys's and the Virginia Company's vision of Virginia. Absorbing the entire chiefdom, ten thousand Powhatans together with their vast territories, into English Virginia was a fundamental element of Sandys's and other leaders' plans. Indians would bring their specialized knowledge to the settlers, such as the cultivation of valuable crops, the location of mines and minerals in the interior, and finding a passage through the mountains to the Pacific or riches in the West. In the absence of thousands of Powhatans to populate and join with the settlers, the English were forced to rely on recruiting large numbers of men and women from England in an attempt to transport an entire settler population across the Atlantic, a feat achieved hitherto only by the Spanish and to a lesser extent the Portuguese. Company leaders recognized this greater role when they stated to the Crown's ministers that they were not merely a company of merchants but were committed to transporting and settling people "in those uninhabited Territories under good government and consequently for the enlargement of his Majesty's Dominions."[20]

Large-scale migration was essential to the colony's future development, but the Company simply did not have sufficient resources to supply the new settlers adequately during the voyage or immediately after arrival. Colonists complained bitterly of ships that were meagerly provisioned and grossly overcrowded. Weakened by malnourishment and prone to sickness from the putrid conditions on board, many new arrivals succumbed within a few months of landing. Lady Margaret Wyatt, the wife of the governor, wrote to her sister from Jamestown that "Few in the Ship that I came in are left alive." During the height of the crisis, starvation and illness carried off so many, old planters as well as newcomers, that George Sandys reported the living were *"hardly able to bury the dead."* For want of adequate shelter, men and women died where they lay outside under bushes and were left unburied for days. Reminiscent of the "starving time" in the colony's early years but on a larger scale, 1622–1623 was the worst year the English endured in Virginia and at least a thousand settlers perished.[21]

———

PLENTY OF CRITICS WERE ON HAND TO FIND FAULT WITH SIR Edwin Sandys, notably powerful grandees of the Virginia Company such as Sir Thomas Smythe and the Earl of War- wick as well as several of the king's ministers. The leading op- position figure in Parliament for more than a decade, Sandys had been a principal rallying point for the county gentry in the House of Commons and spoke to issues that concerned them with an unerring belief in the justice of their cause. Even before the setbacks in Virginia, he and some of his prin- cipal supporters found themselves in trouble with James I and his government for their alleged views on events taking place in Europe, which would eventually have a profound impact on the future of the Company.

In what many members considered a flagrant breach of parliamentary privilege, he and the Earl of Southampton had been imprisoned during the summer recess of the 1621 Parliament, and Sandys was subsequently placed under house arrest at his estate in Northbourne, Kent, as punishment for his alleged overzealousness in opposing royal policies both inside and outside the Commons. Specifically, he was questioned by Crown officials about his opinion of the proposed marriage of the Prince of Wales, Charles, to Infanta Maria of Spain, which was keenly supported by James and his court, and his sympathy for "the Lady Elizabeth," the king's daughter and wife of the Elector Palatine of the Rhine, Frederick V. Sandys, Southampton, and the Virginia colony became briefly embroiled in an international crisis of enormous dimensions.

Elizabeth and Frederick had married eight years earlier; it was the Protestant wedding of the year and an apparent success in James's larger goal of strengthening relations with leading Protestant powers in Europe. In August 1619, Frederick had been offered the crown of Bohemia by rebel nobles in revolt against the Catholic Ferdinand II, soon to be elected the Holy Roman Emperor, and made a fateful error in deciding to accept. His rash action, against the advice of James, sparked a war in Bohemia, the Palatinate, and eventually much of Germany, Flanders, and northern Europe. Later known to history as the Thirty Years' War (1618–1648), the massive convulsion of religious conflict embroiled all the major powers in the most devastating conflict of the era; what amounted to a Europe-wide war of religion.

Frederick's decision was equally disastrous personally. Overwhelmed by Ferdinand's forces, which were supported by veteran units of the Spanish army, Frederick and Elizabeth were forced to flee from Bohemia and also lost their lands in the Palatinate, quickly becoming the objects of pity of English Protestants who were baffled by James's failure to intervene to save them from defeat and humiliation at Catholic hands. Righteous English people called for full-scale intervention in a war they saw not only as a matter of national honor but as a vital sign of the coming of the prophesied thousand-year rule of Jesus Christ on earth. The war was interpreted as a struggle between good and evil on a cosmic scale in which England would play a special role in fighting on the side of Christ and providing a bulwark against Catholicism. "This little island," London preacher Thomas Cooper exclaimed, was the "sanctuary of all the Christian world," by which of course he meant Protestants.

English America would also play a significant role. The dean of St. Paul's, John Donne, believed like Sandys in the "Apostolical" promise of the expansion of English Protestantism in America. Speaking before Virginia Company leaders in November 1622, he assured them that "You shall have made this Island, which is but as the *Suburbs* of the old world, a Bridge, a Gallery to the new; to join all to that world that shall never grow old, the Kingdom of heaven." In this vein, James I was viewed as a new Constantine, "the pacifier of the world and planter of the Gospel in places most remote." A popular tract entitled *Merlin's Prophesie* predicted that the king, the "Western Emperor," would lead the Protestant princes in a holy war against Catholics and die on the battlefield after a great victory.[22]

Yet as it turned out, the king had other ideas. To the

grievous disappointment of his zealous subjects, James chose instead to pursue an alliance with England's old enemy Spain, believing that the marriage of Charles to the infanta would enable a speedy resolution to the conflict and restore his son-in-law to his estates. The king's initiative was desperately unpopular with the people and exasperated members of the Commons during the 1621 Parliament, including Sandys, who were deeply suspicious of Spanish intentions.

From the king's point of view, however, complex diplomatic negotiations that had been in progress for several years were now being jeopardized by the irresponsible behavior of the Commons. James accused "fiery and turbulent spirits" of meddling in "matters far above their capacities which tends to the infringing of our prerogative royal." The House was ordered not to involve itself in discussion about the marriage and to forbear disparaging "the king of Spain, and other of our friends and allies." But further, in an unnecessarily provocative statement of principle and political blunder of major proportions, he underlined to the speaker in reference to the imprisonment of Sandys, Southampton, and other members that "we think ourselves free and able to punish the misbehavior of any member in Parliament as well during the sitting as after." The comment sent shock waves through the House, striking at one of the most sacrosanct of parliamentary rights: freedom of speech—an early hint of the acrimonious disputes between James, Charles I, and Parliament to come.[23]

Virginia Company officials as well as the rank and file were well aware of the significance of the arrest and detention of their two leaders. In the hothouse climate of the early 1620s, with so much at stake at home and abroad, members wondered who was responsible for turning the king against Sandys and Southampton. There were a number of possibilities: the Marquis of Buckingham or perhaps the young prince, who was also closely involved with Buckingham, but Company suspicions fell primarily on the influential Spanish ambassador (influential in James's court at least), Don Diego Sarmiento de Acuña, Count of Gondomar. Rumors circulated in the city that it was he who called James's attention to the frequent meetings of the Virginia Company where, the count said, "too many of his [the king's] Nobility and Gentry resorted to accompany the popular Southampton, and the dangerous Sandys." These meetings, he purportedly warned James, were likely to "prove a seminary for a seditious Parliament." Gondomar apparently believed that politicians associated with Virginia had "further designs than a Tobacco plantation" and once sufficiently strong intended to launch attacks on Spanish possessions in the Indies, which would inevitably bring England into conflict with Spain.[24]

By the early 1620s, Parliament, particularly the House of Commons, viewed itself as indispensable in the maintenance of the people's rights and welfare of the state. The heated deliberations in Parliament about the king's pro-Spanish policy, together with clashes between Company leaders and members of James's court, encouraged intense royal scrutiny of Sandys's larger aims for Virginia. Against the background of the unfolding political crisis in England that pitted Parliament against king, these discussions stimulated a far-reaching debate about key principles of government, authority, and liberty in the home country and the colony.[25]

ANXIOUS TO INVOLVE HIMSELF IN SUCH WEIGHTY MATTERS
was Captain John Bargrave, a well-educated and experienced
man who, following service in the wars in the Netherlands,
had eventually found his way to Virginia and established a
plantation on the south bank of the James River near Martin's
Brandon; he then commenced a career of litigation against
his neighbors and Company officials. In June 1623, seeking
to curry favor with one of James's most powerful ministers,
he wrote a long letter to Lionel Cranfield, Earl of Middlesex
and lord treasurer, which emphasized the dire threat of social
and political turmoil in the colony. The timing of his letter
was determined by the establishment of a royal commission
a few weeks earlier by the king to investigate the calamitous
events in Virginia of the previous year. In Bargrave's opinion,
the root of the problem was that the Company was ruled by
"popular voices" that covered up their secret practices, and
"it is a shame that the Commonweal of Virginia, depending
on the Monarchy here, should be governed so." An ardent
supporter of the monarchy and hierarchy, he was convinced
that the establishment of the General Assembly had given
too much power to ordinary planters who took advantage of
their newly granted influence to pursue policies that benefited themselves rather than the good of the colony.

Problems had first arisen when the Company was led by
Sir Thomas Smythe, Bargrave believed. For a decade, the
colony had labored under harsh regimes that had taught the
planters inhumanity and injustice, which they in turn showed
in their attitudes toward newly arrived servants and free settlers. But the Company's current leaders who had ousted
Smythe, headed by Sandys and the Earl of Southampton,

were as much to blame. Understanding full well that "popular government does directly take away the power of the monarchy," Sandys and his supporters had nonetheless heedlessly sown the seeds of liberty among the settlers and as a consequence had undermined their "discipline, strength and virtue to defend themselves against the domestic enemy," the Powhatans. Company leaders, Bargrave alleged, did so "knowingly and wittingly" against the sovereign power in England, underlining the point by asserting that "*extreme liberty being worse than extreme tyranny* [my italics], as it appeared by *the troubles in Rome after Nero's death.*" He concluded by assuring Middlesex that "I delight not to be an accuser, unless necessity enforce it," which presumably it did in this case.[26]

A few weeks earlier, Sir Nathaniel Rich, cousin and ally of the Earl of Warwick, recorded a private conversation at which Bargrave claimed that Sandys was satisfied that those who went to Virginia should have "no Government put upon them but by their own consents," adding that if his other business concerning the colony were looked into, it would "be found that he aimed at nothing more than to make a free and popular state there." Through long association, Bargrave was convinced "there was not any man in the world that carried a more *malicious* heart to the Government of a Monarchy" than Sandys, for he had heard him say "that if ever God from heaven did constitute and direct a form of Government it was that of Geneva" (a Calvinist republic) and that he had told him he was dissatisfied with the "constitution and frame" of the government in the colony and intended to "*erect a free state in Virginia*" (my italics).

Bargrave reminded Rich that Sandys had persuaded the archbishop of Canterbury to allow the "Brownists and Separatists of England" to move to the colony. In turn, the archbishop had mentioned to him that he "should never like well of Sir E. S [Sandys]: those Brownists by their Doctrine claiming a liberty to disagreeing to the Government of Monarchs." "Brownists" were separatists, named after Robert Browne who in the 1580s had been one of the first preachers to openly advocate separating from the Anglican Church on the grounds that godly Protestants could no longer wait for Elizabeth I's government to carry out the necessary religious reforms to purify the church. Several groups moved to the Netherlands, one of which, later known to history as the Pilgrims, entered into discussions with Sandys in the winter of 1617 to negotiate moving to Virginia. In North America, they aimed to establish a community hundreds of miles north of Jamestown, near the Hudson River, where they could establish their own church and community and live free from the corruptions of old-world society. Sandys had been keen to recruit nonconformists not because he was sympathetic to their religious convictions, as was put about by his critics, but because puritan migration would give a significant boost to the colony's growing population. The Pilgrims, of course, ended up settling in Plymouth, not Virginia, yet questions continued to be raised about Sandys's own religious affiliations.[27]

Bargrave's allegations might simply be dismissed as merely another example of the caustic gossip swirling around and within various factions of the Company at this time. He was not a man of influence, as he acknowledged himself, and any testimony he gave would inevitably be colored by his lengthy involvement in disputes with the Company about his lands and rights in Virginia. Ultimately, his provocative accusations were not included in evidence prepared by the Earl of Warwick's supporters for the king's inquiry into events in Virginia, probably because they were considered too extreme or might bring unwanted attention to the dubious financial conduct of the Smythe faction. Nevertheless, Bargrave's remarks likely reflected a common perception of Sandys and those associated with him. Sandys was undoubtedly enthusiastic about establishing representative government as a vital component of building a commonwealth in the colony. Company leaders had approved of settlers having a say in conducting their own affairs, but in Bargrave's view the impulse had gone too far, opening the way for sedition and rebellion.

The first meeting of the General Assembly, after all, had commenced with prayer and the burgesses taking the oath of supremacy to their "most gracious and dread Sovereign," but it had ended with an entreaty from the burgesses for additional governing powers along with a clear warning to the Company should their request not be granted. John Pory, speaker of the assembly in 1619, had observed that if Company leaders refused their plea, the settlers might take it ill. This "people (who now at length have gotten the reins of former servitude into their own swindge [hands]) would in short time grow so insolent, as they *would shake off all government* [my italics], and there would be no living among them." It was an astonishing comment. First was the assumption of equivalence, assuming the assembly should have a similar right to disallow orders from London just as the Company had the right by its charter to dismiss laws passed at Jamestown, and second was the bald comment that if the Company did not grant their request, the settlers might rebel and resist government altogether.

What Company leaders thought of these potentially incendiary remarks is unrecorded, but at a court held at his house in London on April 13, 1620, Sir Edwin stated briefly that although he had found the acts of the General Assembly "in their greatest part to be very well and judicially carried and performed" they had to be ratified by a General Court of the Company before being "confirmed." The Company—not the settlers, in other words—would make the final determination about the colony's legislation.[28]

Unchecked power threatened to corrupt elites, but the illusion of power among the poorer classes was even more dangerous, Bargrave observed. Because they had little or no stake in society, the landless lower classes were incapable of rule. They formed the great mass of people in all societies, who, owing to their dependence on others, effectively had no political will of their own. As a student of classical political philosophy, Bargrave was mindful of Cicero's warning about demagogues who sought to win popularity among the people by promising an even distribution of property. What could be more "baneful" than that, Cicero asked, considering that the chief reason for the founding of cities and states was to protect private property? Bargrave was not opposed to limited social mobility but only in strictly prescribed forms that maintained stability and hierarchy. Hence, his unshakable faith in monarchy: the sanctity of property and individual property rights could only be guaranteed by the supremacy of the sovereign. For "the kings right no man will doubt but it immediately comes from god, and being the soul . . . of our government, from it we derive all the happiness and unity of our commonwealth. To depart from it or usurp upon the said sovereign power," he cautioned dramatically, "is death."[29]

Included with his letter to Middlesex was a treatise that Bargrave had written the previous year. Adopting the unusual artifice of speaking as the king, *A Forme of Polisie to Plante and Governe Many Families in Virginea* presented his views on the governing of Virginia and more broadly the emerging English empire, which spoke directly to the relationship of England to her colonies. Given that the colony had grown into maturity, he considered the time was right to put an end to Company rule and place it directly under royal authority. In Virginia, he argued, the government had been instituted by a Company to advance the private interests of the merchants and investors who sponsored it, not for the benefit of the settlers but mainly for themselves. Several joint stock companies *"have governed our free subjects in Virginia as if they were their servants"* rather than the king's subjects, he wrote. Company rule had led to confusion over who was the supreme authority as well as to tyranny and corruption. By contrast, the "uniting power" of sovereign authority enforced by the king's officers and courts would ensure good government throughout all English colonies and between England and her dependencies. Colonies "differing in condition" and "severed in distance and place" could thereby be brought under one supreme jurisdiction.[30]

Good government depended on the direct application of sovereign authority, Bargrave reiterated, to the end of guaranteeing security of property. Once again quoting Cicero, he noted that "by the instinct of nature, men were drawn into sociable assemblies," yet the most important reason for men to join together was to look after "their goods." Bargrave's idea of commonwealth was founded on clearly defined and agreed social ranks that formed the major safeguard against "popular liberty." The "mouth of equal liberty therefore must needs be stopped" and social rank among settlers had to be clearly delineated, which thereby "will immovably fix the form of the colony" and protect property. He laid out in detail the hierarchy of ranks from servants and tenants, who had only their labor but "no shares," to landowners ranging from commoners and citizens to "lord patriots," who would have extensive estates in England and rule over particular plantations or corporations in Virginia. Just as in England, the principal governors of the colony would be drawn from the eminent and wealthy.[31]

ALTHOUGH MANY OF THE PROPOSALS WERE IMPRACTICAL, Bargrave's *Polisie* was nonetheless a remarkable document. It spoke not only to fundamentally important political issues of how best to fashion new English societies overseas but also to the role of the monarchy in providing a fixed central authority from which ultimately all power flowed. He understood that the creation of a "perfect commonweal" in individual colonies depended on fashioning suitable social and economic conditions as well as an effective political framework. He proposed a form of government firmly based on sovereign authority that would discourage the concentration of power and office in the hands of the few, which he believed inevitably led to corruption, yet he was equally apprehensive about the potential of unrest from below.

Sandys's purpose was in some regards the same, although considerably more pragmatic. He also sought to grasp the opportunity to create an English society in America that reflected and improved upon that of the mother country. True to his stoicist cast of mind, emphasizing reason and its practical application, his reform program for Virginia embraced elements of humanism, the ancient constitution, commonwealth theory, moderate Anglicanism, and corporate thinking. His approach to reform and the creation of a commonwealth in Virginia was powerfully influenced by his learning, religious beliefs, and experience at the highest levels of commerce and politics over the previous two decades. He, like Bargrave, had reached the conclusion that the colony had matured into a society (as opposed to a garrison or trading outpost), a tiny offshoot and very different kind of English society compared to that of England but one that was nonetheless capable of sustaining its own institutions under the authority of the Company and the king. In mid-November 1620, he had referred to Virginia as a "Commonwealth and . . . ~~Country~~ [sic] Colony"; the word *country* is crossed out but perhaps suggests his line of thought.

Yet for Sandys, the implications of the emerging maturity of the colony were entirely different from Bargrave's. To the latter, the colony had outgrown the Company and should be ruled directly and impartially by the monarch in the best interests of the crown and subjects. To Sandys and his supporters, the colony's rapid development was a measure of the Company's success and therefore the Company should be supported in times of adversity, such as after the massacre, rather than impugned by the king's government for what Company leaders considered unforeseeable setbacks.

Company leaders, such as Lord Cavendish, son of the Earl of Devonshire, strenuously denied allegations that their forms of government, whether in the colony or their Company meetings in London, were "Democraticall and tumultuous." He pointed out that since their administration was subordinate to the absolute authority of the king as was plainly specified in their charter it "must necessarily be Monarchial." It was true, he argued, their government had "some show of a Democraticall form" but only because it was the most effective means of bringing about prosperity in the colony, encouraging support from investors, and therefore achieving "the ends and effect desired by your Majesty: for the benefit, increase, and wealth of these Plantations."

Neither the Company nor Sandys were explicit, but in defending their governing procedures—which included the active involvement of governors, councils, courts, and assemblies—they were merely reiterating accepted wisdom that mixed government was the superior type. More particularly, political practice throughout the Tudor period and James's reign in encouraging an expansion of the responsibilities of Parliament was a clear endorsement of a monarchial system that fully embraced representative government; what some historians have labeled as monarchial republicanism or "a democratic form of government that was also headed by a monarch." Compare this, Cavendish remarked, with ideas put forward by Sandys's political foes, especially Sir Thomas Smythe and the Earl of Warwick, who were intent on reestablishing an oligarchy of powerful merchants such as had mismanaged the Company and colony before 1619.[32]

At issue in 1619 and years down to the decision by James I in 1624 to revoke the Company's charter was what form of government should prevail. The answer was left to James's son Charles I, who succeeded to the throne in late March 1625 and who oversaw the translation of Virginia into England's first royal colony in America. On May 13, eighteen years to the day after the arrival of the first colonists off Jamestown Island, the king vowed to protect and support the colony in the same measure as any other part of his realms. Virginia's government, he declared, would not be committed to any company or corporation, "to whom it may be proper to trust matters of Trade and Commerce, but cannot be fit or safe to communicate the ordering of state affairs, be they of never so mean consequence." Company land grants would be honored, and Charles pledged to maintain all "public Officers and Ministers" at the Crown's charge as well as lending support to the tobacco trade. The pronouncement by the king in 1625 to institute direct rule in America by the dissolution of a commercial company created a powerful precedent regarding Crown authority in the extended polities of the emerging English Atlantic.

Despite Charles's sweeping statement of the supremacy of his "Regal Office," however, England's empire in America evolved in practice as a patchwork of jurisdictions whereby colonies were governed by royal governors, proprietors, and companies in combination with differing forms of legislative bodies. The Crown never adequately defined a vision of a centralized administration for its overseas dominions, which led to considerable ambiguity about relationships between colonists and royal officials that persisted throughout the entire colonial period.[33]

———•———

To Sandys, legitimacy of government stood upon the twin pillars of just laws and the consent of the governed. Consent was vital because private property was at stake. As Lord Cavendish explained to James in April 1623, Virginia had been founded by the king's grace and permission, but the "charge or expense" had been chiefly borne by "the private purses of the Adventurers" who would never have joined the venture if they had been denied a voice "in the regulating and governing of their own business." A century and a half later, a very similar argument would be taken up by colonists to defend their rights against what they viewed as aggressive parliamentary and Crown policies following the French and Indian Wars.[34]

The controversies that engulfed Sandys and the Virginia Company in the aftermath of the Powhatan attack were part of the much broader constitutional crisis gathering on England's horizon. But precision is required here lest the argument is misconstrued. Sandys's and the Company's establishment of representative government in Virginia in 1619 was not the first blow struck for American independence. As already mentioned above, the Company did not intend to inflame Parliament against the king or erect a popular government or republic in Virginia. Nevertheless, it is notable that Sandys was involved in many of the major political confrontations with James about governance, and it is unlikely to be simply a coincidence that, following his imprisonment in 1621, one of the measures passed by the General Assembly two years later stipulated that "no burgesses of the general Assembly shall be arrested during the time of the assembly, a week before and a week after." The connection between discussions about self-government and the rule of law in England and Virginia during this period is patent and significant.

In 1625, after the dissolution of the Company, Sir George Yeardley journeyed to England to plead with the king and privy council "that their liberty of General Assemblies may be continued and confirmed, and that they may have a voice in the election of officers." The following year, privy councilor Sir Dudley Carleton warned the Commons of the risk of displeasing the king who might be forced to "use new counsels" and rely upon his prerogative powers as other kings (absolutists) in Europe were doing, thereby eventually doing without parliaments. Following the highly acrimonious Parliament of 1628–1629, as Carleton had predicted, Charles decided to rule alone without an intention to call a future parliament. If the king adopted an absolutist government, ruling only with the guidance of his ministers, would the same fate eventually befall Virginia in the form of a royal governor ruling without an assembly?[35]

The Virginia Company's and Sandys's insistence that settlers ought to be represented in their own assembly not only established the first representative government in America but also raised fundamental questions about the nature of peoples' rights, consent, and freedoms. Sir Robert Phelips, during a heated debate in the Commons in 1628 on the

Crown's arbitrary imprisonment of subjects, stated tersely, "We are now upon the point of liberty; first let us understand the thing, then the right, and lastly the violation put upon it. The condition of a free man is to live where there is not *dominum regale,* but *dominum regale politicum,* and this is the state of England." Phelips was referring to Sir John Fortescue's critically important distinction between absolute kingship (*dominum regale*) and those kings who ruled with parliaments and upheld the ancient constitution and rule of law to protect the people and their rights (*dominum regale politicum*). "The "point of liberty" was not only protection from external or internal oppression, David Harris Sacks writes, but was the essential underpinning of a polity governed by "representation and consent." It was *the* fundamental principle of the constitution that the English in the mid-seventeenth century and American colonists 120 years later would fight to uphold.[36]

Six

Inequality and Freedom

My Master Atkins has sold me for £15 like a damned slave.

—*Thomas Best (1623)*

Magna Charta . . . will have no sovereign.

—*Sir Edward Coke (1628)*

The foundation of English liberty, and of all free government, is a right in the people to participate in their legislative council.

—*First Continental Congress (1774)*

H OW BEST TO CONTAIN THE INFLUENCE OF OVERMIGHTY subjects, the greedy "caterpillars of the commonweal," was a question that had faced free societies from ancient times onward. For Company and royal officials alike, the challenge posed by the grandees of Virginia was all the more intractable given the colony's remoteness from central government in London and the rapid concentration of political power in wealthy planters' hands. Over the next century and a half, colonial elites would jealously protect their political privileges and independence, which they lauded in terms of traditional English freedoms. Yet at the same time, the majority of Virginia's population—poor tenant farmers, white servants, and enslaved Africans—found themselves mired in deep-rooted poverty with little or no hope of joining the ranks of the middling and wealthy. The escalating demand for labor made the recruitment of poor, mostly young, male laborers a necessity that in turn created a highly unbalanced society. A census ordered by crown officials in 1625 revealed that 70 percent of the adult population of English settlements was made up of servants and enslaved Africans. For them, the sheer struggle for survival was all-consuming. Stark inequality soon emerged as one of the principal characteristics of the colony and had a lasting influence.[1]

SIR EDWIN SANDYS AND HIS SUPPORTERS HAD BEEN ACUTELY aware of the possible exploitation of the poor and vulnerable by rich planters in Virginia. The whole point of the reforms of 1619 was to end the rapacious activities of governors such as Captain Samuel Argall, charged openly by Nicholas Ferrar of tolerating "Rapines, extortions, and oppressions." During the government of Sir Thomas Smythe and Argall, settlers had been plundered mercilessly, Ferrar wrote, and corruption at the highest levels of the Company was rife. Even the wealthy and influential occasionally fell afoul of Argall and his powerful backers in London, who were concerned more with their own private gain than the public good. After Lord De La Warr's death at sea in the summer of 1618, lawsuits regarding the subsequent embezzlement of his goods and servants worth thousands of pounds ended up in the king's courts for years. Captain Edward Brewster, who spoke up against Argall in the matter, was condemned to death for his opposition by a martial court convened by Argall in James-town. Goods sent by the Company were routinely pillaged by the governor and his coterie so that the "Colony was cheated and robbed." For Sandys, the arbitrary government of Virginia and plundering of the public store was the very antithesis of a commonwealth, which persuaded him that nothing less than root and branch changes to the management of the Company were necessary to save the colony.[2]

Critical to the effort to establish the new state that San-dys and the Company had in mind was the appointment of virtuous and effective governors who would implement the necessary reforms. Commonwealths could not flourish with-out just rulers and honorable magistrates. The governor and his principal officers were the agents of change in Virginia for policies formulated by Sandys, his deputies, and the Com-pany's council in London. But despite an elaborate system of oversight to ensure regular reports and compliance with Company plans, evidenced by the enormous volume of papers generated by the leadership in this period, serious difficulties arose. Some were predictable and largely unavoidable. Sheer distance and the vagaries of winds and weather disrupted trade and communications. Crossing thousands of miles of ocean was hazardous: ships were unseaworthy, sickness might break out, and navigation was sometimes uncertain. Similarly, conditions in the colony might periodically be unsuited for the arrival of hundreds of settlers owing to the season, "pestilence," lack of adequate food, or places for them to lodge. These were challenges all colonizers faced, whether Spanish, French, or English, but the Virginia Company was the first English enterprise to attempt mass transportation of settlers and the creation of a transplanted English society in America. In addition, expectations in London of what should have been achieved were often wildly unrealistic, as successive governors from Sir George Yeardley onward frequently pointed out.

Invariably, the poor suffered most. Less than six months after Sandys took over governing the Company, John Pory sent an enthusiastic letter to England reporting the rapid progress of the colony. After first highlighting tobacco as the planters' primary source of wealth, he immediately corrected himself: "Our principal wealth, (I should have said) consists in servants." To the wealthy and well placed, it quickly became apparent that the more servants they could command, the more money could be made. All the major officeholders requested servants, ostensibly to support the cost of their office but in reality to provide them with handsome incomes.

Colony officials soon realized that trafficking in servants was as lucrative as selling goods imported from England. John Rolfe remarked that there had been "many complaints against the Governors, Captains, and Officers in Virginia, for buying and selling men and boys." Most of the Company tenants who arrived on the *Bona Nova* in November 1619, for example, were rented out for a year to wealthy planters such as Samuel Mathews instead of being put to work on Company (public) lands as originally intended. Company leaders later complained that whereas it had been claimed that placing the men "with old planters" was for their health and to learn tobacco husbandry, they had been "so unmercifully used that it was the greatest cause of our Tenants discontent." Company tenants and "lawful servants" had been forced to work for planters or had had their contracts altered without their consent, which in England, Rolfe commented, would have been held "a thing most intolerable."

Reports of wrongdoing and the poor treatment of servants severely tarnished the reputation of the colony. In the spring of 1620, a story circulating in Plymouth, England, reported that nine hundred settlers had died in the previous twelve months and that "the people are used with more slavery than if they were under the Turk." Alderman Robert Johnson, one of Sandys's archrivals closely associated with Sir Thomas Smythe, calculated that between April 1619 and March 1622 some three thousand people had died for "want of houses, pestering [pestilent] ships, shortness and badness of food."

Most servants' circumstances became even more desperate after the Indian massacre of 1622 and harrowing winter that followed. Richard Frethorne arrived at Martin's Hundred at a particularly bad time early in 1623. Shortly after arrival, he wrote back to his parish minister in England begging for food and clothes: "I am in a most miserable and pitiful Case [state], for want of meat and want of clothes." He asked his minister to speak to his parishioners to raise a small donation for clothes and food and ended with a plea "to be freed out of this Egypt." A few weeks later, he wrote to his parents describing scurvy and the "bloody flux" (dysentery) and short-age of provisions: "Since I came out of the ship, I never ate anything but peas and loblolly (that is water gruel)." It would be "most pitiful if you did know as much as I, when people cry out day, and night, Oh that they were in England with-out their limbs and would not care to lose any limb to be in England again, yea though they beg from door to door." If "you love or respect me as your Child, release me from this bondage, and save my life," he pleaded. Whether his parents were able to save him is unknown, but more likely he died in the summer or fall. Thomas Nicolls, a surveyor who worked at Martin's Hundred, complained that "lying Virginians" who told misleadingly optimistic stories about prospects in Vir-ginia had encouraged many servants to adventure themselves. They were the "chief causers of their [the servants'] deaths," Nicolls charged, who went to their graves "cursing them most bitterly who sent them out." He also died that year.[3]

SOCIAL CONDITIONS IN VIRGINIA, AS LATER IN OTHER COLO-nies, encouraged the rise of powerful local elites. The stripping away of layers of provincial English customs and traditions that had moderated relations between rulers and the ruled, together with the abridging of English judicial in-stitutions, central and local, created a political and social terrain more susceptible to unconstrained elite dominance than in England. Whereas English counties were governed by scores of titled and gentry families, many of whom had lived in their "countries" (regions) for centuries, the size of local elites in Virginia was tiny. Consequently, small groups of wealthy men were able to dominate their respective localities and the colony's governance.[4]

A couple of dozen men, including Sir George Yeardley, cape (head) merchant Abraham Piersey, and Captain William Pierce, who had amassed large fortunes and lucrative offices, made up Virginia's early ruling group. At his death, Piersey owned thousands of acres along the James River, a store and house in Jamestown, and a total of thirty-nine servants and slaves comprising "the best Estate that was ever yet known in Virginia." During the turmoil following the 1622 massacre, he and other members of the elite such as Captain William Tucker and Samuel Mathews also accumulated, both fairly and fraudulently, huge areas of prime land together with cattle and goods from the estates of those who had died or gone back to England.

After the godly George Thorpe's death in the massacre, one of the promoters of Berkeley Hundred, where Thorpe had lived, reported that Thorpe's cattle and servants had been taken to Yeardley's house, but he did not know what had happened to them. The failure of Sandys's commonwealth and the end of Company rule offered plenty of opportunities for wealthy planters to expand their influence and power. No effective remedy to check their influence could be mounted in the colony or from England. With all the major offices of government under their control, together with the General Assembly and court, the colony's leaders increased their already considerable political authority and as a result profited handsomely.[5]

At the same time, wealthy planters continued to cling to an elevated view of Virginia and themselves as holding a special place within the king's realms and affections. The colony was, in their eyes, at least from 1619, far more significant than simply a commercial undertaking managed by a collection of merchants purely for profit. For Sandys and other Company leaders, it represented a new Protestant state in America, an unambiguous expression of English greatness just as Spain had established a great empire in the New World. After the end of the Company, planters looked forward to a fresh beginning under the new king that would confirm their special standing, which his proclamation of March 1625 formally acknowledging Virginia as part of his "Royal Empire" seemed to promise.[6]

Ironically, political institutions such as the General Assembly established by the Company to promote broad-based involvement in government became a principal means by which wealthy planter-merchants consolidated their power. They were no longer accountable, insofar as they had ever been, to Company oversight, and complaints about the corruption of leading officials by lesser planters were met with contempt and the meting out of brutal punishments. Over the next several decades, wealthy planters in the General Assembly gradually adopted more parliamentary privileges based on English precedents and strengthened their powers as the colony's highest court. Officeholders gained extensive legislative experience at provincial level and took on growing responsibilities in localities as county magistrates and sheriffs, much like their counterparts in England. Given their governing experience, they saw themselves not as merely advisors to royal governors but as indispensable partners in running the affairs of the colony.

One early test of their influence arose with the appointment of governor Sir John Harvey, who arrived in Virginia in 1630 and soon became mired in endless disputes with his councilors who, instead of providing assistance "stand contesting and disputing my authority, averring that I can do nothing but what they shall advise me, and that my powers extend no further than a bare casting voice." The struggle came to a head a few years later when a group of councilors forcibly removed Harvey from office and packed him off to England to face censure. It was a lesson not lost on future royal governors. Lacking financial or military resources to impose their authority, governors ruled largely with the approval of leading planters, not the other way around. Although the worse abuses of elite dominance were confronted in a large-scale revolt, Bacon's Rebellion of 1676–1677, and the temporary imposition of military rule by the English government that followed, Virginia's wealthy and well-connected planters continued to exert enormous influence over domestic and imperial affairs down to the American Revolution.[7]

POVERTY AND INEQUALITY WERE WORSENED IMMEASURABLY BY the evolution of slavery and racial prejudice, which emphasized early English America's racial divide. When the *White Lion* and the *Treasurer* cast anchor at Point Comfort and sold most of the Angolans they had looted from the Portuguese slave ship they captured in the Gulf of Mexico, planters had been eager to buy them. Sandys was outraged, but more because he was aware of the damage the incident would do to his fragile relationship with James I, who was actively pursuing a pro-Spanish foreign policy at the time than out of any moral scruple. He showed little unease about the well-being of the Angolan men and women who were sold into slavery or about the fact that the Company's own officers, Yeardley and Piersey, had acquired the majority of them. Sandys did not support the inclusion of African slaves in his commonwealth—he believed plenty of willing workers were available in England and hopefully among the Powhatans—but he took no steps to censure the governor or anyone else in authority for profiting from the transaction. From 1619, the highest officers and wealthiest settlers, including the governor, led the way as slaveholders, setting the tone for the rest of planter society over the next 246 years.[8]

Virginia planters followed the example of their plantation-owning counterparts in the Hispanic Atlantic world who over the previous century had acquired hundreds of thousands of African captives. By the early seventeenth century, approaching forty thousand African slaves worked in the ports and rural hinterlands of the Spanish Caribbean. In the same period, massive numbers of Angolans were transported to Brazil and Spanish America, underlining historian David Wheat's point that Portugal's colonization of Angola and the colonization of South America and the Caribbean "mutually reinforced one another." The English in Bermuda, Virginia, and then the Caribbean quickly adopted Portuguese and Spanish models of slavery, as well as the racial attitudes that sanctioned them. Much of the vocabulary of English racism was adopted from Spanish America.[9]

With the growth of tobacco as England's initial great transatlantic staple crop, big planters sought to acquire more

Africans and, as they arrived in larger numbers after 1670, began to lay down harsh discriminatory legislation to police and protect their human property. Some ten thousand slaves were forcibly transported to the colony between 1670 and 1700, most from ports of Upper Guinea and the Bight of Biafra in West Africa. In the huge new statehouse built at Jamestown in this period, no more than a few hundred yards from the site of the church where the first General Assembly was held, burgesses and councilors sat regularly to create legislation that would strip Africans and African Americans of their basic human rights. It was a vicious cycle: from an English perspective, the growing presence of slaves toiling in tobacco fields was a significant marker of the difference between colonial society and the mother country, a difference that in turn permitted the drastic curtailments of rights and liberties of Africans and their descendants that would never have been allowed to occur in England.

The tenor of the legislation was chilling. After 1669, as already noted, a planter who killed a slave during corporal punishment could not be charged with murder or a felony; it became lawful to kill or wound a runaway slave who resisted arrest; any slave who lifted a hand against a "Christian" would receive thirty lashes; and a slave who was emancipated or a white man or woman who married an African American would have to leave the colony within a few months. The rights of the tiny number of free blacks were severely restricted also. Finally, in the first major piece of legislation passed in the new capitol in Williamsburg, the comprehensive slave code of 1705 brought together acts of the previous forty years and formally sanctioned an increasingly blunt delineation of Virginia's racial system by including Indians and a new legal definition of racial difference, "mulatto." It affirmed that all enslaved men, women, and children were defined in law as chattel. At the time of their passage, the laws applied to 13,000 enslaved men, women, and children; fifty years later, the number had risen to over 100,000, or nearly half the total population of the colony, and by the American Revolution, the number had doubled again to more than 200,000. Within three-quarters of a century, the entire social terrain of Virginia had been transformed and a massive and permanent enslaved class of laborers created, a trend followed by other southern mainland colonies such as South Carolina and Georgia.[10]

The arrival of the *White Lion* and *Treasurer* in 1619 may seem a long way from Thomas Jefferson's Virginia, but several important points are worth emphasizing. Slavery originated in Virginia with the arrival of the first Africans in 1619. Although the colony did not emerge as a "slave society," by which is meant a society where a large proportion of the population is enslaved, until the end of the century nonetheless the colony's planters were among the first in the English Atlantic to reveal a strong and lasting preference for enslaved labor. Second, the fundamental elements of a slave system, supported initially by common practice and then subsequently by formal legislation, were established by well-connected planters in the half century after 1619. Third, the arrival of two privateers shortly after the conclusion of the first assembly underlines a highly significant development that worked upon early Virginia and the Company in this period. The plunder of Spanish shipping and possessions in the Caribbean by the English from island bases, such as Bermuda, had been a familiar and successful method of pillaging the wealth of the Indies for generations and represented a viable alternative to the founding of a self-sufficient mainland colony such as Sir Edwin Sandys envisaged. This tension was underscored within the Company by the rivalry and ultimately disastrous rift between Sandys and the Earl of Warwick, who espoused two quite different visions of empire. A fourth point, critically important, is that in recognizing the appalling impersonal forces that worked upon the lives of African and Indian victims of violence, slavery, degrading legislation, and harsh work regimes, we should not overlook their humanity or the importance of their own agency. Enslaved Africans and their descendants, Philip Morgan writes, "actively participated in their destiny *and* were victims of a brutal dehumanizing system. Subject to grinding daily exploitation, caught in the grip of powerful forces that were often beyond their power to control, slaves nevertheless strove to create order in their lives, to preserve their humanity, to achieve dignity, and to sustain dreams of a better future." They endured in the hope that their lives would eventually improve or if not theirs, then perhaps their children's or those of future generations.[11]

THE DISASTROUS SETBACKS OF 1622–1623 IN VIRGINIA AND England had led to the end of the Company, but old John Ferrar, Sir Edwin Sandys's loyal deputy and steadfast friend, ultimately lived to see a commonwealth in Virginia. In 1649, thirty years after he and Sandys had launched their reforms, he wrote *A Perfect Description of Virginia* in which he related the felicity of the colony. Approximately fifteen thousand English settlers now lived in Virginia, he reported, and thousands of livestock of all kinds, hogs both tame and wild "innumerable," and poultry "without number." Recalling the Company's efforts to encourage a diversified economy, he described how planters sowed "many hundred Acres of *Wheat,* as good, and fair, as any in the world, and great increase." He listed barley for making excellent malt, six public brew-houses, and the planters' own "strong and good" beer; all sorts of crops, fruits and vines, mulberry trees for silk, herbs, medicinal plants, birds, meats, and fish.

Virginia tobacco continued to be esteemed in all places, and although the price per pound was low, a man could make a good living from it. Indigo production returned ten times as much as tobacco, and the planters hoped "to supply all Christendom," worth thousands of pounds. Iron ore was found in abundance throughout the colony and could be easily transported along the great rivers. Overall, such was the flourishing trade that thirty "sail of ships," employing nearly a thousand mariners, arrived annually, mostly from England but also from New England and the Netherlands. Within three decades, Virginia had grown from a few small, struggling settlements to a wealthy and thriving province.

Ferrar took particular pleasure in describing the estate of "worthy" Samuel Mathews, a planter who had first arrived in Virginia about 1618 and had more than three decades' experience in the colony. He was the very exemplar of a "deserving Commonwealthsman." He had held all the major offices of state and had been a major figure in government, politics, and economic developments throughout his long career. At his extensive plantation on the James River, Mathews Manor, he owned a fine house and kept weavers and shoemakers as well as forty slaves, many of whom he was bringing up to crafts. He produced English grains, wheat and barley, beef cattle, dairy cows, and hogs, much of which was for provisioning oceangoing shipping en route upriver to Jamestown. Lt. Col. Mathews, Ferrar concluded, was a "true lover of *Virginia*" and his estate a miniature of what the colony's economy under the administration of the Company could have eventually developed into, featuring a wide range of commodities, development of crafts, and plentiful work for thousands of English settlers who would come.

But of particular interest is less his assessment of the colony's developing society and economy, which was unashamedly favorable, as his view of the dissolution of the Company. From the safe haven of a generation later, Ferrar was able to voice his opinion, and he chose not to hold back. Time was, he wrote of the early 1620s, that our statesmen "had store of Gondomores [Count Gondomar's] gold to destroy and discountenance the Plantation of *Virginia,* and he effected it in great part, by dissolving the Company, wherein most of the Nobility, Gentry, Corporate Cities, and most Merchants of England, were Interested and Engaged; after the expense of some hundreds of thousands of pounds." The reason was plain; the Spaniard had admitted it himself: he had been commanded by his master Philip IV of Spain to bring about the downfall of Virginia before the colony grew so powerful that English settlers would begin moving into Philip's West Indies and "his Mexico" by sea and land. Tragically, owing

to his misguided faith in Gondomar and the possibility of a
Spanish alliance, James I and his courtiers had gone along
with the plan leading to the Company's ruin and setting back
the colony's potential development for decades.

In the light of the scale of the disaster that befell the Company, Ferrar can doubtless be forgiven a touch of exaggeration
in his account of what had happened and the consequences,
but there is also a good deal of truth in his reading of events.
The Virginia Company was the only mercantile company of
the era to be dissolved by quo warranto proceedings, enabled
by authority of the king's absolute powers. Parliament had no
say in the matter. A long-lasting, powerful, private company
that had invested tens of thousands of pounds was abolished
by a legal instrument of the royal prerogative.

From this point of view, Ferrar's mention of nobles, gentry, corporations, and merchants "Interested and Engaged" in
the venture was not therefore simply an effort to emphasize
the Company's impressive and widespread support but rather
a means of drawing attention to the Company itself being an
expression of England's commonwealth. The Company represented the leading political and economic classes of English
society, oversaw the interests of its members (investors and
settlers) for the common good, and governed through fair and
open procedures in London and Jamestown, enabling those
who had invested to have a voice. It had a specific focus on
developing transatlantic trade, but it also had the responsibility of governing England's first colony on behalf of Company
members, settlers, and the nation. The dissolution of the
Company had been an assault on the English commonwealth
and a violation of the ancient constitution that would have

lasting implications, the first of a series of major attacks by the Stuart monarchy on the liberties of the people.[12]

—•—

MOST OF THE ENGLISH RULING CLASS WAS DEEPLY INFLU-enced by the concept of the ancient constitution. An almost mystical formulation of custom and the common law precedents from time out of mind, it served as a vital guide for monarchs and the governing classes in confronting vexing political issues of their own age. In a mixed constitution and commonwealth such as England's, balance was vital, especially between sovereign powers and the people's liberties. For, Sir Edward Coke explained, "as the subject owes to the king his true and faithful allegiance and obedience so the sovereign is to govern and protect his subjects." This was the unwritten but universally assumed compact between a just Christian monarch and his or her people.[13]

The broad constitutional discussions that took place in this period related to the ancient constitution would ultimately raise questions of the most fundamental kind. What was the proper balance between sovereign authority and subjects' rights? What would happen if consensus were lost? How were the liberties of a free people defined and preserved? In terms of the gathering political crisis that would frustrate James I and ultimately overwhelm Charles, the abolition of the Company was a minor matter, but as a symptom of a troubling trend toward royal absolutism or, even worse, the likelihood of closer ties to Spain and possibly other Catholic states, the calculated destruction of the Company took on a much wider dimension. Ten years before Parliament presented the Petition of Right (1628)—a comprehensive list of grievances intended to persuade Charles to cease taxing and imprisoning his subjects without regard to the law—the major reforms introduced by Sandys and his supporters emphasized the Company's determination to apply the principles of the ancient constitution and rule of law in Virginia. In its preamble, the Company's great charter spoke of creating a "laudable form of Government by Magistracy and just Laws . . . for the happy guiding and governing of the people." These laws were "not to be chested or hidden like a candle under a bushel, *but in form of a Magna Charta* [my italics] to be published to the whole colony." All settlers "though never so mean," had the right to appeal to the law for "speedy remedy."

The desire to implement these measures at the same time that issues of governance and law were coming under intense scrutiny in England was not coincidental; it occurred because Sandys and many of the leading supporters of the Company had also been prominent critics of Crown policy in the fractious parliamentary sessions of James's reign. What occurred at Jamestown in 1619 was a highly significant moment in the increasingly heated political ferment of the early seventeenth century that marked the beginning of a far-reaching Anglo-American debate about sovereignty and representative government.[14]

Shortly after John Ferrar had written his *Perfect Description,* Charles I went to his death still affirming his sacred duty to govern and protect his people. Viewed as the instigator of two civil wars against his people during the 1640s, Parliament and the army led by Oliver Cromwell saw no alternative but to put the king on trial for his crimes. With all trust between the warring parliamentarians and royalists long gone, the king was subsequently convicted and sentenced to execution. The people's "Liberty and Freedom," he declared from the scaffold, "consists in having of Government those Laws, by which their Life and their goods may be most their own." Few in the crowd at Whitehall on that cheerless winter's day would have disagreed, yet the reason he stood on the point of execution was precisely because by raising armies against Parliament and engaging in war, he had patently failed to defend his people's rights and property.

A few years earlier, in language that once again few of his opponents would have found controversial, Charles and his advisors had offered one of the clearest expositions of the virtues of a mixed constitution of "absolute monarchy, aristocracy, and democracy." He set out persuasively the reciprocal responsibilities of each of the three constitutional groups— king, lords, and commons—and confirmed that monarchs may not use their powers to oppress those "for whose good he has it." But the main point of his argument revolved around the threat to law and order from below, not from the top. If the powers of the sovereign were first undermined, followed by those of the aristocracy, lords, and bishops, and then the privileges of the House of Commons, who would be left to govern? His prediction was bleak:

> At last the Common people (who in the meantime must be flattered, and to whom License must be given in all their wild humors, how contrary [what]soever to established Law, or their own real Good) discover this *arcanum*

imperii [secret empire] That all this was done by them, but not for them, grow weary of Journey-work, and set up for themselves, call Parity and Independence, Liberty; devour that Estate which had devoured the rest; Destroy all Rights and Proprieties, all distinctions of Families and Merit; And by this means this splendid and excellently distinguished form of Government, end in a dark equal Chaos of Confusion, and the long Line of Our many noble Ancestors in a Jack Cade, or a Wat Tyler.[15]

Charles's forceful case against limiting the powers of monarchs took on greater significance following his death. The abolition of the House of Lords and creation of the English Republic in 1649 seemed to bear out his prediction and became a classic statement justifying nonresistance to absolutist rulers or even tyrants. Beset, as Thomas Hobbes put it two years after Charles's death, "with those who contend on the one side for too great Liberty, and on the other side for too much Authority, 'tis hard to pass between the points of both unwounded." Regarding the latter, should or could subjects protect themselves from those monarchs who by turning to absolutism were *themselves* the major risk to the people's liberties? If absolute monarchs chose to interpret their prerogative powers broadly in ways that were contrary to accepted constitutional norms and traditional assumptions, what remedies remained to defend the people's ancient rights and freedoms?[16]

Ultimately, at the core of these questions was the issue of accountability. How could (or should) kings be held accountable? James I wrote expansively about his divine regal powers but usually tempered his more extreme utterances by underlining his duty under God to protect his subjects' lives and property. Yet his grand pronouncements of principle rarely matched his actions, no more than did his son's, as England's ruling classes discovered during the complete breakdown of constitutional relations that led to war in the three kingdoms, military rule, and the short-lived English commonwealth of 1649–1653.[17]

———

THE ACCOUNTABILITY OF MONARCHS, STATUTORY LIMITS ON sovereign power, and the protection of subjects' rights evolved as the central constitutional propositions of the seventeenth and eighteenth centuries. They were voiced in the fiery political debates of the 1610s and 1620s that swirled around Westminster and Whitehall, were heard in the great merchant houses of the City of London, and for a brief period echoed in the governor's council and General Assembly on the other side of the Atlantic at Jamestown. They would be taken up by parliamentarians, soldiers, and godly revolutionaries during the British Civil Wars of the mid-seventeenth century, and again by Americans in revolt who were determined to rid themselves of British rule and kings altogether. Kings and queens, Thomas Paine declared grandly in 1776, had reduced the world to "blood and ashes"—it was time to throw off the yoke of monarchy and create a republican self-government where the law "was king" and the people sovereign.[18]

Epilogue

After 1619

ACROSS FOUR HUNDRED YEARS, THE CONTRASTING LEGA-
cies of 1619 are still with us. The arrival of Europeans
and Africans in English America and their encounters with
Indian peoples created a highly diverse society in which the
terms of engagement as well as consequences for different
peoples were starkly unequal. For Native Americans, the
rapid growth of white settler populations was catastrophic
on a hemispheric scale. Wars and European diseases dec-
imated their numbers, causing massive regional depopula-
tions and in some areas almost complete social collapse. In
early Virginia, Indian peoples knew the English had come, as
the great chief Wahunsonacock put it, "not for trade, but to
invade . . . and possess" the country. Sanctioned by specious
laws and racist ideology, the Powhatan wars in Virginia were
merely the first episode in the use of extreme violence that
involved mass killings, dispossession, and enslavement of

Indians repeated over and over again across British America and, later, the United States.[1]

For Africans and their descendants, the experience of European colonization was similarly tragic. The grinding inhumanity of slavery in mainland English America lasted for nearly two and a half centuries until the carnage of the Civil War brought it to an end at Appomattox Court House, fewer than 150 miles from where the first Africans arrived at (incongruously) Point Comfort. From the mid-seventeenth century onward, as the material conditions of most whites rose dramatically—reflected by increasing wealth, better standards of living, and a life expectancy far longer than enjoyed even by their counterparts in Europe—those of African Americans languished. Whether by force, legislation, or marginalization, African Americans and Indian peoples were systematically excluded from enjoying the benefits of their own labor and consigned to the lowest substrata of poverty.

The extreme inequality, impoverishment, and de facto segregation that divide different American communities are among the most intractable social problems that face modern society. While our national credo espouses opportunity for all, the consequences of long-term discrimination and racism remain clearly evident around us. Applying any measure of net wealth, income, or social well-being, Native American peoples and African Americans are among the poorest citizens in the United States today. Throughout the nation, one in four Native Americans and African Americans live in poverty compared to one in ten whites. In addition, the former have been gravely hampered by inadequate and poor-quality public services, leading to significantly lower educational attainments and greater health and social welfare challenges. We "remain two Americas," a recent report by the Stanford Center on Poverty and Inequality stated: a high-poverty America for African Americans and Native Americans and "a (relatively) low-poverty America for whites." At the same time as the United States emerged as a beacon of freedom and eventually assumed leadership of the free world, domestically the impact of bigotry and intolerance has continued to disfigure the lives of countless millions of people of color. Poverty filtered by race highlights the gross inequalities among our nation's diverse peoples, a striking and persistent feature of our social landscape that reaches far back into the past.[2]

——•——

AND YET, 1619 ALSO EMBODIES A LEGACY OF QUITE DIFFERent meaning: the inception of the most important political development in American history, the rise of democracy. What began at Jamestown during those torrid few days of summer would have momentous consequences. Shortly before he died on July 4, 1826, Thomas Jefferson composed one of his greatest tributes to liberty in a last letter to posterity. Referring to the still novel American form of government, he wrote, "May it be to the world, what I believe it will be (to some parts sooner, to others later, but finally to all), the signal of arousing men to burst the chains under which monkish ignorance and superstition had persuaded them to bind themselves, and to assume the blessings and security of self-government." By "the grace of God," he concluded, "these are grounds of hope for others," and, he might have added, for us. The felicity of self-government and its benefits were held out to future generations of peoples around the globe.[3]

In fact, the spread of self-government had begun long before. Originating in the English parliaments of the early seventeenth century, the principle that just government relied on the consent of the governed and the rule of law applied to everyone irrespective of social status was transferred to Virginia as part of the Company's sweeping reforms of 1619. Every subsequent British American colony established its own representative assembly and judicial system that would secure and protect settlers' lives, liberties, and properties. From colonial New England to the West Indies, historian Jack P. Greene comments, America proved to be "an extraordinarily fertile ground for parliamentary governance.

By the time of the American Revolution, most colonies had enjoyed self-government for more than a century and were able to translate their governing institutions into republican forms relatively easily; the habit of self-rule and exercise of extensive fiscal and lawmaking powers had been the norm for so long. A deeply ingrained sense of independence on the part of wealthy elites at colony and state levels emerged early and became the basis for the growth of powerful local political institutions modulated by their own regional cultures. Colonial and then state legislatures developed as the bedrock of the American political system, a finely tuned balance of local and central powers that gave expression to and celebrated citizens' collective rights and liberties. Today, these freedoms, together with the federal and state constitutions that enshrine them, constitute the foundational principles of American democracy.[4]

Epilogue

Sir Edwin Sandys believed passionately that the creation of a commonwealth was the best means of establishing just laws and a fair and equitable society in America. In November 1622, six months after news of the Indian attack that had devastated the colony reached London, the poet and dean of Paul's Church, John Donne, preached movingly to leaders of the Company, "Those amongst you that are old now, shall pass out of this world with this great comfort, that you contributed to the beginning of that Common Wealth" in Virginia. Sandys's dream of creating a commonwealth in the interests of settlers and Indians proved short-lived. But the twin pillars of democracy—the rule of law and representative government—survived and flourished. It was his greatest legacy to America. What was lost was his steadfast conviction that serving the common good served all.[5]

Acknowledgments

I WOULD LIKE TO THANK MY COLLEAGUES OF THE JAMESTOWN Rediscovery Foundation for their support throughout the writing of this book. The archaeological investigations by the Jamestown Rediscovery team at this world-class historic site have been inspirational, and it has been a privilege to work alongside such a talented group of archaeologists and educators who have brought the story of early Jamestown to the public in all its vivid detail. I am grateful to William M. Kelso; Jamie May, who expertly drew the maps; Michael Lavin, who helped with the production of images; and Mary Anna Hartley and David Givens for their leadership of the excavations at the 1617 Church and the Angela site, respectively. During the research, the staffs of the John D. Rockefeller Jr. Library at the Colonial Williamsburg Foundation, the Swem Library of the College of William and Mary, the Library of Virginia, the Virginia Museum of History and Culture, and the National Archives, UK, have provided invaluable assistance.

I have learned a great deal from numerous scholars whose recent work has shaped my own thinking, in particular Jack P.

Greene, Andrew Fitzmaurice, Alexander Haskell, Paul Musselwhite, Philip D. Morgan, Paul Halliday, Peter Mancall, James Rice, Warren M. Billings, Lauren Working, Edmond Smith, Misha Ewen, Nicholas Canny, Linda Heywood, E. M. Rose, John Coombs, James Walvin, and Michael Jarvis. Lara Heimert at Basic Books has been a superb editor, and I am most grateful for her insightful critiques of the manuscript. I owe a debt of thanks also to Leah Stecher for her skillful editing and to Stephanie Summerhays and other staff involved in bringing the book to completion.

My family has been a continual source of support throughout the research and writing. I thank them with all my heart. The book is dedicated to my wife, Sally, and to Liz, Ben, and Alice, with much love.

Notes

Introduction: 1619

1. Susan Myra Kingsbury, ed., *The Records of the Virginia Company of London* (hereafter *RVC*), 4 vols. (Washington, DC: 1906–1935), 3:98–99. An excellent transcription and facsimile of John Pory's report of the first General Assembly can be found in William J. Van Schreeven and George H. Reese, eds., *Proceedings of the General Assembly of Virginia, July 30–August 4, 1619* (Jamestown, VA: 1969).

2. Engel Sluiter, "New Light on the '20. and Odd Negroes' Arriving in Virginia, August 1619," *William and Mary Quarterly* (hereafter *WMQ*), 3rd ser., 54 (1997): 395–398; Linda M. Heywood and John K. Thornton, *Angolans, Atlantic Creoles, and the Foundation of the Americas, 1585–1660* (Cambridge: 2007), 5–7; Kingsbury, *RVC*, 3:243.

3. Warren M. Billings, *A Little Parliament: The Virginia General Assembly in the Seventeenth Century* (Richmond, VA: 2004), xvi, 5–10; Christopher Tomlins, *Freedom Bound: Law, Labor, and Civic Identity in Colonizing English America* (Cambridge: 2010), 401–508; Philip D. Morgan, "Virginia Slavery in Atlantic Context, 1550 to 1650," in *Virginia 1619: Slavery, Freedom, and the Construction of English America*, ed. Paul Musselwhite, James Horn, and Peter C. Mancall (Chapel Hill, NC: forthcoming).

4. See Edmund S. Morgan, *American Slavery, American Freedom: The Ordeal of Colonial Virginia* (New York: 1975), 5–6, 386–387.

5. For a popular and influential account of the Pilgrims, see Nathaniel Philbrick's best-seller *Mayflower: A Story of Courage, Community, and War* (New York: 2006), 5, passim. Nancy Isenberg critiques the Plymouth myth in *White Trash: The 400-Year Untold History of Class in*

America (New York: 2016), 5–8. The quote (not the sentiment) is from Lauren Working, "'The Savages of Virginia Our Project': The Powhatan in Jacobean Political Thought," in *Virginia 1619,* ed. Musselwhite, Horn, and Mancall; Theodore K. Rabb, *Jacobean Gentleman: Sir Edwin Sandys, 1561–1629* (Princeton, NJ: 1998).

6. Rabb, *Jacobean Gentleman,* 344–352; Noel Malcolm, "Hobbes, Sandys, and the Virginia Company," *Historical Journal* 24 (1981): 297–321; [Arthur Wodenoth], *A Short Collection of the Most Remarkable Passages from the Originall to the Dissolution of the Virginia Company* (London: 1651), 18–19; Peter Peckard, *Memoirs of the Life of Mr. Nicholas Ferrar* (Cambridge: 1790), 115–116, 144; Conrad Russell, *King James VI & I and His English Parliaments,* ed. Richard Cust and Andrew Thrush (Oxford: 2012); S. L. Adams, "Foreign Policy and the Parliaments of 1621 and 1624," in *Faction and Parliament: Essays on Early Stuart History,* ed. Kevin Sharpe (Oxford: 1978), 146–147; Andrew Fitzmaurice, "The Company–Commonwealth," in *Virginia 1619,* ed. Musselwhite, Horn, and Mancall; Alexander B. Haskell, *For God, King, and People: Forging Commonwealth Bonds in Renaissance Virginia* (Chapel Hill, NC: 2017), 187–239.

7. James Horn, *A Land as God Made It: Jamestown and the Birth of America* (New York: 2005), 241–248.

8. Winthrop D. Jordan, *White Over Black: American Attitudes Toward the Negro, 1550–1812* (Chapel Hill, NC: 1968); Alden T. Vaughan, *Roots of American Racism: Essays on the Colonial Experience* (Oxford: 1995); C. S. Everett, "'They Shalbe Slaves for Their Lives': Indian Slavery in Colonial Virginia," in *Indian Slavery in Colonial America,* ed. Alan Gallay (Lincoln, NE: 2009), 67–108.

9. Kingsbury, *RVC,* 4:223, 416; Brent Tarter, *The Grandees of Government: The Origins and Persistence of Undemocratic Politics in Virginia* (Charlottesville, VA: 2013), 3–87; Morgan, *American Slavery, American Freedom,* 108–130; David Brion Davis, *Inhuman Bondage: The Rise and Fall of Slavery in the New World* (Oxford: 2006), 124–156, 175–204, 297–322; Stuart Banner, *How the Indians Lost Their Land: Law and Power on the Frontier* (Cambridge, MA: 2005), passim.

Chapter 1: Jamestown

1. Samuel M. Bemiss, *The Three Charters of the Virginia Company of London . . . 1606–1621* (Williamsburg, VA: 1957), 1–12; Karen Ordahl Kupperman, *The Jamestown Project* (Cambridge, MA: 2007), 12–42, 183–217; Lansdowne MS 160, ff. 356–357, British Library, London, UK. The proposal was likely written in January 1608 with the intention of expanding support for Jamestown following what appeared initially to be its

successful establishment. My transcription is from the original MS, Virginia Colonial Records Project, John D. Rockefeller Jr. Library, Colonial Williamsburg Foundation, microfilm.

2. Two English colonies were created by the charter of April 10, 1606. One, in the mid-Atlantic corresponding to an area that stretched from Cape Fear in North Carolina to New York, was named the first colony of Virginia. The other, which included New England but reached as far south as the Chesapeake Bay, was called the second colony of Virginia. Together they represented the twin centers of English activity of the previous twenty years and were sponsored by London and West Country political and mercantile interests, respectively. Theodore K. Rabb, *Enterprise and Empire: Merchant and Gentry Investment in the Expansion of England, 1575–1630* (Cambridge, MA: 1967); Susan Myra Kingsbury, ed., *The Records of the Virginia Company of London* (hereafter *RVC*), 4 vols. (Washington, DC: 1906–1935), 3:240, 256; *A Declaration of the State of the Colonie and Affaires in Virginia. . . .* (London: 1620), 19.

3. William S. Powell, *John Pory, 1572–1636: The Life and Letters of a Man of Many Parts* (Chapel Hill, NC: 1977), 6–75; Kingsbury, *RVC*, 3:220–221.

4. Kingsbury, *RVC*, 3:221–222.

5. John Rolfe, *A True Relation of the State of Virginia Lefte by Sir Thomas Dale Knight in May Last 1616* (Charlottesville, VA: 1971), 7–10; William Thorndale, "The Virginia Census of 1619," *Virginia Genealogical Society* 33 (1995): 155–170.

6. Philip L. Barbour, ed., *The Jamestown Voyages under the First Charter, 1606–1609*, 2 vols. (Cambridge: 1969): 1:49–51.

7. Sebastian Munster, *A Treatyse of the Newe India, with Other New Founde Landes and Ilandes....*, trans. Richard Eden (London: 1553), sig. aa iii^z—aa iiii^v. For examples of Spanish activities, see Charles Hudson, *Knights of Spain, Warriors of the Sun: Hernando de Soto and the South's Ancient Chiefdoms* (Athens, GA: 1997), 2, 89, 130, 176–178,189, 203; David B. Quinn, ed., *New American World: A Documentary History of North America to 1612*, 5 vols. (New York: 1979), 2:543–544, 546, 548. For French explorations of the Florida coast, see Sarah Lawson, *A Foothold in Florida: The Eye-Witness Account of Four Voyages Made by the French to that Region and the Attempt at Colonization, 1562–1568* (East Grinstead, England: 1992), 5, 94–95, 127. For English activities, see David B. Quinn, *England and the Discovery of America, 1481–1620* (New York: 1974); E. G. R. Taylor, ed., *The Original Writings and Correspondence of the Two Richard Hakluyts*, 2 vols. (London: 1935), 2:254, 283–289, and David B. Quinn, ed., *The Roanoke Voyages, 1584–1590*, 2 vols. (London: 1955), 1:263–264, 268–270, 273–275, 2:761–765.

8. Barbour, *Jamestown Voyages*, 1:110–113.

9. Barbour, *Jamestown Voyages,* 1:46–48; Philip L. Barbour, ed., *The Complete Works of Captain John Smith,* 3 vols. (Chapel Hill, NC: 1986), 2:139–140, 3:236.

10. Barbour, *Jamestown Voyages,* 1:214–234 (reference to "a Parliament," 227). The original is in Lambeth Palace Library, MS 250, ff. 382r–395v. Jocelyn R. Wingfield, *Virginia's True Founder: Edward Maria Wingfield and His Times, 1550–1631* (North Charleston, SC: 2007), and offers a spirited defense of Wingfield's conduct in Virginia. Ratcliffe's real name was Sicklemore, which suggests he had adopted an alias because he was sending secret reports back to England to a high-placed patron. He and Smith both served as presidents and were also subsequently overthrown, the latter in an attempt on his life that left him grievously wounded and unable to remain in Virginia.

11. Alexander Brown, *The First Republic in America* (Boston: 1898), 73–74, 83; Alexander Brown, *The Genesis of the United States,* 2 vols. (New York: 1890), 1:341–342; *A True and Sincere Declaration of the Purposes and Ends of the Plantation Begun in Virginia....,* in *Jamestown Narratives: Eyewitness Accounts of the Virginia Colony. The First Decade: 1607–1617,* ed. Edward Wright Haile (Champlain, VA: 1988), 356–371; Barbour, *Jamestown Voyages,* 2:274–277.

12. Bemiss, *Three Charters,* 27–28, 42–54. Sir Thomas Smythe was to exert great influence on the affairs of the colony over the next decade and beyond. The council was named formally His Majesty's Council for the Company of Adventurers for Virginia, sometimes shortened to simply His Majesty's Council.

13. Bemiss, *Three Charters,* 55–75; Darrett B. Rutman, "The Virginia Company and Its Military Regime," in *The Old Dominion: Essays for Thomas Perkins Abernethy,* ed. Darrett B. Rutman (Charlottesville, VA: 1964), 1–20; Kingsbury, *RVC,* 3:15; John M. Collins, *Martial Law and English Laws, c. 1500–c. 1700* (Cambridge: 2016), 29–133. Lord De La Warr was thirty-two when he was appointed. He had distinguished himself in the wars in the Netherlands and Ireland, served in Parliament, and was a member of the king's privy council.

14. David H. Flaherty, ed., *Lawes Divine, Morall and Martiall, etc.* (Charlottesville, VA: 1969). For a discussion of the laws, see David Thomas Konig, "'Dale's Laws' and the Non-Common Law Origins of Criminal Justice in Virginia," *American Journal of Legal History* 26 (1982): 354–375; Edward L. Bond, *Damned Souls in a Tobacco Colony: Religion on Seventeenth-Century Virginia* (Macon, GA: 2000), 83–92; Paul Philip Musselwhite, "Towns in Mind: Urban Plans, Political Culture, and Empire in the Colonial Chesapeake, 1607–1722" (PhD diss., College of William and Mary, 2011), 23–33; and generally Alexander B. Haskell, "'The Affections of the People': Ideology and the Politics of State Building

in Colonial Virginia, 1607–1754" (PhD diss., Johns Hopkins University, 2004), 1–137.

15. Brown, *Genesis*, 1:238–240, 248–253; Kent History and Library Center, Maidstone, Kent, England, Sandwich Borough Records, Sa/ ZB2/64-68; Bemiss, *Three Charters*, 27–54. The Company also urged the City of London and merchant guilds to make voluntary contributions to help "ease the city and suburbs of a swarm of unnecessary inmates [migrants], as a continual cause of dearth and famine, and the very original cause of all the plagues that happen in this kingdom."

16. Bemiss, *Three Charters*, 42–43, 60–61, 65–67.

17. Quinn, *New American World*, 5:238–248; Andrew Fitzmaurice, "The Commercial Ideology of Colonization in Jacobean England: Robert Johnson, Giovanni Botero, and the Pursuit of Greatness," *William and Mary Quarterly* (hereafter *WMQ*), 3d ser., 64 (2007): 791–820; Alexander B. Haskell, *For God, King, and People: Forging Commonwealth Bonds in Renaissance Virginia* (Chapel Hill, NC: 2017), 138–139, 146–149; Edmond Smith, "A Merchant Colony: Reinterpreting the Virginia Plantation in its Global Context, 1609–1618," *WMQ*, 3d ser. (forthcoming).

18. For promoters of American ventures in the 1570s and 1580s who emphasized commercial benefits, see Quinn, *New American World*, 3:27–34 (Christopher Carleill), 49–53 (Sir George Peckham), and 61–123 (the two Richard Hakluyts).

19. Promotional literature of the 1570s and 1580s had highlighted spreading the gospel as one of the many benefits that would follow the founding of English colonies in America. See John Parker, "Religion and the Virginia Colony, 1609–10," in *The Westward Enterprise: English Activities in Ireland, the Atlantic and America, 1480–1650*, ed. K. R. Andrews, N. P. Canny, and P. E. H. Hair (Liverpool: 1978), 247–248, 257; Bond, *Damned Souls*, 1–29; Brown, *Genesis*, 1:290, 313–314, 369, 463; Edward D. Neill, *The English Colonization of America During the Seventeenth Century* (London: 1871), 71; Carla Gardina Pestana, *Protestant Empire: Religion and the Making of the British Atlantic World* (Philadelphia, PA: 2009), 67–69; Douglas Bradburn, "The Eschatological Origins of the English Empire," in *Early Modern Virginia: Reconsidering the Old Dominion*, ed. Douglas Bradburn and John C. Coombs (Charlottesville, VA: 2011), 17–36.

20. Lauren Working, "'The Savages of Virginia Our Project': The Powhatan in Jacobean Political Thought," and Nicholas Canny, "Race, Conflict, and Exclusion in Ulster, Ireland, and Virginia," in *Virginia 1619: Slavery, Freedom, and the Construction of English America*, ed. Paul Musselwhite, James Horn, and Peter C. Mancall (Chapel Hill, NC: forthcoming); Nicholas Canny, *Making Ireland British, 1580–1650* (Oxford: 2001), 203–204.

21. Population estimates are derived from Christian F. Feest, in Bruce G. Trigger, ed., *Northeast* (Washington, DC: 1978), 241–242, 255–256; E. Randolph Turner, "Socio-Political Organization within the Powhatan Chiefdom and the Effects of European Contact, A.D. 1607–1646," in *Cultures in Contact: The European Impact on Native Cultural Institutions in Eastern North America, A.D. 1000–1800,* ed. William W. Fitzhugh (Washington, DC: 1985), 193; William Strachey, *The Historie of Travell into Virginia Britania (1612),* ed. Louis B. Wright and Virginia Freud (London: 1953), 57; J. Frederick Fausz, "Patterns of Anglo-Indian Aggression and Accommodation along the Mid-Atlantic Coast, 1584–1634," in *Cultures in Contact,* ed. Fitzhugh, 226–236; Helen C. Rountree, *The Powhatan Indians of Virginia: Their Traditional Culture* (Lincoln, NE: 1989), 7–15; Frederic W. Gleach, *Powhatan's World and Colonial Virginia: A Conflict of Cultures* (Lincoln, NE: 1997), 22–28; April Lee Hatfield, "Spanish Colonization Literature, Powhatan Geographies, and English Perceptions of Tsenacommacah/Virginia," *Journal of Southern History* 69 (2003): 245–283; Daniel K. Richter, "Tsenacommacah and the Atlantic World," in *The Atlantic World and Virginia, 1550–1624,* ed. Peter C. Mancall (Chapel Hill, NC: 2007), 29–65; Martin D. Gallivan, *The Powhatan Landscape: An Archaeological History of the Algonquian Chesapeake* (Gainesville, FL: 2016), passim. The tidewater is the coastal region below the fall line where the rivers are tidal. It extends about a hundred miles from the Virginia coast inland to the piedmont. The *piedmont* is the term used to describe the gently sloping plateau that runs up to the Blue Ridge Mountains, the eastern chain of the Appalachians.

22. Barbour, *Complete Works,* 1:53, 55; Strachey, *Historie,* 37, 56–57, 60–61; Robert Beverley, *The History and Present State of Virginia,* ed. Louis B. Wright (Chapel Hill, NC: 1947), 45, 61; J. Frederick Fausz, "Opechancanough: Indian Resistance Leader," in *Struggle and Survival in Colonial America,* ed. David G. Sweet and Gary B. Nash (Berkeley, CA: 1981), 23; James D. Rice, "Escape from Tsenacommacah: Chesapeake Algonquians and the Powhatan Menace," in *The Atlantic World,* ed. Mancall, 97–140; Barbour, *Jamestown Voyages,* 1:93; Barbour, *Complete Works,* 1:147, 2:97–99. I have made no effort to provide a thorough description of the Powhatan's society, spiritual beliefs, economy, or culture. For such studies, see in particular works by Helen Rountree, Frederic Gleach, Martin D. Gallivan, James Rice, and, more broadly, Bernard Bailyn, *The Barbarous Years: The Peopling of British North America: The Conflict of Civilizations, 1600–1675* (New York: 2012), 3–31.

23. Barbour, *Jamestown Voyages,* 1:95, 133–138. Generally, see James Horn, "Imperfect Understandings: Rumor, Knowledge, and Uncertainty in Early Virginia," in *The Atlantic World,* ed. Mancall, 513–540. The remains of one of the settlers killed in the Indian attack, a young man of

approximately fifteen years of age, have been discovered by the archaeologists of Jamestown Rediscovery at the original site.

24. Lorri Glover and Daniel Blake Smith, *The Shipwreck that Saved Jamestown: The* Sea Venture *Castaways and the Fate of America* (New York: 2008), 49–123, 171–193.

25. Barbour, *Jamestown Voyages*, 2:283–284.

26. The best account of the war remains John Frederick Fausz's "The Powhatan Uprising of 1622: A Historical Study of Ethnocentrism and Cultural Conflict" (PhD diss., College of William and Mary, 1977), 267–285, and his "An 'Abundance of Blood Shed on Both Sides': England's First Indian War, 1609–1614," *Virginia Magazine of History and Biography* (hereafter *VMHB*) 98 (1990): 3–56; Mark Nicholls, "George Percy's 'Trewe Relacyon': A Primary Source for the Jamestown Settlement," *VMHB* 113 (2005): 247–248, 264–265.

27. Horn, *Land as God Made It,* 157–178; Nicholls, "George Percy's 'Trewe Relacyon,'" 243–252, 269; James Horn, William M. Kelso, Douglas Owsley, and Beverley Straube, *Jane: Starvation, Cannibalism, and Endurance at Jamestown* (Richmond, VA: 2013); Brown, *Genesis*, 1:363; Haile, *Jamestown Narratives,* 702. In addition, approximately fifty to sixty colonists survived at Fort Algernon downriver from Jamestown.

28. Nicholls, "George Percy's 'Trewe Relacyon,'" 252–254; Matthew Jennings, *New Worlds of Violence: Cultures and Conquests in the Early American Southeast* (Knoxville, TN: 2011), 97–109.

29. Fausz, "An 'Abundance of Blood,'" 30–42; Haile, *Jamestown Narratives,* 553–556. The remains of Captain William West, a relation of Lord De La Warr, were discovered in the chancel of the first church (1608) at Jamestown in 2013. He was killed in fighting at the falls in the winter of 1610–1611 and his body returned to James Fort, where he was buried with honor; see Jamestown Rediscovery, *Holy Ground: Archaeology, Religion, and the First Founders of Jamestown* (Richmond, VA: 2016) for a brief account of the discovery and identification of West and three other men buried in the chancel.

30. Haile, *Jamestown Narratives,* 434–435, 708, 711; Nicholls, "George Percy's 'Trewe Relacyon,'" 252; Bond, *Damned Souls,* 1–4, 22–23; Brown, *Genesis,* 1:361–373.

31. Ralph Hamor, *A True Discourse of the Present State of Virginia* (London: 1615), 2–16; Horn, *Land as God Made It,* 211–223; Fausz, "An 'Abundance of Blood,'" 43–49.

32. The original site of the church was discovered in 2010 by Jamestown Rediscovery archaeologists. See William M. Kelso, *Jamestown: The Truth Revealed* (Charlottesville, VA: 2017), 167–171; Rolfe, *True Relation,* 12–14. Pocahontas/Rebecca called herself Matoaka, which was her Powhatan adult name. Pocahontas was her nickname (diminutive) as a girl.

33. Brown, *Genesis,* 2:639–640, 774–779; *A Briefe Declaration of the Present State of Things in Virginia* (London: 1616), 5; Haile, *Jamestown Narratives,* 757; Strachey, *Historie,* 21–22; Hamor, *True Discourse,* 24, 34; Barbour, *Complete Works,* 2:262.

34. Brown, *Genesis,* 2:789–790; Lyon Gardiner Tyler, ed., *Narratives of Early Virginia, 1606–1625* (New York: 1966), 422–424; Bemiss, *Three Charters,* 89–92. Newgate was one of London's most notorious prisons. See Dale to Salisbury, August 17, 1611, Public Record Office, CO1/1, f. 95 (VCRP 622) and Haile, *Jamestown Narratives,* 748, 765–766. The term *hundred* was derived from an ancient English (late Saxon) administrative unit below the level of the county associated with the militia, maintenance of justice, and tax collection.

35. Irene A. Hecht, "The Virginia Colony, 1607–1640: A Study in Frontier Growth" (PhD diss., University of Washington, 1969), 68–74; Brown, *Genesis,* 2:783; Rolfe, *True Relation,* 3, 6–11. The settlements were: (1) Henrico, on the north side of the James River, where 38 men and boys lived, most of whom were farmers together with a few laborers, all of whom farmed for themselves. (2) Bermuda Nether Hundred, on the south bank, five miles as the crow flies downriver from Henrico, where 119 men and women lived, most of the whom were laborers contracted to work for three years producing pitch, tar, potashes, and charcoal. (3) At West and Sherley Hundred, located a few miles below Bermuda Hundred, were 25 men employed in cultivating tobacco, while (4) on Jamestown Island were 50 settlers, of which two-thirds were farmers tending their crops and looking after the Company's livestock. (5) Near the entrance to the James River, the settlement at Kecoughtan had 20 men, half of whom were farmers. Finally, across the Chesapeake Bay (6) near Cape Charles on the Eastern Shore was Dale's Gift, where 17 men fished and produced salt. See Dale's concerns in his letter of June 18, 1614, in Hamor, *True Discourse,* 57–59, cited by Smith, "A Merchant Colony."

Chapter 2: The Great Reforms

1. Philip J. Stern, "Companies: Monopoly, Sovereignty, and the East Indies," in *Mercantilism Reimagined: Political Economy in Early Modern Britain and its Empire,* ed. Philip J. Stern and Carl Wennerlind (Oxford: 2014), 179.

2. Philip L. Barbour, ed., *The Jamestown Voyages under the First Charter, 1606–1609,* 2 vols. (Cambridge: 1969), 1:24; John T. Juricek, "English Territorial Claims in North America under Elizabeth and the Early Stuarts," *Terrae Firma* 7 (1976): 7–22. Stuart Banner considers the complexity of the issue and contrasting opinions in *How the Indians Lost Their Land: Law and Power on the Frontier* (Cambridge, MA: 2005), 10–48.

3. Ralph Hamor, *A True Discourse of the Present State of Virginia* (London: 1615), 17; I owe this point to Paul Musselwhite, "Private Plantation: The Political Economy of Land in Early Virginia," in *Virginia 1619: Slavery, Freedom, and the Construction of English America,* ed. Paul Musselwhite, James Horn, and Peter C. Mancall (Chapel Hill, NC: forthcoming); Wesley Frank Craven, *Dissolution of the Virginia Company: The Failure of a Colonial Experiment* (Gloucester, MA: 1964), 35; William Bradford, *Of Plymouth Plantation, 1620–1647,* ed. Francis Murphy (New York: 1981), 133–134.

4. Hamor, *True Discourse,* 31–32; John Rolfe, *A True Relation of the State of Virginia Lefte by Sir Thomas Dale Knight in May Last 1616* (Charlottesville, VA: 1971), 9–10.

5. *A Briefe Declaration of the Present State of Things in Virginia, and of a Division to Be Now Made, of Some Part of Those Lands in Our Actuall Possession. . . .* (London: 1616), 5–6; Alexander Brown, *The Genesis of the United States,* 2 vols. (New York: 1890), 2:776–779; Wesley Frank Craven, *The Southern Colonies in the Seventeenth Century, 1607–1689* (Baton Rouge, LA: 1970), 116–120.

6. An early map of the James River shows the location of Argall's Town; see Michael Jarvis and Jeroen van Driel, "The Vingboons Chart of the James River, Virginia, circa 1617," *William and Mary Quarterly,* 3d ser., 54 (1997): 386; Charles E. Hatch, *The First Seventeen Years: Virginia, 1607–1624* (Charlottesville, VA: 1957), 18, 35–39, 104–105; Susan Myra Kingsbury, ed., *The Records of the Virginia Company of London* (hereafter *RVC*), 4 vols. (Washington, DC: 1906–1935), 3:68, 103; Lorena S. Walsh, *Motives of Honor, Pleasure, and Profit: Plantation Management in the Colonial Chesapeake, 1607–1763* (Chapel Hill, NC: 2010), 38–46.

7. David Thomas Konig, "Colonization and the Common Law in Ireland and Virginia, 1569–1634," in *The Transformation of Early American History: Society, Authority, and Ideology,* ed. James A. Henretta, Michael Kammen, and Stanley N. Katz (New York: 1991), 83–85; Musselwhite, "Reshaping Plantation"; Kingsbury, *RVC,* 1:303.

8. C. M. MacInnes, *The Early English Tobacco Trade* (London: 1926), 27–36, 47–48; Jeffrey Knapp, "Elizabethan Tobacco," in *New World Encounters,* ed. Stephen Greenblatt (Berkeley, CA: 1993), 272–312; Craven, *Southern Colonies,* 123–124; Bernard Bailyn, *The Barbarous Years: The Peopling of British North America: The Conflict of Civilizations, 1600–1675* (New York: 2012), 79; Walsh, *Motives of Honor,* 38; Hamor, *True Discourse,* 24; Philip L. Barbour, ed., *The Complete Works of Captain John Smith,* 3 vols. (Chapel Hill, NC: 1986), 2:262–263; Irene A. Hecht, "The Virginia Colony, 1607–1640: A Study in Frontier Growth" (PhD diss., University of Washington, 1969), 79–80. For Bermuda's early predominance, see Michael J. Jarvis, *In the Eye of All Trade: Bermuda,*

Bermudians, and the Maritime Atlantic World, 1680–1783 (Chapel Hill, NC: 2010), 26–29. Virginia's production did not overtake Bermuda's until the mid-1620s.

9. Ken MacMillan, *Sovereignty and Possession in the English New World: The Legal Foundations of Empire, 1576–1640* (Cambridge: 2006), 29–41; Paul D. Halliday, *Habeus Corpus: From England to Empire* (Cambridge, MA: 2010), 156; Daniel J. Hulsebosch, "The Ancient Constitution and the Expanding Empire: Sir Edward Coke's British Jurisprudence," *Law and History Review* 21 (2003): 439–482; Mary Dewar, ed., *De Republica Anglorum by Sir Thomas Smith* (Cambridge: 1982), 88; Robert Zaller, *The Discourse of Legitimacy in Early Modern England* (Stanford, CA: 2007), 1–50, 223–354; Ellis Sandoz, ed., *The Roots of Liberty: Magna Carta, Ancient Constitution, and the Anglo-American Tradition of the Rule of Law* (Columbia, MO: 1993), passim; Charles M. Gray, "Parliament, Liberty, and the Law," in *Parliament and Liberty: From the Reign of Elizabeth to the English Civil War*, ed. J. H. Hexter (Stanford, CA: 1992), 155–200, 304–309.

10. Johann P. Sommerville, ed., *King James VI and I: Political Writings* (Cambridge: 1994), 64–65; Samuel M. Bemiss, *The Three Charters of the Virginia Company of London . . . 1606–1621* (Williamsburg, VA: 1957), 1, 51, 86–87; Philip L. Barbour, ed., *The Jamestown Voyages under the First Charter, 1606–1609*, 2 vols. (Cambridge: 1969), 1:35. In the charter of 1612, laws and ordinances passed for the welfare of the plantation were simply stated not to be "contrary to the laws and statutes of this our realm of England"; MacMillan, *Sovereignty and Possession*, 89–96.

11. Bemiss, *Three Charters*, 47; David Thomas Konig, "'Dale's Laws' and the Non-Common Law Origins of Criminal Justice in Virginia," *American Journal of Legal History* 26 (1982): 354–375, and Konig, "Colonization and the Common Law," 70–92, 276–280; Halliday, *Habeus Corpus*, 137–157; Nicholas Canny, *Making Ireland British, 1580–1650* (Oxford: 2001), 59–164; Bailyn, *The Barbarous Years*, 39–40.

12. Kingsbury, *RVC*, 2:51–56. A scathing attack on Smythe and Argall was written by Nicholas Ferrar in 1624, *Sir Thomas Smith's Misgovernment of the Virginia Company*, ed. D. R. Ransome (Cambridge: 1990), 3–15; Craven, *Dissolution*, 45. For the corruption of public officials and abuse of martial law in Ireland in 1590, see Canny, *Making Ireland British*, 91. Lord De La Warr, who was still the lord governor and captain general of Virginia, was to replace the deputy governor, Captain Samuel Argall, in the summer of 1618 but died at sea en route to the colony. Yeardley departed for Jamestown in January 1619. Alexander Brown, *The First Republic of America: An Account of the Origins of the Nation. . . .* (New York: 1898), 281–283; National Archives UK, C24, 486.

13. Ferrar Papers (hereafter FP) 93, December 5, 1618, *Virginia*

Company Archives (hereafter *VCA*), Adam Mathew Digital (2007); Theodore K. Rabb, *Jacobean Gentleman: Sir Edwin Sandys, 1561–1629* (Princeton, NJ: 1998), 3–54; Andrew Thrush and John P. Ferris, eds., *The House of Commons, 1604–1629*, 6 vols. (Cambridge: 2010), 6:502–508; Sir John Fortescue's *De Laudibus Legnum Angliae* was translated into English nearly a century later by Richard Mulcaster, Sandys's headmaster at Merchant Taylors' School. Thrush and Ferris, *The House of Commons*, 6: see entry for Sir Edwin Sandys; Andrew Fitzmaurice, "Introduction: Neither Neo-Roman nor Liberal Empire," *Renaissance Studies* 26 (2012): 479–482; Richard Tuck, *Philosophy and Government, 1572–1651* (Cambridge: 1993), 146–151. Hooker's staunchly Anglican work defended the Elizabethan Church settlement against Puritan critics who continued to seek far-reaching reforms to bring English religious practice into closer conformity with that of Reformed Protestantism elsewhere in Europe, notably Presbyterianism. Careful to avoid a direct challenge, Hooker underlined the continuing importance of liturgy and communal prayer and put much more emphasis than Puritans on the value of preaching and sermons.

14. Pauline Croft, *King James* (New York: 2003), 48–86; Margaret Atwood Judson, *The Crisis of the Constitution: An Essay in Constitutional and Political Thought in England, 1603–1645* (New York: 1964), 17–106; J. H. Hexter, ed., *Parliament and Liberty: From the Reign of Elizabeth to the English Civil War* (Stanford, CA: 1992), passim; Burgess, *The Politics of the Ancient Constitution*, 151–156; Sommerville, *King James VI and I: Political Writings;* Conrad Russell, *King James VI & I and His English Parliaments*, ed. Richard Cust and Andrew Thrush (Oxford: 2012), passim. See also Glenn Burgess, *Absolute Monarchy and the Stuart Constitution* (New Haven, CT: 1996); James S. Hart, *The Rule of Law, 1603–1660* (Edinburgh: 2003), 79–81; David Harris Sacks, "Parliament, Liberty, and the Commonweal," in *Parliament and Liberty*, ed. Hexter, 85–121; Rabb, *Jacobean Gentleman*, 92–173; Robert Zaller, *The Discourse of Legitimacy in Early Modern England* (Stanford, CA: 2007), 318–328, 480–487, 502–506, 586–609.

15. Rabb, *Jacobean Gentleman*, 319–325; Wesley Frank Craven, *Dissolution of the Virginia Company: The Failure of a Colonial Experiment* (Gloucester, MA: 1964), 88. Important recent exceptions include the work of Andrew Fitzmaurice, Paul Musselwhite, and Lauren Working. See also Alexander Haskell, "Like 'the Roote and Body of a Tree': The Renaissance Ideal of the Public and the Creation of Virginia's General Assembly," in *Virginia 1619*, ed. Musselwhite, Horn, and Mancall, and his *For God, King, and People: Forging Commonwealth Bonds in Renaissance Virginia* (Chapel Hill, NC: 2017), 137–198.

16. Brown, *Genesis*, 2:890–891, 1061–1063; Thrush and Ferris, *House of Commons*, 3:463–465, 4:17–18, 245–247; G. P. V. Akrigg,

Shakespeare and the Earl of Southampton (Cambridge, MA: 1968); Stephen Greenblatt, *Will in the World: How Shakespeare Became Shakespeare* (New York: 2004), 227–232.

17. Kingsbury, *RVC*, 3:98–109, 482–484; FP 93, December 5, 1618, *VCA*, Adam Mathew Digital (2007); Jon Kukla, *Political Institutions in Virginia, 1618–1660* (New York: 1989), 40–48.

18. William S. Powell, *John Pory, 1572–1636: The Life and Letters of a Man of Many Parts* (Chapel Hill, NC: 1977), 25–30; Kingsbury, *RVC*, 1:350–351, 2:404, 3:98–109, 158, 473, 478, 482–484; Craven, *Dissolution*, 41–54, 73–75; Warren M. Billings, *A Little Parliament: The Virginia General Assembly in the Seventeenth Century* (Richmond, VA: 2004), 5–7; Brown, *First Republic*, 456; Konig, "Colonization and the Common Law," 86; Craven, *Southern Colonies*, 129–131; see in particular Musselwhite, "Towns in Mind," 34–51; H. R. McIlwaine, ed., *Journals of the House of Burgesses of Virginia, 1619–1658/59* (Richmond, VA: 1915), 36.

19. FP 93, December 5, 1618, *VCA*.

20. Kingsbury, *RVC*, 3:473, 478, 482–484; Billings, *A Little Parliament*, 149–171; Paul D. Halliday, "Brase's Case: Making Slave Law as Customary Law in Virginia's General Court, 1619–1625," in *Virginia 1619*, ed. Musselwhite, Horn, and Mancall; Jon Kukla, *Political Institutions in Virginia, 1618–1660* (New York: 1989), 43–45; Brown, *First Republic*, 456.

21. FP 93, December 5, 1618, *VCA*; Kukla, *Political Institutions*, 48–50; Billings, *A Little Parliament*, 7–10; Craven, *Dissolution*, 67–73; Haskell, *For God, King, and People*, 196–198; MacMillan, *Sovereignty and Possession*, 32–33.

22. Despite its importance, few comprehensive accounts of the first General Assembly exist, but see McIlwaine, *Journals*, 36; Kingsbury, *RVC*, 4:449; Billings, *A Little Parliament*, 7–10. An excellent transcription with a facsimile of the document is provided in William J. Van Schreeven and George H. Reese, eds., *Proceedings of the General Assembly of Virginia, July 30–August 4, 1619* (Jamestown, VA: 1969).

23. Kingsbury, *RVC*, 3:119, 154–155; National Archives UK, C24, 486. In Anglican churches, the *choir* is traditionally the western part of the chancel. The church was built on the instructions of Samuel Argall, and excavations of the 1617 church by Jamestown Rediscovery archaeologists have revealed it was approximately fifty feet long and twenty wide with cobblestone and brick foundations, timber frame and plaster walls, and a wooden or thatch roof. The interior would also have been plastered. Appropriately, carpenters transported by Lord De La Warr were put "to work about the church," where he was buried in mid-August 1618, National Archives, UK, C24/486. Peter Wilson Coldham, "The Voyage of the *Neptune* to Virginia, 1618–1619, and the Disposition of its Cargo,"

Virginia Magazine of History and Biography (VMHB) 87 (1979): 33, 40, 43; Jon Kukla, *Political Institutions in Virginia, 1618–1660* (New York: 1989): 51–52.

24. Kingsbury, *RVC*, 3:155–156.

25. Kingsbury, *RVC*, 3:156–158, 162–164; Van Schreeven and Reese, *Proceedings*, 21; Kukla, *Political Institutions*, 53–55; Konig, "Colonization and the Common Law," 84–85.

26. Helen C. Rountree, *The Powhatan Indians of Virginia: Their Traditional Culture* (Norman, OK: 1989), 114–116; William Strachey, *The Historie of Travell into Virginia Britania (1612)*, eds. Louis B. Wright and Virginia Freud (London: 1953), 77.

27. Kingsbury, *RVC*, 3:158–159; Powell, *Pory*, 87–90; James Rice, "'These Doubtful Times, Between Us and the Indians': Indigenous Politics and the Jamestown Colony in 1619," in *Virginia 1619*, ed. Musselwhite, Horn, and Mancall.

28. Kingsbury, *RVC*, 3:160–175; Powell, *Pory*, 90–93. The examination of Robert Poole is preserved in the Ferrar Papers and provides evidence of the careful preparation of cases that came before the General Assembly acting as a court. See FP 113, July 13, 1619, *VCA*; J. Frederick Fausz, "Middlemen in Peace and War: Virginia's Earliest Indian Interpreters, 1608–1632," *Virginia Magazine of History and Biography* 5 (1987): 41–64.

29. Craven, *Dissolution*, 43–50; Brown, *First Republic*, 305–307; Elizabeth McClure Thomson, ed., *The Chamberlain Letters: A Selection of Letters of John Chamberlain concerning Life in England from 1597 to 1626* (New York: 1965), 218–219; Kingsbury, *RVC*, 3:118–120, 123, 125–126.

30. Kenneth R. Andrews, *Trade, Plunder, and Settlement: Maritime Enterprise and the Genesis of the British Empire, 1480–1630* (Cambridge: 1984), 280–340; Mark G. Hanna, *Pirate Nests and the Rise of the British Empire, 1570–1740* (Chapel Hill, NC: 2015), 63–77.

31. Kingsbury, *RVC*, 3:176–177. Yeardley dissolved the assembly shortly afterward. The next meeting did not take place until November–December 1621, McIlwaine, *Journals*, 17. A revealing description of the first General Assembly held in Bermuda in August 1620 can be found in C. F. E. Hollis Hallett, ed., *Butler's History of the Bermudas: A Contemporary Account of Bermuda's Earliest Government* (Bermuda: 2007), 153–163.

32. *A Declaration of the State of the Colony and Affaires in Virginia. . . .*, June 22, 1620, in Kingsbury, *RVC*, 3:309–311; Konig, "Dale's Laws," 365, 368–375. Even if settlers were unable to avail themselves of the common law, the adoption by the Company of those "Laws of *England*" suitable for use in the colony was a means of importing

traditional laws that had shaped collective and individual English rights for centuries.

33. Kingsbury, *RVC*, 3:170, 177; Halliday, "Brase's Case"; Billings, *A Little Parliament*, 5–23, and more generally Warren M. Billings, "The Transfer of English Law to Virginia, 1606–1650," in *The Westward Enterprise: English Activities in Ireland, the Atlantic, and America, 1480–1650*, ed. K. R. Andrews, N. P. Canny, and P. E. H. Hair (Liverpool: 1978), 215–244.

Chapter 3: First Africans

1. Philip D. Morgan, "Virginia Slavery in Atlantic Context, 1550 to 1650," in *Virginia 1619: Slavery, Freedom, and the Construction of English America*, ed. Paul Musselwhite, James Horn, and Peter C. Mancall (Chapel Hill, NC: forthcoming); David Wheat, *Atlantic Africa and the Spanish Caribbean, 1570–1640* (Chapel Hill, NC: 2016), 12.

2. Alex Borucki, David Eltis, and David Wheat, "Atlantic History and the Slave Trade to Spanish America," *American Historical Review* (hereafter *AHR*) 120 (2015): 440. Approximately 275,000 men and women were forcibly taken from Africa and transported to Spanish and Portuguese America in the sixteenth century, *The Trans-Atlantic Slave Trade Data Base*. Nick Hazlewood, *The Queen's Slave Trader: John Hawkyns, Elizabeth I, and the Trafficking in Human Souls* (New York: 2002), 309–314; Mark G. Hanna, *Pirate Nests and the Rise of the British Empire, 1570–1740* (Chapel Hill, NC: 2015), 70–77; April Lee Hatfield, *Atlantic Virginia: Intercolonial Relations in the Seventeenth Century* (Philadelphia: 2004), 137–138; Engel Sluiter, "New Light on the '20. and Odd Negroes' Arriving in Virginia, August 1619," *William and Mary Quarterly* (hereafter *WMQ*), 3rd ser., 54 (1997): 395–398.

3. Sluiter, "New Light," 395–398. Accounting for 24 African boys sold in Jamaica and the 60 African captives taken by Jope and Elfrith, the death toll was at least 120, a third of the total who boarded ship in Luanda. Wheat, *Atlantic Africa*, 78–81; Susan Myra Kingsbury, ed., *The Records of the Virginia Company of London* (hereafter *RVC*), 4 vols. (Washington, DC: 1906–1935), 3:219, 243. John Pory reported a few months earlier that "the occasion of this ship's [*White Lion*] coming hither was an accidental consortship in the West Indies with the *Treasurer*, an English man of war also, licensed by a commission from the Duke of Savoy to take Spaniards as lawful prize." Piersey was an influential and wealthy settler who first arrived in the colony three years earlier and was in charge of the colony's magazine (store) exchanging goods sent by the Company for settlers' tobacco, Martha W. McCartney, *Virginia Immigrants and Adventurers, 1607–1635: A Biographical Dictionary* (Baltimore:

2007), 548–549. Whether the Africans went ashore at Point Comfort and how and by whom they were transported upriver are unknown.

4. Kingsbury, *RVC*, 1:367, 3:243. Sir Edwin Sandys characterized Bermuda in May 1620 as "much frequented with men of War and Pirates" and "if there be not a strict course taken herein it will be made another Algiers." Algiers was a major base of operations for the Barbary pirates who preyed on European shipping and sold enslaved Christians to the Turks. Heywood and Thornton estimate that approximately one hundred Africans were in Bermuda by 1620, "a sizable part of the population of the island," Linda M. Heywood and John K. Thornton, *Angolans, Atlantic Creoles, and the Foundation of the Americas, 1585–1660* (Cambridge: 2007), 5–7, 28; Wesley Frank Craven, *An Introduction to the History of Bermuda*, 2nd ed. (Bermuda: 1990), 91–93; Michael J. Jarvis, *In the Eye of All Trade: Bermuda, Bermudians, and the Maritime Atlantic World, 1680–1783* (Chapel Hill, NC: 2010), 29; Michael Guasco, *Slaves and Englishmen: Human Bondage in the Early Modern Atlantic World* (Philadelphia: 2014), 119, 199–201. Tim Hashaw argues that Rolfe deliberately sought to mislead Sandys owing to his loyalty to Captain Samuel Argall, who had authorized the *Treasurer* to raid the West Indies, *The Birth of Black America: The First African Americans and the Pursuit of Freedom at Jamestown* (New York: 2007), 86–91; E. M. Rose, "The Conflicted Politics of Slavery: The First Africans in British North America," in *Virginia 1619*, ed. Musselwhite, Horn, and Mancall.

5. *Virginia Colonial Records Project* (hereafter *VCRP*), Survey Report (hereafter SR) 1106, number 261, from the Manchester Papers; C. F. E. Hollis Hallett, ed. *History of the Bermudas: A Contemporary Account of Bermuda's Earliest Government* (Bermuda: 2007), 120, 127–128; Heywood and Thornton, *Angolans, Atlantic Creoles*, 7–8; William Thorndale, "The Virginia Census of 1619," *Virginia Genealogical Society* 33 (1995): 168. The census was taken in early March 1620.

6. Sluiter, "New Light," 395–398; John Thornton, "The African Experience of the '20. and Odd Negroes' Arriving in Virginia in 1619," *WMQ*, 3rd ser., 55 (1998): 421–434. For the view that the first Africans came from the Spanish Caribbean, see, for example, Wesley Frank Craven, *Red, White, and Black: The Seventeenth Century Virginian* (Charlottesville, VA: 1971), 80–82. Craven notes, however, that there is little evidence for the assumption and refers also to Captain Arthur Guy's seizure of "an Angola man [ship] with many Negroes" brought to Virginia in 1628.

7. Heywood and Thornton, *Angolans, Atlantic Creoles*, 52–53, 215–217; Joseph C. Miller, *Way of Death: Merchant Capitalism and the Angolan Slave Trade, 1730–1830* (Madison, WI: 1988), 10–11, 24, 28–29, 36–37, 148; John Thornton, *Africa and Africans in the Making of*

the Atlantic World, 1400–1800 (Cambridge: 1998), xxvi–xxxvi, 91, 93–94, 96–97, 118; John K. Thornton, *A Cultural History of the Atlantic World, 1250–1820* (Cambridge: 2012), 77.

8. Ira Berlin, "From Creoles to African: Atlantic Creoles and the Origins of African-American Society in Mainland North America," *WMQ*, 3rd ser., 53 (1996): 251–288; Ira Berlin, *Many Thousands Gone: The First Two Centuries of Slavery in North America* (Cambridge, MA: 1998), 29–46; Linda M. Heywood and John K. Thornton, "Central African Leadership and the Appropriation of European Culture," in *The Atlantic World and Virginia, 1550–1624,* ed. Peter C. Mancall (Chapel Hill, NC: 2007),194–224; Heywood and Thornton, *Angolans, Atlantic Creoles,* passim; John C. Coombs is cautious about the "Atlantic Creoles" theory, see "Beyond the 'Origins Debate': Rethinking the Rise of Virginia Slavery," in *Early Modern Virginia: Reconsidering the Old Dominion,* ed. Douglas Bradburn and John C. Coombs (Charlottesville, VA: 2011), 255–263. See also James H. Sweet, *Recreating Africa: Culture, Kinship, and Religion in the African-Portuguese World, 1441–1770* (Chapel Hill, NC: 2003), 115–117, and James H. Sweet, "African Identity and Slave Resistance in the Portuguese Atlantic," in *The Atlantic World and Virginia,* ed. Mancall, 246–247.

9. Linda Heywood, "The Angolan Background to the '20 and Odd Negars," in *Virginia 1619,* ed. Musselwhite, Horn, and Mancall; A. J. R. Russell-Wood, "The Portuguese Atlantic, 1415–1808," in *Atlantic History: A Critical Appraisal,* ed. Jack P. Greene and Philip D. Morgan (Oxford: 2009), 90–91; Thornton, *A Cultural History of the Atlantic World,* 81–82; David Eltis and David Richardson, *Atlas of the Transatlantic Slave Trade* (New Haven, CT: 2010), 136–137, maps 92 and 95.

10. Thornton, "The African Experience," 421–434. Thornton readily concedes that the "20. and odd" could have come from elsewhere in the region where conflict took place in this period. Heywood and Thornton, *Angolans, Atlantic Creoles,* 82–123, 227; Heywood, "The Angolan Background"; Linda Heywood, *Njinga of Angola: Africa's Warrior Queen* (Cambridge, MA: 2017), 1–61; Wheat, *Atlantic Africa,* 95–101.

11. Thornton, "The African Experience," 426, 431, 434; Sweet, *Recreating Africa,* 162; Thornton, *Africa and Africans,* 154–156. The Jagas led by Imbe Kalandula embraced Central African concepts of witchcraft and were viewed as witches by the people they terrorized, Heywood and Thornton, *Angolans, Atlantic Creoles,* 93; Robert J. Allison, ed., *The Interesting Narrative of the Life of Olaudah Equiano, Written by Himself* (New York: 1995), 56; Sluiter, "New Light," 397; Eltis and Richardson offer estimates of mortality rates for the second half of the seventeenth century, but they may have been higher in earlier decades, *Atlas of the Transatlantic Slave Trade,* 167, 169, maps 116, 117; Herbert S. Klein, Stanley

L. Engerman, Robin Haines, and Ralph Shlomowitz, "Transoceanic Mortality: The Slave Trade in Comparative Perspective," *WMQ*, 3rd ser., 58 (2001): table VI (a), 114; James Walvin, *Crossings: Africa, the Americas, and the Atlantic Slave Trade* (London: 2013), passim; Morgan, "Virginia Slavery."

12. Martha W. McCartney, "A Study of Africans and African Americans on Jamestown Island and at Green Spring, 1619–1803" (a report for the National Park Service and Colonial Williamsburg: 2003), 36; John Camden Hotten, ed., *The Original Lists of Persons of Quality; Emigrants; Religious Exiles; Political Rebels; Serving Men Sold for a Term of Years* (Baltimore: 2007), 172–174, 178, 182, 185, 217–218, 222, 224, 229, 241, 244, 257.

13. *VCRP*, SR 1106, number 289 from the Manchester Papers; James Horn, *A Land as God Made It: Jamestown and the Birth of America* (New York: 2005), 255, 260–261, 268. Hashaw points out that no Africans were killed in the attack despite heavy losses among planters and their white servants, especially at Bennett's plantation, *Birth of Black America*, 159, but this is not certain. Coombs, "Beyond the 'Origins Debate,'" 247–250.

14. Richard Ligon, *A True and Exact History of the Island of Barbados. . . .* (London: 1970), 44; Heywood and Thornton, *Angolans, Atlantic Creoles*, 169–236, 242–243; Thornton, *A Cultural History*, 328–330; Sweet, *Recreating Africa*, 13–14,104–115. Some recent historians consider the cultural encounters in Kongo as a striking example of an "Atlantic Creole" culture: the fusion of European and African cultures. Such creole cultures, historians have emphasized, borrowed as much from regional African societies as they drew from the Portuguese.

15. The literature on this subject is vast, but for summaries of the debate, see Winthrop D. Jordan, *White Over Black: American Attitudes Toward the Negro, 1550–1812* (Chapel Hill, NC: 1968), 3–98; Alden T. Vaughan, *Roots of American Racism: Essays on the Colonial Experience* (Oxford: 1995), 136–174; Coombs, "Beyond the 'Origins Debate,'" 239–278. Depending on their age and circumstances, indentured or poor white laborers without contracts usually served from four to seven years, after which they were freed and sometimes given certain "freedom dues" consisting typically of provisions, clothing, basic tools, and even the right to a small area of land, see James Horn and Philip D. Morgan, "Settlers and Slaves: European and African Migrations to Early Modern British America," in *The Creation of a British Atlantic World*, ed. Elizabeth Manke and Carole Shammas (Baltimore: 2005), 27–28.

16. Coombs, "Beyond the 'Origins Debate,'" 239–278; T. H. Breen and Stephen Innes, *"Myne Owne Ground": Race and Freedom on Virginia's Eastern Shore, 1640–1676* (Oxford: 1980), 19–35; Vaughan, *Roots of*

American Racism, 136–174; Thomas D. Morris, *Southern Slavery and the Law, 1619–1860* (Chapel Hill, NC: 1996), 8–19; [John Ferrar], *A Perfect Description of Virginia.* . . . (London: 1649), 3.

17. Hashaw argues that the three Africans, Antonio, Mary, and John Pedro, who arrived in Virginia after 1620 were originally taken from the *São Joã Bautista,* landed on Bermuda, then transported to Sir Robert Rich in England in 1621 before being returned to Virginia, *Birth of Black America,* 130–131, 140–151, 212–217, 299–300. The evidence, however, is circumstantial. Clayton Coleman Hall, ed., *Narratives of Maryland, 1633–1684* (New York: 1967), 305. For Anthony Johnson, see Breen and Innes, *"Myne Owne Ground,"* 7–18, 68–109.

18. James H. Sweet, "The Iberian Roots of American Racist Thought," *WMQ,* 3rd ser., 54 (1997): 157–158. The old slave market house in Lagos, Portugal, still exists.

19. Gustav Ungerer, *The Mediterranean Apprenticeship of British Slavery* (Madrid: 2008), 70–95; Miranda Kaufmann, *Black Tudors: The Untold Story* (London: 2017); David Olusoga, *Black and British: A Forgotten History* (London: 2017), 44–66; Onyeka, *Blackamoores: Africans in Tudor England, Their Presence, Status and Origins* (London: 2013), xii–xv, 1–40, 52, 211–238; Guasco, *Slaves and Englishmen,* 11–79; Richard Hakluyt, *The Principal Navigations, Voyages, Traffiques, and Discoveries of the English Nation,* 8 vols. (Glasgow: 1904), 6:167–170, 176; William S. Powell, *John Pory, 1572–1636: The Life and Letters of a Man of Many Parts* (Chapel Hill, NC: 1977), 12–17; Jordan, *White Over Black,* 33–34; David Brion Davis, "'Constructing Race': A Reflection," *WMQ,* 3rd ser., 54 (1997): 7–18.

20. Borucki, Eltis, and Wheat, "Atlantic History," 433–461; Hatfield, *Atlantic Virginia,* 138; Hazlewood, *The Queen's Slave Trader,* 309–314.

21. Morgan, "Virginia Slavery"; Jonathan A. Bush, "The British Constitution and the Creation of American Slavery," in *Slavery and the Law,* ed. Paul Finkelman (New York: 1997), 379–418; Guasco, *Slaves and Englishmen,* 208; Lorena S. Walsh, *Motives of Honor, Pleasure, and Profit: Plantation Management in the Colonial Chesapeake, 1607–1763* (Chapel Hill, NC: 2010), 116.

22. Kingsbury, *RVC,* 3:243; H. R. McIlwaine, ed., *Minutes of the Council and General Court of Colonial America,* 2nd ed. (Richmond, VA: 1979), 66–69, 71–73; and Paul D. Halliday's insightful, "Brase's Case: Making Slave Law as Customary Law in Virginia's General Court, 1619–1625," in *Virginia 1619,* ed. Musselwhite, Horn, and Mancall; Edmund S. Morgan, *American Slavery, American Freedom: The Ordeal of Colonial Virginia* (New York: 1975), 119.

23. McCartney, "A Study of Africans and African Americans," 37; Hashaw, *Birth of Black America,* 106–109; McCartney, *Virginia Immigrants*

and Adventurers, 484–485; *VCRP,* SR 6153, ff. 560v–561r; National Archives, UK, Principal Probate Registry Class, Will Register Books, 9 Ridley, 1ᵛ·ʳ; Virginia Historical Society, Richmond, Virginia, MSS 2y327a.

24. Coombs, "Beyond the 'Origins Debate,'" 247, 254–258.

25. *VCRP,* SR 1106, number 289; John C. Coombs, "Building the Machine: The Development of Slavery in Early Colonial Virginia" (PhD diss., College of William and Mary, 2003), 38, 41–42; James Horn, *Adapting to a New World: English Society in the Seventeenth-Century Chesapeake* (Chapel Hill, NC: 1994), 172. Two ships brought approximately 165 enslaved Africans (some from the Bight of Biafra on the west coast of Africa) in the 1650s. Guasco, *Slaves and Englishmen,* 199–209; Virginia Bernhard, "Beyond the Chesapeake: The Contrasting Status of Blacks in Bermuda, 1616–1663," *Journal of Southern History* 54 (1988): 545–564; Karen Ordahl Kupperman, *Providence Island: The Other Puritan Colony, 1630–1641* (Cambridge: 1993), 172. Providence Island lies off the coast of Nicaragua. The first law in English America that was explicitly racially motivated was passed by the assembly of Bermuda in 1623: "An act to restrain the insolences of the Negroes" restricted the free movement of Africans and denied men the right to carry weapons, Craven, *History of Bermuda,* 94. Simon P. Newman, *A New World of Labor: The Development of Plantation Slavery in the British Atlantic* (Philadelphia: 2013), 189–257; John Wareing, *Indentured Migration and the Servant Trade from London to America, 1619–1718* (Oxford: 2017), 42.

26. Vaughan, *Roots of American Racism,* 157; Hotten, *The Original Lists,* 172–174, 178, 182, 185.

27. Hotten, *The Original Lists,* 180, 204, 205, 209, 211, 212, 217, 218, 222, 235, 239, 258, 261; Joyce E. Chaplin, "Race," in *The British Atlantic World, 1500–1800,* ed. David Armitage and Michael J. Braddick (New York: 2002), 154–172; William Waller Hening, ed., *The Statutes at Large Being a Collection of All the Laws of Virginia....,* 13 vols. (Charlottesville, VA: 1969), 1:146; Rebecca Anne Goetz, *The Baptism of Early Virginia: How Christianity Created Race* (Baltimore: 2012), 73, 78–79.

28. Kathleen M. Brown, *Good Wives, Nasty Wenches, and Anxious Patriarchs: Gender, Race, and Power in Colonial Virginia* (Chapel Hill, NC: 1996), 116–133; McIlwaine, *Minutes of the Council and General Court,* 477; Coombs, "Building the Machine," 138–150; Hening, *Statutes at Large,* 1:226, 242, 292, 2:170, 195, 260, 267, 270, 280–281, 288, 299–300.

29. Morgan, "Virginia Slavery."

30. Eltis and Richardson estimate 388,000 Africans arrived in British North America, 1619–1860, *Atlas of the Transatlantic Slave Trade,* 89, 200, 205, map 137; Heywood and Thornton, *Angolans, Atlantic Creoles,* 169–293; Michael Mullin, *Africa in America: Slave Acculturation and*

Resistance in the American South and the British Caribbean, 1736–1831 (Urbana, Il: 1992), 13–74; Philip D. Morgan, *Slave Counterpoint: Black Culture in the Eighteenth-Century Chesapeake and Lowcountry* (Chapel Hill, NC: 1998), part 3; Sweet, *Recreating Africa,* passim.

31. The site of Captain William Pierce's house and his three- to four-acre lot on Jamestown Island where Angela lived in 1624 and 1625 still exists. It has been the subject of recent archaeological excavations and research by the National Park Service in collaboration with the Jamestown Rediscovery archaeological team led by David Givens.

Chapter 4: Commonwealth

1. Susan Myra Kingsbury, ed., *The Records of the Virginia Company of London* (hereafter *RVC*), 4 vols. (Washington, DC: 1906–1935), 1:423, 3:307. Sir Thomas Gates and Sir Thomas Dale had earlier attempted to found a civil society "based on labor, worship, and Christian morality," backed by strict discipline and martial law that had failed; see Edward L. Bond, *Damned Souls in a Tobacco Colony: Religion on Seventeenth-Century Virginia* (Macon, GA: 2000), 83–92.

2. Glenn Burgess, "England and Scotland," in *European Political Thought, 1450–1700: Religion, Law and Philosophy,* ed. Howell A. Lloyd, Glenn Burgess, and Simon Hodson (New Haven, CT: 2007), 336–337; Glenn Burgess, *British Political Thought, 1500–1660* (London: 2009), 19–20, 22, 26; Andy Wood, *Riot, Rebellion, and Popular Politics in Early Modern England* (New York: 2002), 25–26; *The Boke Named the Gouernour Devised by Sir T. E., Knyght* (London: 2010); C. H. Williams, ed., *English Historical Documents, 1485–1558* (London: 1971), 295–302; David Rollison, *A Commonwealth of the People: Popular Politics and England's Long Social Revolution, 1066–1649* (Cambridge: 2010), passim. Expressed in many different forms over the course of the fifteenth and sixteenth centuries, humanist or neo-Roman thought evolved as the application of ancient Greek and Roman learning to contemporary issues and policy, particularly in matters of governance, law, and the well-being of society; see Burgess, *British Political Thought,* 1–27; Andrew Fitzmaurice, *Humanism and America: An Intellectual History of English Colonization, 1500–1625* (Cambridge: 2003), 1–19; Andrew Fitzmaurice, "'Every Man, That Prints, Adventures': The Rhetoric of the Virginia Company Sermons," in *The English Sermon Revised: Religion, History and Literature, 1600–1750,* ed. Lori Anne Ferrell and Peter McCullough (Manchester: 2000), 24–42.

3. Francis Grigor, ed., *Sir John Fortescue's Commendation of the Laws of England: The Translation into English of De Laudibus Legnum Angliae* (London: 1917), 16, 22, 26–28, 56–63; Thomas Smith, *De Republica*

Anglorum, ed. Mary Dewar (Cambridge: 1982), 49, 57, 78, 88; Henry S. Turner, "Corporations: Humanism and Elizabethan Political Economy," in *Mercantilism Reimagined: Political Economy in Early Modern Britain and its Empire,* ed. Philip J. Stern and Carl Wennerlind (Oxford: 2014), 156–161; Burgess, "England and Scotland," 339–342, 352–353; Glenn Burgess, *The Politics of the Ancient Constitution: An Introduction to English Political Thought 1603–1642* (University Park, PA: 1992); Steve Hindle, *The State and Social Change in Early Modern England, 1550–1640* (New York: 2002), 24–27.

4. Wood, *Riot, Rebellion, and Popular Politics,* 29–89; Mark Nicholls, *A History of the Modern British Isles, 1529–1603: The Two Kingdoms* (Oxford: 1999), 113–161; Anthony Fletcher and Diarmaid MacCulloch, *Tudor Rebellions,* 5th ed. (London: 2008), 28–101; Ethan H. Shagan, *Popular Politics and the English Reformation* (Cambridge: 2002), passim; C. H. Williams, ed., *English Historical Documents, 1485–1558* (London: 1971), 268–273, 293–333; Burgess, *British Political Thought,* 20–25.

5. Rollison, *Commonwealth of the People,* 342–350; Phil Withington, *Society in Early Modern England: The Vernacular Origins of Some Powerful Ideas* (Cambridge: 2010), 143, 149–150; Lloyd, Burgess, and Hodson, *European Political Thought,* 337–338; Williams, *English Historical Documents,* 268–273, 293–333; Thomas Smith, *A Discourse of the Common Weal of this Realm of England,* ed. Elizabeth Lamond (Cambridge: 1929), 1, 57–59; Henry S. Turner, *The Corporate Commonwealth: Pluralism and Political Fictions in England, 1516–1651* (Chicago: 2016), ch. 2; Keith Wrightson, *Earthly Necessities: Economic Lives in Early Modern Britain* (New Haven, CT: 2000), 149–158.

6. David Beers Quinn, ed., *The Voyages and Colonizing Enterprises of Sir Humphrey Gilbert,* 2 vols. (London: 1940), 2:361; Richard Hakluyt was known as *the younger* to distinguish him from his older cousin of the same name, *Divers Voyages Touching the Discovery of America. . . .* (London: 1582), 8; E. G. R. Taylor, ed., *The Original Writings and Correspondence of the Two Richard Hakluyts,* 2 vols. (London: 1935), 2:233–234, 315; Jack P. Greene, *The Intellectual Construction of America: Exceptionalism and Identity from 1492 to 1800* (Chapel Hill, NC: 1993), 39–46. See, for example, *Ease for Overseers of the Poor* (London: 1601), Gerard de Malynes, *Saint George for England, Allegorically Described* (London: 1601), and Francis Trigge, *To the Kings Most Excellent Majestie: The Humble Petition of Two Sisters the Church and Common-wealth: For the Restoring of Their Ancient Commons and Liberties, which Late Inclosure with Depopulation, Uncharitably Hath Taken Away* (London: 1604).

7. Withington, *Politics of Commonwealth;* Andrew Fitzmaurice, "The Company–Commonwealth," in *Virginia 1619: Slavery, Freedom, and the Construction of English America,* ed. Paul Musselwhite, James Horn, and

Peter C. Mancall (Chapel Hill, NC: forthcoming); Alexander B. Haskell, *For God, King, and People: Forging Commonwealth Bonds in Renaissance Virginia* (Chapel Hill, NC: 2017), 106–198.

8. Wood, *Riot, Rebellion, and Popular Politics*, 25–28; Williams, *English Historical Documents*, 268, 295–296; Burgess, *Ancient Constitution*, 5–6, 131–134; Burgess, *British Political Thought*, 20–25, 96–97; Alexander B. Haskell, "'The Affections of the People': Ideology and the Politics of State Building in Colonial Virginia, 1607–1754," (PhD diss., Johns Hopkins University, 2004), 25–26; FP 121, July 1619, VCA, "A Project from M[aste]r Caswell for Creating Noblemen in Virginia," cited by Lauren Working. Robert Gray, *Good Speede to Virginia* (London: 1609), Dr. Gray was rector of St. Benet Sherehog and neighbor of John Ferrar, the deputy treasurer of the Virginia Company in Sithes Lane, London; FP 166, April 1620, VCA.

9. Theodore K. Rabb, *Enterprise and Empire: Merchant and Gentry Investment in the Expansion of England, 1575–1630* (Cambridge, MA: 1967), 22–101, 104, 128; Samuel M. Bemiss, *The Three Charters of the Virginia Company of London . . . 1606–1621* (Williamsburg, VA: 1957), 28–42, 79–85; Kingsbury, *RVC*, 3:231–232, 317–340; Lauren Working, "'The Savages of Virginia Our Project': The Powhatan in Jacobean Political Thought," in *Virginia 1619*, ed. Musselwhite, Horn, and Mancall. Nonetheless, rumblings of disapproval about Yeardley's appointment continued to surface in both London and Jamestown, see for example a petition sent to the Company's Council in 1619/1620 from "sundry ancient adventurers" requesting "some man of quality sent [to be] governor into Virginia," VCRP, SR 1106, number 247, from the Manchester Papers.

10. H. R. McIlwaine, ed., *Journals of the House of Burgesses of Virginia, 1619–1658/59* (Richmond, VA: 1915), 36; Cicero, *On the Commonwealth*, trans. George Holland Sabine and Stanley Barney Smith (New York: 1976), bk. 2, XLII; Haskell, *For God, King, and People*, 196–198.

11. Edmund Spenser, *A Veue of the Present State of Irelande*, 1596, Rawlinson MS, Renascence Editions, University of Oregon (1997). Spenser attended the same school as Sandys, Merchant Taylors, London. Audrey Horning, *Ireland in the Virginia Sea: Colonialism in the British Atlantic* (Chapel Hill, NC: 2013), 244–253; Paul Philip Musselwhite, "Towns in Mind: Urban Plans, Political Culture, and Empire in the Colonial Chesapeake, 1607–1722," (PhD diss., College of William and Mary, 2011), 33–36; David Armitage, *The Ideological Origins of the British Empire* (Cambridge: 2000), 48–55; Robert Johnson, *Nova Britannia. . . .* in *New American World: A Documentary History of North America to 1612*, 5 vols., ed. David B. Quinn (New York: 1979), 5:246–247; Andrew Fitzmaurice, "The Commercial Ideology of Colonization in Jacobean England: Robert Johnson, Giovanni Botero, and the Pursuit of Greatness," *William*

and Mary Quarterly (hereafter *WMQ*), 3d ser., 64 (2007): 791–820; Phil Withington, *The Politics of Commonwealth: Citizens and Freemen in Early Modern England* (Cambridge: 2008), 66; Francis Trigge, *The Humble Petition of Two Sisters: The Church and the Common-wealth. . . .* (London: 1604).

12. Musselwhite, "Towns in Mind," 43; Withington, *Politics of Commonwealth,* 11, 87–123; Diego Quaglioni and Vittor Ivo Comparato, "Italy," in *European Political Thought,* ed. Lloyd, Burgess, and Hodson, 92; Tuck, *Philosophy and Government,* 67.

13. Kingsbury, *RVC,* 3:100, 209; Martha W. McCartney, *Virginia Immigrants and Adventurers, 1607–1635: A Biographical Dictionary* (Baltimore: 2007), 30–31, 35–74; Ralph Hamor, *A True Discourse of the Present State of Virginia* (London: 1615), 29–34; John Rolfe, *A True Relation of the State of Virginia Lefte by Sir Thomas Dale Knight in May Last 1616* (Charlottesville, VA: 1971), 9–10; William M. Kelso, *Jamestown: The Truth Revealed* (Charlottesville, VA: 2017), passim.

14. Kingsbury, *RVC,* 1:256, 270, 3:259, 307–312, 493; Robert C. Johnson, "The Transportation of Vagrant Children from London to Virginia, 1618–1622," in *Early Stuart Studies: Essays in Honor of David Harris Wilson,* ed. Howard S. Reinmuth Jr. (Minneapolis, MN: 1970), 137–151; Paul Griffiths, *Lost Londons: Change, Crime, and Control in the Capital City, 1550–1660* (Cambridge: 2008), 284–286; Thomas Scanlan, *Colonial Writing and the New World, 1583–1671: Allegories of Desire* (Cambridge: 1999), 119–121; Edward Wright Haile, ed., *Jamestown Narratives: Eyewitness Accounts of the Virginia Colony: The First Decade, 1607–1617* (Champlain, VA: 1998), 718–720; Gray, *Good Speede,* B2v, B3v.

15. Kingsbury, *RVC,* 1:258, 392–393, 420, 446, 483, 3:278, 315, 474, 477, 502, 581–581, 634, 640, 651, 661, 4:23–24, 174–182; J. C. Harrington, *Glassmaking at Jamestown: America's First Industry* (Richmond, VA: 1952), 9–10.

16. David R. Ransome, "'Shipt for Virginia': The Beginnings in 1619–1623 of the Great Migration to the Chesapeake," *VMHB* 103 (1995): 443–458; David R. Ransome, "Wives for Virginia, 1621," *WMQ,* 3d ser., 43 (1991): 3–18; FP 306, August 1621, *VCA;* FP 309, September 1621, *VCA.*

17. Kingsbury, *RVC,* 3:99–101.

18. FP 93, December 5, 1618, *VCA.*

19. Kingsbury, *RVC,* 1:266–267, 3:307–312; Samuel Purchas, *Hakluytus Posthumus, or His Pilgrimes: Contayning a History of the World in Sea Voyages and Lande Travells by Englishmen and Others,* 20 vols. (Glasgow: 1905), 19:150.

20. At Berkeley Hundred, a private plantation founded in 1619, four hundred acres of common land was to be fenced and used for growing

corn, wheat, tobacco, and vines as well as for housing cattle sent by the Berkeley Company, Kingsbury, *RVC*, 1:270–271, 3:200. Wrightson, *Earthly Necessities*, 149–155; Williams, *English Historical Documents*, 268–273, 293–333; *Journal of the Common Council of London, 1618*, ff.374v. The children served as servants (apprentices) until twenty-one or until the girls married and were then placed on Company lands as tenants, at which time they would receive a house with corn and cattle and earn half the yearly profit.

21. The site of the first Anglican Church built in America (1608) was discovered at Jamestown in 2010 by William M. Kelso and the Jamestown Rediscovery team of archaeologists; see Kelso, *The Truth Revealed*, 167–184. The second church of 1617–1618 has also been investigated by the Jamestown team led by Mary Anna Hartley. FP 93, December 5, 1618, *VCA*; Kingsbury, *RVC*, 3:164–165, 172–173, 208–209, 276–277.

22. Matthew 22:37–40; Withington, *Society in Early Modern England*, 138–139; Eamon Duffy, *The Stripping of the Altars: Traditional Religion in England, 1400–1580*, 2nd ed. (New Haven, CT: 2005), 92–95,131–154; Rollison, *A Commonwealth of the People*, 163–165.

23. Fitzmaurice, "Every Man, That Prints, Adventures," 24–42; Alexander Brown, *The Genesis of the United States*, 2 vols. (Boston: 1891), 1:366, 368, 369; John Parker, "Religion and the Virginia Colony, 1609–10," in *The Westward Enterprise: English activities in Ireland, the Atlantic and America, 1480–1650*, ed. K. R. Andrews, N. P. Canny, and P. E. H. Hair (Liverpool: 1978), 247–248, 257; Rebecca Anne Goetz, *The Baptism of Early Virginia: How Christianity Created Race* (Baltimore: 2012), 21–34; Bond, *Damned Souls*, 1–29; James Horn, *A Land as God Made It: Jamestown and the Birth of America* (New York: 2005), 138–141; Avihu Zakai, *Exile and Kingdom: History and Apocalypse in the Puritan Migration to America* (Cambridge: 1992), 61–68, 94–115; Scanlan, *Colonial Writing*, 93–122; Douglas Bradburn, "The Eschatological Origins of the English Empire," in *Early Modern Virginia: Reconsidering the Old Dominion*, ed. Douglas Bradburn and John C. Coombs (Charlottesville, VA: 2011), 17–36.

24. Hooker's quotation is cited in Bond, *Damned Souls*, 57. In fact, Sandys and the Company did not scruple at encouraging former Leiden Separatists (Pilgrims) and other Puritans to settle in Virginia.

25. W. B. Patterson, *King James VI and I and the Reunion of Christendom* (Cambridge: 1997), 1, 26, 34, 260–364; Louis B. Wright, *Religion and Empire: The Alliance between Piety and Commerce in English Expansion, 1558–1625* (Chapel Hill, NC: 1943), 107; Fitzmaurice, "The Commercial Ideology of Colonization," 791–820.

26. Rabb, *Jacobean Gentleman*, 18–46, esp. 38; [Edwin Sandys], *A*

Relation of the State of Religion . . . in the Severall States of Those Westerne Parts of the Worlde (London: 1605), R3ii–R3iii.

27. Hamor, *True Discourse*, 11–16; Purchas, *Hakluytus Posthumus*, 19:106–107.

28. Kingsbury, *RVC*, 1:538–541, 3:102, 128–129, 147, 165–166, 276–277.

29. FP 93, December 5, 1618, *VCA*; Patterson, *King James VI and I*, 260–292; Kingsbury, *RVC*, 1:247–248, 278–279.

30. Kingsbury, *RVC*, 1:379, 3:123–124, 305, 307, 379–381, 397–400, 446–448, 469–470, 584. Eric Gethyn-Jones, *George Thorpe and the Berkeley Company: A Gloucestershire Enterprise in Virginia* (Gloucester, England: 1982), 153–158, 168–174, 181–185, 188–189, 224–227.

31. Smith's citing of Utopia was a reference to Sir Thomas More's book of the same name; see David Armitage, *The Ideological Origins of the British Empire* (Cambridge: 2000), 50. For the Smiths' venture in Ards Peninsula, Ulster, see Horning, *Ireland in the Virginia Sea*, 65–68, and Hiram Morgan, "The Colonial Venture of Sir Thomas Smith in Ulster, 1571–1575," *Historical Journal* 28 (1985): 261–278. Smith was the same man who wrote *De Republica Anglorum*.

32. Kingsbury, *RVC*, 3:537, 546; Purchas, *Hakluytus Posthumus*, 19:149; David B. Quinn, ed., "A List of Books Purchased for the Virginia Company," *VMHB* 77 (1969): 347–360.

Chapter 5: Tumult and Liberty

1. Susan Myra Kingsbury, ed., *The Records of the Virginia Company of London* (hereafter *RVC*), 4 vols. (Washington, DC: 1906–1935), 1:613, 628–629, 3:581–589. The General Assembly met in late November and early December 1621, shortly after Wyatt arrived in the colony. Patrick Copland, *Virginia's God be Thanked, or a Sermon of Thanksgiving for the Happie Successe of the Affayres in Virginia this Last Yeare* (London: 1622).

2. Kingsbury, *RVC*, 3:551; Philip L. Barbour, ed., *The Complete Works of Captain John Smith*, 3 vols. (Chapel Hill, NC: 1986), 2:293–298. The Reverend Joseph Mead, an influential scholar of religion at Christ College, Cambridge, reported in mid-July that between 300 and 329 settlers were killed; later he suggested 340; Robert C. Johnson, "The Indians Massacre of 1622: Some Correspondence of the Reverend Joseph Mead," *Virginia Magazine of History and Biography* (hereafter *VMHB*) 71 (1963): 408–409. The fullest account of the attack is by J. Frederick Fausz, "The Powhatan Uprising of 1622: A Historical Study of Ethnocentrism and Cultural Conflict" (PhD diss., College of William and Mary, 1977), 353–403.

3. Kingsbury, *RVC*, 3:612.

4. Kingsbury, *RVC*, 3:666–667; Robert C. Johnson, "A Poem on the Late Massacre in Virginia by Christopher Brooke," *VMHB* 72 (1964): 262; Fausz, "Powhatan Uprising," 431–434.

5. Kingsbury, *RVC*, 3:623, 656–657, 4:38, 41, 58, 515–516; Barbour, *Complete Works,* 2:308.

6. Kingsbury, *RVC*, 3:564, 669–671, 683.

7. Diarmaid MacCulloch, *The Reformation: A History* (New York: 2005), 337–340; Geoffrey Parker describes the "sack of Antwerp" as one of the "worst atrocities of the sixteenth century," in *The Dutch Revolt* (Ithaca, NY: 1977), 178; Jonathan I. Israel, *The Dutch Republic: Its Rise, Greatness, and Fall, 1477–1806* (Oxford: 1995), 185; Eugene Lyon, *The Enterprise of Florida: Pedro Menéndez de Avilés and the Spanish Conquest of 1565–1568* (Gainesville, FL: 1976), 100–130; John T. McGrath, *The French in Early Florida: In the Eye of the Hurricane* (Gainesville, FL: 2000), 133–155; Johnson, "The Indians Massacre of 1622," 408–409.

8. Kingsbury, *RVC*, 3:542, 550–551, 553, 559, 666. Tzvetan Todorov, *The Conquest of America: The Question of the Other* (New York: 1984), 50; Peter Hulme, *Colonial Encounters: Europe and the Native Caribbean, 1492–1797* (London: 1986), 45–87, 138–173; Anthony Pagden, *European Encounters with the New World: From Renaissance to Romanticism* (New Haven, CT: 1993), passim; Jack P. Greene, *The Intellectual Construction of America: Exceptionalism and Identity from 1492–1800* (Chapel Hill, NC: 1993), 15–25; Karen Ordahl Kupperman, *Indians and English: Facing Off in Early America* (Ithaca, NY: 2000), 16–74; David Beers Quinn, ed., *The Roanoke Voyages, 1584–1590,* 2 vols. (London: 1955), 1:108.

9. Kingsbury, *RVC*, 3:556–560, 562–563; Fausz, "Powhatan Uprising," 421–432; Bartolomé de Las Casas, *An Account, Much Abbreviated, of the Destruction of the Indies, with Related Texts,* ed. Franklin W. Knight (Indianapolis, IN: 2003), 2–86; "Letter of Sir Francis Wyatt, Governor of Virginia, 1621–1626," *William and Mary Quarterly* (hereafter *WMQ*), 2d ser., 6 (1926): 118–119. The brief history of the *Destruction of the Indies* and *History of the Indies* were published in 1552 and 1566, respectively. During the second half of the century, both were translated into other languages, including English, and were highly influential. Las Casas provided a scathing critique of what he viewed as the sadistic violence inflicted by Spanish colonists on innocent Indian peoples in the Americas, which he witnessed firsthand. For an account of the violence of Hernando de Soto's expedition and the subsequent collapse of Mississippian society in the mid-sixteenth century, see Robbie Ethridge, *From Chicaza to Chickasaw: The European Invasion and the Transformation of the Mississippian World, 1540–1715* (Chapel Hill, NC: 2010), 42–59; April Lee Hatfield, "Spanish Colonization Literature, Powhatan Geographies, and

English Perceptions of Tsenacommacah/Virginia," *Journal of Southern History* 69 (2003): 277–278.

10. Johnson, "A Poem on the Late Massacre," 282–292; Fausz, "Powhatan Uprising," 434; Alden T. Vaughan, *Roots of American Racism: Essays on the Colonial Experience* (Oxford: 1995), 124.

11. Hulme, *Colonial Encounters*, 154.

12. Pope Alexander VI's three bulls (charters) of the 1490s provided the legal basis of Spain's claim to the Americas, together with first discovery and conquest. See Anthony Pagden, *Lords of All the World: Ideologies of Empire in Spain, Britain and France, c.1500–c.1800* (New Haven, CT: 1995), 29–52; James Muldoon, "Papal Responsibility for the Infidel: Another Look at Alexander VI's *Inter Caetera*," *Catholic Historical Review* 64 (1978): 168–184; David Beers Quinn, ed., *The Voyages and Colonizing Enterprises of Sir Humphrey Gilbert*, 2 vols. (London: 1940), 2:450, 453; Robert Johnson, *Nova Britannia. . . .* (London: 1609); Robert Gray, *Good Speede to Virginia* (London: 1609), sig. C3iᵛ. For an overview, see Stuart Banner, *How the Indians Lost Their Land: Law and Power on the Frontier* (Cambridge, MA: 2007), passim.

13. Kingsbury, *RVC*, 3:671–673, 683, 4:451; Hulme, *Colonial Encounters*, 172.

14. Kingsbury, *RVC*, 2:678, 4:9–10; Barbour, *Complete Works*, 2:310.

15. Geoffrey Parker, *The Military Revolution: Military Innovation and the Rise of the West, 1500–1800*, 2nd ed. (Cambridge: 1996), 6–44; Kingsbury, *RVC*, 3:665, 676, 678–679; D. A. Tisdale, *Soldiers of the Virginia Colony, 1607–1699: A Study of Virginia's Military, Its Origins, Tactics, Equipment, and Development* (Petersburg, VA: 2000), 1–31, 81–161. Archaeological investigations at James Fort, Jamestown, have unearthed armor, weapons, and arrow points that confirm the arms sent from the Tower of London arrived. For broader perspectives, see John McGurk, *The Elizabethan Conquest of Ireland: The 1590s Crisis* (New York: 1997), 227–235, and Guy Chet, *Conquering the American Wilderness: The Triumph of European Warfare in the Colonial Northeast* (Boston: 2003).

16. Kingsbury, *RVC*, 2:482, 486, 4:61, 89, 98, 102, 108–109, 221–222, 507–508; Barbour, *Complete Works*, 2:320–321; Johnson, "The Indians Massacre of 1622," 410; Fausz, "Powhatan Uprising," 487–490, 493, 509–512. Opechancanough mounted one last attack in 1644, during which approximately four hundred to five hundred settlers were killed.

17. H. R. McIlwaine, ed., *Journals of the House of Burgesses of Virginia, 1619–1658/59* (Richmond, VA: 1915), 38; Samuel Purchas, *Hakluytus Posthumus, or Purchas His Pilgrims....*, 20 vols. (Glasgow: 1905–1907), 19:224, 228–231, 246, 266; Hulme, *Colonial Encounters*, 158.

18. Kingsbury, *RVC*, 3:672, 705–707; C. S. Everett, "'They Shalbe Slaves for Their Lives': Indian Slavery in Colonial Virginia," in *Indian*

Slavery in Colonial America, ed. Alan Gallay (Lincoln, NE: 2009), 69; Kristalyn Marie Shefveland, *Anglo-Native Virginia: Trade, Conversion, and Indian Slavery in the Old Dominion, 1646–1722* (Athens, GA: 2016), 6–79; H. R. McIlwaine, ed., *Minutes of the Council and General Court of Colonial Virginia,* 2nd ed. (Richmond, VA: 1979), 111; Andrés Reséndez, *The Other Slavery: The Uncovered Story of Indian Enslavement in America* (New York: 2016), passim.

19. Helen C. Rountree, *Pocahontas's People: The Powhatan Indians of Virginia Through Four Centuries* (Norman, OK: 1990), 84–91.

20. Kingsbury, *RVC,* 2:325.

21. Kingsbury, *RVC,* 2:375, 4:65, 147, 151, 160–161, 216, 231–235; Wesley Frank Craven, *Dissolution of the Virginia Company: The Failure of a Colonial Government* (Gloucester, MA: 1964), 200–220. George Sandys estimated no fewer than five hundred settlers died from an "extreme sickness" during the bitterly cold winter of 1623, a figure later adopted by royal commissioners sent to investigate the colony.

22. Rabb, *Jacobean Gentleman,* 241–269; Robert Zaller, *The Discourse of Legitimacy in Early Modern England* (Stanford, CA: 2007), 610–620; Thomas Cogswell, *The Blessed Revolution: English Politics and the Coming of War, 1621–1624* (Cambridge: 1989), 12–53, 298; S. L. Adams, "Foreign Policy and the Parliaments of 1621 and 1624," in *Faction and Parliament: Essays on Early Stuart History,* ed. Kevin Sharpe (Oxford: 1978), 146–147; Geoffrey Parker, *Global Crisis: War, Climate Change and Catastrophe in the Seventeenth Century* (New Haven, CT: 2103), 211; W. B. Patterson, *King James VI and I and the Reunion of Christendom* (Cambridge: 1997), 293–335; Alastair Bellany and Thomas Cogswell, *The Murder of King James I* (New Haven, CT: 2015), 1–5; Geoffrey Parker, ed., *The Thirty Years' War,* 2nd ed. (London: 1997), 43–61; Patrick Collinson, *The Birthpangs of Protestant England: Religious and Cultural Change in the Sixteenth and Seventeenth Centuries* (London: 1988), 5, 17; Avihu Zakai, *Exile and Kingdom: History and the Apocalypse in the Puritan Migration to America* (Cambridge: 1992), 109–118; John Donne, *A Sermon Upon the VIII Verse of the 1: Chapter of the Acts of the Apostles* (London: 1622).

23. Pauline Croft, *King James* (Basingstoke: 2003), 103–121; Patterson, *King James VI and I,* 309; G. P. V. Akrigg, ed., *Letters of King James VI and I* (Berkeley, CA: 1984), 377–378; Conrad Russell, *The Fall of the British Monarchies, 1637–1642* (Oxford: 1991), 100–123, 206–236.

24. Noel Malcolm, "Hobbes, Sandys, and the Virginia Company," *Historical Journal* 24 (1981): 300–301; [Arthur Wodenoth], *A Short Collection of the Most Remarkable Passages from the originall to the dissolution of the Virginia Company* (London: 1651), 18–19; Peter Peckard, *Memoirs of the Life of Mr. Nicholas Ferrar* (Cambridge: 1790), 115–116,

144; Alexander Brown, *The First Republic of America: An Account of the Origins of the Nation. . . .* (New York: 1898), 269–270, 439–440; Cogswell, *Blessed Revolution,* 302–307; Craven, *Dissolution of the Virginia Company,* 9–11, 319–320. Craven is right to be skeptical about placing too much emphasis on the influence of Gondomar in bringing about the collapse of the Company, but it is clear from reports of 1625, as well as accounts from several decades later during the Interregnum, when it was safe to publish criticisms of Stuart foreign policy (Wodenoth above), that he played a prominent role in promoting James's pro-Spanish policy and was extremely hostile toward Virginia and Bermuda; see, for example, Kingsbury, *RVC,* 4:539–540.

25. Alexander B. Haskell, *For God, King, and People: Forging Commonwealth Bonds in Renaissance Virginia* (Chapel Hill, NC: 2017), 192–213, 218–220, 233–234; David Underdown, *A Freeborn People: Politics and the Nation in Seventeenth-Century England* (Oxford: 1996), 20–44; Robert Zaller, *The Parliament of 1621: A Study in Constitutional Conflict* (Berkeley, CA: 1971); Conrad Russell, *King James VI & I and His English Parliaments,* ed. Richard Cust and Andrew Thrush (Oxford: 2012), 177–187; Cogswell, *Blessed Revolution,* 17–20.

26. Kingsbury, *RVC,* 4:223–224; Martha W. McCartney, *Virginia Immigrants and Adventurers, 1607–1635: A Biographical Dictionary* (Baltimore: 2007), 109–110; Haskell, *For God, King, and People,* 225–227.

27. Kingsbury, *RVC,* 4:194–195; Rabb, *Jacobean Gentleman,* 320–321; Malcolm Gaskill, *Between Two Worlds: How the English Became Americans* (New York: 2014), 61–64; Horn, *Land as God Made It,* 241–243; Thomas Locke to William Trumbull, August 28, 1618, Berkshire Record Office, Trumbull Manuscripts, *VCRP,* 07127, no. 101.

28. Kingsbury, *RVC,* 1:336, 3:155, 177.

29. Kingsbury, *RVC,* 4:416; Cicero, *On Obligations,* trans. P. G. Walsh (Oxford: 2000), 80. John Bargrave, *A Treatise Shewing Howe to Erect a Publique and Increasing Treasurie, A Commentary on the Lawes of Virginia* (ca. 1622), the Henry E. Huntington Library, Huntington Mss. HM 962. I am most grateful to Paul Musselwhite for sharing his transcript of the document.

30. Kingsbury, *RVC,* 4:408–411, 424–429; Peter Thompson, "Aristotle and King Alfred in America," in *Thomas Jefferson, the Classical World, and Early America,* ed. Peter S. Onuf and Nicholas P. Cole (Charlottesville, VA: 2011), 200–205; Haskell, *For God, King, and People,* 227–232. From internal evidence, the *"Polisie"* appears to have been written before news of the Indian massacre reached England. It was one of a series of tracts on a variety of topics penned by Bargrave (I owe this point to Paul Musselwhite).

31. Kingsbury, *RVC,* 4:415–416, 424–429.

32. Craven, *Dissolution of the Virginia Company*, 276–285; Kings-bury, *RVC*, 2:358–359. See, for example, Cicero, *On the Commonwealth*, trans. George Holland Sabine and Stanley Barney Smith (New York: 1976), 133–134, and Francis Grigor, ed., *Sir John Fortescue's Commenda-tion of the Laws of England: The Translation into English of De Laudibus Legnum Angliae* (London: 1917), 28, 59–61; Andrew Fitzmaurice, "The Company–Commonwealth," in *Virginia 1619: Slavery, Freedom, and the Construction of English America*, ed. Paul Musselwhite, James Horn, and Peter C. Mancall (Chapel Hill, NC: forthcoming).

33. Kingsbury, *RVC*, 1:423; Thomas Cary Johnson, introduction to *A Proclamation for Setling the Plantation of Virginia* (Charlottesville, VA: 1946). Despite Charles I's remarks concerning commercial companies and their fitness to undertake "state-affaires," he continued to grant char-ters, as for example to the New England Company in 1628 and the Mas-sachusetts Bay Company the following year.

34. Kingsbury, *RVC*, 2:359. By adventurers, the Company meant in-vestors and colonists. Paul Christianson, "Ancient Constitution in the Age of Sir Edward Coke and John Selden," in *The Roots of Liberty: Magna Carta, Ancient Constitution, and the Anglo-American Tradition of the Rule of Law*, ed. Ellis Sandoz (Columbia, MO: 1993), 122–125.

35. Kingsbury, *RVC*, 4:582; Thomas J. Wertenbaker, *Virginia Under the Stuarts, 1607–1688* (New York: 1958), 62; Glenn Burgess, *The Politics of the Ancient Constitution: An Introduction to English Political Thought 1603–1642* (University Park, PA: 1992), 181; Zaller, *Discourse of Legiti-macy*, 620–700; Stephen D. White, *Sir Edward Coke and "the Grievances of the Commonwealth," 1621–1628* (Chapel Hill, NC: 1979), 213–275; J. H. Baker, *The Reinvention of Magna Carta, 1216–1616* (Cambridge: 2017), 335–409; Kevin Sharpe, *The Personal Rule of Charles I* (New Haven, CT: 1992), passim. See also J. R. Tanner, *English Constitutional Conflicts of the Seventeenth Century, 1603–1689* (Cambridge: 1962), 68–70.

36. Sir Robert Phelips is quoted in David Harris Sacks, "Parliament, Liberty, and the Commonweal," in *Parliament and Liberty: From the Reign of Elizabeth to the English Civil War*, ed. J. H. Hexter (Stanford, CA: 1992), 120–121; Grigor, *Sir John Fortescue's Commendation*, 22, 55–56.

Chapter 6: Inequality and Freedom

1. Keith Wrightson, *Earthly Necessities: Economic Lives in Early Mod-ern Britain* (New Haven, CT: 2000), 151; Irene W. D. Hecht, "The Vir-ginia Muster of 1624/5 as a Source for Demographic History," *William and Mary Quarterly* (hereafter *WMQ*), 3d ser., 30 (1973): 70–71, 77–78, 89.

2. Nicholas Ferrar in 1624, *Sir Thomas Smith's Misgovernment of the Virginia Company*, ed. D. R. Ransome (Cambridge: 1990), 4–5, 7–10; Peter Wilson Coldham, "The Voyage of the Neptune to Virginia, 1618–1619, and the Disposition of Its Cargo," *Virginia Magazine of History and Biography* (hereafter *VMHB*), 87 (1979): 30–67. Fortunately for Brewster, the sentence was commuted to banishment from Virginia.

3. William Thorndale, "A Passenger List of the 1619 *Bona Nova*," *Virginia Genealogical Society* 33 (1995): 3–11; Philip L. Barbour, ed., *The Complete Works of Captain John Smith*, 3 vols. (Chapel Hill, NC: 1986), 2:268, 284; Susan Myra Kingsbury, ed., *The Records of the Virginia Company of London* (hereafter *RVC*), 4 vols. (Washington, DC: 1906–1935), 1:319–329, 334–335, 3:221, 226–227, 246, 262–265, 275, 489, 536–537, 4:41, 58–59, 62, 175, 231–232, 235; Martha W. McCartney, *Virginia Immigrants and Adventurers, 1607–1635: A Biographical Dictionary* (Baltimore: 2007), 517.

4. James Horn, *Adapting to a New World: English Society in the Seventeenth-Century Chesapeake* (Chapel Hill, NC: 1994), 104, 118–119, 147–148, 425–427; Jack P. Greene, "The Exclusionary Legacy of Subjecthood in Making and Remaking the Atlantic World: English-Speaking America as a Case for Historical Reflection" (keynote address, Rice University, 2014), 17; Warren M. Billings, *A Little Parliament: The Virginia General Assembly in the Seventeenth Century* (Richmond, VA: 2004), 87–113, 149; Edmund S. Morgan, *American Slavery, American Freedom: The Ordeal of Colonial Virginia* (New York: 1975), 124–126; David Thomas Konig, "'Dale's Laws' and the Non-Common Law Origins of Criminal Justice in Virginia," *American Journal of Legal History* 26 (1982): 369–375; Paul D. Halliday, in "Brase's Case: Making Slave Law as Customary Law in Virginia's General Court, 1619–1625," in *Virginia 1619: Slavery, Freedom, and the Construction of English America*, ed. Paul Musselwhite, James Horn, and Peter C. Mancall (Chapel Hill, NC: forthcoming), puts forward a strong argument about the unchecked powers of magistrates that characterized the making of customary law in Virginia after 1619.

5. Kingsbury, *RVC*, 3:221–222; Virginia M. Meyer and John Frederick Dorman, eds., *Adventurers of Purse and Person: Virginia, 1607–1624/5* (Richmond, VA: 1987), 478–480; Kent History and Library Center, Maidstone, Kent, England, U269/1, OV 15, August 27, 1631; Morgan, *American Slavery, American Freedom*, 108–129.

6. Morgan, *American Slavery, American Freedom*, 124–126; Alexander B. Haskell, *For God, King, and People: Forging Commonwealth Bonds in Renaissance Virginia* (Chapel Hill, NC: 2017), 258–259; Kingsbury, *RVC*, 2:325; Thomas Cary Johnson, introduction to *By the King: A Proclamation for Setling the Plantation of Virginia* (Charlottesville, VA: 1946).

7. Quoted in Haskell, *For God, King, and People*, 262; Billings, *A Little Parliament*, 12–35; Thornton J. Mills III, "The Thrusting Out of Governor Harvey: A Seventeenth-Century Rebellion," *VMHB*, 76 (1968): 11–26; Warren M. Billings, ed., *The Old Dominion in the Seventeenth Century: A Documentary History of Virginia, 1606–1700*, rev. ed. (Chapel Hill, NC: 2007), 50, 296–299, 310–318; Douglas Bradburn, "The Visible Fist: The Chesapeake Tobacco Trade in War and the Purpose of Empire, 1690–1715," *WMQ* 68 (2011): 361–386; James D. Rice, *Tales From a Revolution: Bacon's Rebellion and the Transformation of Early America* (Oxford: 2012).

8. Wesley Frank Craven, *Dissolution of the Virginia Company: The Failure of a Colonial Experiment* (Gloucester, MA: 1964), 131–136; Kingsbury, *RVC*, 3:219–220.

9. David Wheat, *Atlantic Africa and the Spanish Caribbean, 1570–1640* (Chapel Hill, NC: 2016), 17; Philip D. Morgan, "Virginia Slavery in Atlantic Context, ca. 1550 to ca. 1650," in *Virginia 1619*, ed. Musselwhite, Horn, and Mancall.

10. Philip D. Morgan, *Slave Counterpoint: Black Culture in the Eighteenth-Century Chesapeake and Lowcountry* (Chapel Hill, NC: 1998), 59–66; William Waller Hening, ed., *The Statutes at Large Being a Collection of All the Laws of Virginia....*, 13 vols. (Charlottesville, VA: 1969), 1:270, 2:280–281, 299–300, 481–482, 491–492, 3:86–88, 102–103, 250–259, 269–270, 333–335, 447–462.

11. Barbados emerged as the first slave society in the English Atlantic. By 1650, the enslaved population was about thirteen thousand, a third of the population of the island; see Philip D. Morgan, "British Encounters with Africans and African-Americans, circa 1600–1780," in *Strangers within the Realm: Cultural Margins of the First British Empire*, ed. Bernard Bailyn and Philip D. Morgan (Chapel Hill, NC: 1991),173; Morgan, *Slave Counterpoint*, xxiv; Mark G. Hanna, *Pirate Nests and the Rise of the British Empire, 1570–1740* (Chapel Hill, NC: 2015), 70–77; Carla Gardina Pestana, *The English Atlantic in an Age of Revolution, 1640–1661* (Cambridge, MA: 2004), 183–212.

12. John Ferrar, *A Perfect Description of Virginia. . . .* (London: 1649); it was evidently written either the previous year or in the first part of January 1649 since Charles I is mentioned in the text. McCartney, *Virginia Immigrants and Adventurers*, 483–485; Billings, *A Little Parliament*, 20–22; Kingsbury, *RVC*, 2:325. Mathews had remained a stalwart supporter of the Virginia Company, served with Ferrar in the early 1630s on a royal commission (Dorset) to consider reviving it and was one of the four leading councilors who plotted to send Sir John Harvey back to England.

13. Glenn Burgess, *The Politics of the Ancient Constitution: An Introduction to English Political Thought, 1603–1642* (University Park, PA:

1992), 3–7; J. P. Kenyon, ed., *The Stuart Constitution: Documents and Commentary* (Cambridge: 1969), 82–85.

14. Kingsbury, *RVC,* 3:98–99; Ferrar Papers 93, December 5, 1618, *Virginia Company Archives,* Adam Mathew Digital (2007). As noted above, even before the collapse of the Company, and especially following, the laws and institutions put in place by Sandys's great reforms eventually became the means by which wealthy planter elites were able to pursue their own interests largely unrestrained by the English government or royal governors often to the detriment of the poor and vulnerable, Halliday, "Brase's Case."

15. Martyn Bennett, *The Civil Wars in Britain and Ireland, 1638–1651* (Oxford: 1997), 142–255; *King Charles His Speech Made upon the Scaffold at Whitehall-Gate, Immediately before His Execution, on Tuesday the 30 of Jan. 1648* (London: 1649), 9–10; Kenyon, *Stuart Constitution,* 21–23. Wat Tyler was one of the leaders of the Peasants' Revolt of 1381 and Jack Cade the leader of the rebellion of 1450.

16. Thomas Hobbes, *Leviathan,* ed. C. B. Macpherson (Harmondsworth, Middlesex: 1968), 75.

17. John Morrill, *The Nature of the English Revolution* (London: 1993), 285–305; Austin Woolrych, *Britain in Revolution, 1625–1660* (Oxford: 2002), 234–559; Blair Worden, *The English Civil Wars, 1640–1660* (London: 2009), passim; Michael Braddick, *God's Fury: A New History of the English Civil Wars* (London: 2009), 241–580; Pestana, *The English Atlantic,* 1–117.

18. James T. Kloppenberg, *Toward Democracy: The Struggle for Self-Rule in European and American Thought* (Oxford: 2016), 94–363; Richard Tuck, *The Sleeping Sovereign: The Invention of Modern Democracy* (Cambridge: 2015), 63–120, 181–248.

Epilogue: After 1619

1. Philip L. Barbour, ed., *The Complete Works of Captain John Smith,* 3 vols. (Chapel Hill, NC: 1986), 2:245. Generally, Francis Jennings, *The Invasion of America: Indians, Colonialism, and the Cant of Conquest* (Chapel Hill, NC: 1975); Jennings, *The Founders of America, from the Earliest Migrations to the Present* (New York: 1994), 233–411; Ned Blackhawk, *Violence Over the Land: Indians and Empires in the Early American West* (Cambridge, MA: 2006); Matthew Jennings, *New Worlds of Violence: Cultures and Conquests in the Early American Southeast* (Knoxville, TN: 2011); Andrés Reséndez, *The Other Slavery: The Uncovered Story of Indian Enslavement in America* (New York: 2016); Carol Smith-Rosenberg, *This Violent Empire: The Birth of an American Identity* (Chapel Hill, NC: 2010).

2. Philip D. Morgan, "Slaves and Poverty," in *Down and Out in Early America,* ed. Billy G. Smith (University Park, PA: 2004), 93–131; Thomas M. Shapiro, *Toxic Inequality: How America's Wealth Gap Destroys Mobility, Deepens the Racial Divide, and Threatens Our Future* (New York: 2017), 13, and note 9, 228; Stephen M. Caliendo, *Inequality in America: Race, Poverty, and Fulfilling Democracy's Promise,* 2nd ed. (New York: 2017); Melvin Oliver and Thomas M. Shapiro, *Black Wealth / White Wealth: A New Perspective* (New York: 2006), appendix A. Douglas A. Blackmon argues persuasively that a form of quasi slavery persisted on a massive scale in the Deep South for three-quarters of a century after emancipation, see *Slavery by Another Name: The Re-Enslavement of Black Americans from the Civil War to World War II* (New York: 2008); Valerie Wilson and William D. Rodgers III, "Black-White Wage Gaps Expand with Rising Wage Inequality," *Economic Policy Institute,* September 20, 2016; Linda M. Burton, Marybeth Mattingly, Juan Pedroza, and Whitney Welsh, *State of the Union 2017: Poverty,* Stanford Center on Poverty and Inequality (Stanford, CA: 2017); Renee Stepler, "5 Key Takeaways about Views of Race and Inequality in America," Pew Research Center, June 27, 2016.

3. Thomas Jefferson to Roger Weightman, Monticello June 24, 1826, in Merrill D. Peterson, ed., *Thomas Jefferson, Writings* (New York: 1984), 1516–1517.

4. Jack P. Greene, "The Exclusionary Legacy of Subjecthood in Making and Remaking the Atlantic World: English-Speaking America as a Case for Historical Reflection" (keynote address, Rice University, 2014), 2, 11–22, 27–30; Michael Kammen, *Deputyes and Libertyes: The Origins of Representative Government in Colonial America* (New York: 1969), passim; Michael Kammen, *Spheres of Liberty: Changing Perceptions of Liberty in American Culture* (Madison, WI: 1986), passim. The extensive powers assumed by local elites and legislatures, one of the principal institutional strengths of the British imperial system and subsequently of the American Union, carried with them opportunities for wholesale and systematic abuse of African Americans and Native Americans, see for example, David Brion Davis, *Inhuman Bondage: The Rise and Fall of Slavery in the New World* (Oxford: 2006), 298–306; Blackmon, *Slavery by Another Name;* Michelle Alexander, *The New Jim Crow: Mass Incarceration in the Age of Colorblindness* (New York: 2010); Helen C. Rountree, *Pocahontas's People: The Powhatan Indians of Virginia Through Four Centuries* (Norman, OK: 1990), 219–242; Edwin Black, *War Against the Weak: Eugenics and America's Campaign to Create a Master Race,* 2nd ed. (Washington, DC: 2012); Nancy Isenberg, *White Trash: The 400-Year Untold History of Class in America* (New York: 2016), 192–205.

5. Today, four states—Virginia, Kentucky, Pennsylvania, and Massachusetts—together with the territory of Puerto Rico, continue to call themselves *commonwealths* although the term retains little or nothing of its original political and social meaning. John Donne, *A Sermon Preached to the Honorable Company of the Virginian Plantation, 13th November, 1622* (London: 1622), 17.

Index

Michael Lavin

James Horn is president and chief officer of the Jamestown Rediscovery Foundation (Preservation Virginia), responsible for the management of Historic Jamestowne, the original site of the first permanent English colony in America. He is the author and editor of seven books on colonial America and is a regular contributor to radio and TV programs, including the History Channel, *Nova, Time Team America,* and PBS. He lives in Richmond, Virginia.